Fruits of Her Plume

Fruits of Her Plume

**Essays on Contemporary
Russian Woman's Culture**

edited by

Helena Goscilo

M.E. Sharpe
Armonk, New York
London, England

Library of Congress Cataloging-in-Publication Data

Fruits of her plume : essays on contemporary Russian women's culture /
edited by Helena Goscilo.

p.   cm.
Includes index
ISBN 1-56324-125-0.—ISBN 1-56324-126-9 (pbk)
1. Russian literature—Women authors—History and criticism.
2. Russian literature—20th century—History and criticism.
3. Russia (Federation)—Intellectual life.
I. Goscilo, Helena, 1945–
PG2997.F78   1993
891.709'9267'0904—dc20
93-22088
CIP

Printed in the United States of America

The paper used in this publication meets the minimum requirements of
American National Standard for Information Sciences—
Permanence of Paper for Printed Library Materials,
ANSI Z 39.48-1984.

MV (c)   10   9   8   7   6   5   4   3   2   1

MV (p)   10   9   8   7   6   5   4   3   2   1

To the vivid memory of
the late
Inna Varlamova
Svetlana Mikhailova
Irina Velembovskaia

CONTENTS

LIST OF PHOTOGRAPHS

ACKNOWLEDGMENTS

In addition to the institutions and individuals acknowledged in my essay, I thank those organizations that have underwritten my research in contemporary Russian women's culture: the National Endowment for the Humanities, IREX, Pushkinskii Dom, the Kennan Institute, the Humanities Center at Research Triangle Park, and the Russian and East European Studies Center (REES) at the University of Pittsburgh. Work conducted with their support has fed into my own writing as well as into the editing of this volume.

Three of the essays in this volume—those by Svetlana Boym, Caryl Emerson, and Natal'ia Ivanova—are reworkings of talks presented at the conference "Glasnost in Two Cultures," organized by Domna Stanton at the Humanities Center, New York University. I am indebted to Domna and to the Center for making that forum available.

The capable staff at M.E. Sharpe and especially Patricia Kolb—flexible, decisive, and unflappable—likewise have my warmest appreciation.

A special word of gratitude to all of the contributors and to those Russian friends who unfailingly respond with unobtrusive generosity to even the quirkiest queries and requests: Nadezhda Azhgikhina, Ol'ga Lipovskaia, Svetlana Mikhailova, and Elena Trubilova.

Finally, my customary thank you to Bożenna Goscilo, sister and personal editor extraordinaire, for questioning my hypotheses, curbing my wild flights, and shaving the carbuncles off my prose.

ABOUT THE EDITOR AND CONTRIBUTORS

Helena Goscilo, currently the Chairwoman of the Slavic Department at the University of Pittsburgh, specializes in Romanticism, contemporary Russian literature and culture, and Slavic women's writing. Her publications include articles on Pushkin, Lermontov, Tolstoi, Bulgakov, and Tolstaia, as well as *Russian and Polish Women's Fiction* (University of Tennessee Press, 1985); *Balancing Acts* (Indiana University Press, 1989; Dell, 1991); *Glasnost: An Anthology of Literature* (Ardis, 1990)—with Byron Lindsey; *The Wild Beach and Other Stories* (Ardis, 1992)—also with Lindsey; *Skirted Issues: The Discreteness and Indiscretions of Russian Women's Prose* (*Russian Studies in Literature*, Spring 1992); *Lives in Transit* (Ardis, 1993). She is working on three monographs, devoted respectively to recent women's fiction, Tat'iana Tolstaia, and Liudmila Petrushevskaia.

Svetlana Boym, Assistant Professor of Comparative Literature at Harvard University and the author of *Death in Quotation Marks: Cultural Myths of the Modern Poet* (1991), is currently writing a book on kitsch.

Richard Chapple, who has published on Dostoevskii, most notably *A Dostoevsky Dictionary* (1983), chairs the Department of Modern Languages and Literatures at Florida State University.

Caryl Emerson, Professor of Slavic at Princeton University, has written widely on Bakhtin, Pushkin, Russian opera, and various aspects of Russian culture. Her numerous publications include translations of Bakhtin (*The Dialogic Imagination,* with Michael

Holquist, 1981), as well as *Boris Godunov: Transpositions of a Russian Theme* (1986) and *Mikhail Bakhtin: Creation of a Prosaics,* coauthored with Saul Morson (1990). She is currently finishing a monograph on Mussorgsky.

John R. Givens is an associate instructor at the University of Washington whose research has focused on Vasilii Shukshin.

Darra Goldstein of Williams College has published extensively on such diverse topics in Russian culture as Russian homes, Georgian and Russian cuisine (*A la Russe: A Cookbook of Russian Hospitality*), and modern Russian poetry. In addition to translating Nadezhda Teffi's prose, *All about Love* (1985), Darra Goldstein has recently completed a study of the absurdist poet N. Zabolotskii.

Beth Holmgren, a specialist in Polish and Russian literature in the Slavic Department at the University of North Carolina in Chapel Hill, has several articles on Gombrowicz and Terts to her credit. Her book on women's autobiography, *Women's Works in Stalin's Time: On Lidiia Chukovskaia and Nadezhda Mandelstam,* is slated for publication later this year (Indiana University Press). Recent projects include articles on mass literature by and for women and a volume of essays on Russian women's popular culture, coedited with Helena Goscilo.

Natal'ia Ivanova, currently on the staff of *Znamia* (The Banner), is one of Moscow's most prolific commentators on the contemporary literary scene. Among her publications are a booklength study of Trifonov's prose and several collections of literary criticism—*Tochka zreniia* [Point of View], *Osvobozhdenie ot strakha* [Freedom from Fear], and *Voskreshenie nuzhnykh veshchei* [The Resurrection of Necessary Things, 1990].

Jerzy Kolodziej is Director of the Summer Slavic Workshop at Indiana University. A specialist in Polish and Russian fiction, he has written on Zamiatin.

Thomas Lahusen, Chairman of Slavic at Duke University and author of *The Concept of the "New Man": Forms of Address and Society in Nineteenth-Century Russia* (1982) and sundry articles on Polish and Russian literature, is currently writing a monograph on the Zhdanovite model of socialist realism.

Nadya L. Peterson of the University of Pennsylvania specializes in contemporary Russian fiction. In addition to a major study of fantastic realism, she has written on gender in Chekhov and Nina Sadur. Her current projects include a volume on eroticism in Russian women's fiction.

Stephanie Sandler, Associate Professor of Russian and of Women's and Gender Studies at Amherst College, is the author of *Distant Pleasures: Alexander Pushkin and the Writing of Exile* (1989) and coeditor, with Jane Costlow and Judith Vowles, of *Sexuality and the Body in Russian Culture* (1993). She is completing a book on cultural rituals associated with "Pushkin places" in Russia.

Nicholas Žekulin, Professor in the German and Slavic Studies Department at the University of Calgary, has expertise in both Russian literature and music. His publications range over Turgenev, women's prose, and opera productions.

INTRODUCTION

Helena Goscilo

"Punctuality," as the saying goes, "is the courtesy of kings." Yet tardiness, however ill bred, offers inestimable advantages. A latecomer to a feast, for instance (once the ritual of apologies and explanations has run its course), automatically eludes some potential hazards. With the edge of ravenous appetite in the more punctual guests blunted, she need not scramble in unseemly fashion for the most enticing dishes. Nor need she initiate fumbling conversation, for by then, presumably, talk is purling along as uninhibitedly as the wine that has mellowed the company into tolerant affability. Perhaps most important, by observing the effects of the meal on those already at table, she may circumvent the excesses and errors in choice of the gathering's more "kingly" members.

As with dilatory guests, so with Slavists. Arriving only now at the prolonged and clamorous feast of gender studies, they are ideally positioned to reap the potential benefits of informed judiciousness enabled by belatedness. Without wading into the intellectual combat that split pioneering feminists into alienated factions, they may weigh the pros and cons, for example, of the universalizing French concept of *écriture féminine* elaborated by Luce Irigaray and Hélène Cixous, as opposed to the strongly empiricist tendencies of American feminists and the Marxist-socialist element (especially in film studies) of the British pragmatists—both of whom emphasize the historical and social reality of women's experience.[1] They may also gauge with the coolness of hindsight the relative merits of dominant trends within feminism, some of which have settled into their own brand of orthodoxy: the Lacanian revision of Freud, for instance, which animates the research of Juliet Mitchell and especially of Jane Gallop; Carolyn Heilbrun's theories of androgyny; and notions of body representation (mainly in the visual media) influenced by Laura Mulvey's article on the male gaze (1975)—indebted, in its turn, to John Berger's trenchant analysis of art production and consumption (*Ways of Seeing*, 1972).[2] In short, unlike academics in other national literatures who laid the theoretico-critical groundwork for feminist and gender studies, Slavists embarking on a feminist course need not generate fundamental principles *ab ovo*. Their task consists rather of assimilation, development, and adaptation.

The accelerated boom in feminist scholarship since the early 1970s has produced a plethora of reassessments, reconstellations, and indefatigable meta-commentary. Just how extensive a menu of proliferating feminisms confronts the unwary neophyte may be deduced from the mammoth anthology of selected criticism signally titled *Feminisms* and from surveys of feminist scholarship such as Janet Todd's *Feminist Literary History* (1988) and Janet Wolff's more recent *Feminine Sentences* (1990).[3] In light of this *embarras des richesses*, it is unstartling to hear some Western academics elide "postfeminism" with all the other post-isms currently in vogue (post-Marxism, postcommunism, poststructuralism, postcolonialism, postmodernism, etc.). This reflex identification of (over?)abundance with exhaustion implies that Slavists have finally joined a feast that has petered out or is in the process of doing so. Whether such a view accurately reflects the current situation each reader of this volume will have to decide for herself.

Within Russian studies, the majority of book-length feminist (or, more precisely, gender) projects have come from historians, sociologists, and economists rather than specialists in literature.[4] In fact, among Slavists the program of cultural reclamation launched in the initial stages of Anglo-American feminism, when scholars rescued numerous literary texts from arguably undeserved oblivion, still remains in its embryonic phase. Yet even without (re)turning to the past in order to salvage a *by*passed tradition, they have no shortage of material, for the last decade has witnessed the ascendancy of Slavic women in multiple spheres of artistic creation that historically have devalued them as a deductible addendum: literature, film, and the pictorial arts.

Asked whom they consider today's foremost Russian writer or film director, even male respondents acknowledge Liudmila Petrushevskaia, Tat´iana Tolstaia, Kira Muratova, and Lana Gogoberidze (a Georgian) as the most powerful and original practitioners of their craft.[5] Indeed, any roster of contemporary figures meriting serious attention would be incomplete without such names as Ol´ga Bulgakova, Tat´iana Nazarenko, Natal´ia Nesterova, and Larisa Zvezdochetova in art; Nina Gorlanova, Elena Makarova, Tat´iana Nabatnikova, Valeriia Narbikova, Marina Palei, Nina Sadur, Bella Ulanovskaia, Liudmila Ulitskaia, Larisa Vaneeva, and Svetlana Vasilenko in fiction and drama; and Zoia Ezrokhi, Elena Ignatova, Nina Iskrenko, Inna Lisnianskaia, Olesia Nikolaeva, Elena Shvarts, and Tat´iana Shcherbina in poetry. While women's social, political, and economic status has steadily deteriorated during the *glasnost´* and post-*glasnost´* era, in the realm of cultural creativity women undisputedly have come into their own. This volume of essays, then, may be said to engage not only women's artistic production but also the most colorful and thought-provoking examples of recent Russian culture.[6]

The essays collected here examine women's works in order to identify the distinguishing traits of gendered cultural products and of the individual talents that gave them birth. The theoretical and critical positions of the contributors diverge dramatically and, I believe, fruitfully. While Caryl Emerson's polemical essay argues forcefully against the advisability of harnessing Bakhtinian concepts to women's issues, Natal´ia Ivanova demonstrates how Mikhail Bakhtin's notion of carnival may be productively applied to the prose of Tolstaia and Petrushevskaia. Nicholas Žekulin posits the gynocentric parasitism of women's writing during the early 1980s, focusing on its gendered "localization" of themes universalized in malestream fiction and thereby rendered acceptable. The implication of women in domesticity analyzed by Žekulin reverberates in Svetlana Boym's investigation of the links between kitsch and the "feminine" as exemplified in several works by Tolstaia, Gogoberidze, and Zvezdochetova. This same complex, shifting relationship between the domestic/familial and the artistic also underpins the essays by Beth Holmgren and Stephanie Sandler: the first traces the complex construction of an identity undertaken by the wife and widow of the acclaimed "great poet" Osip Mandel'shtam,[7] while the second explores the way in which three lyric poets use retrospection and a female viewpoint to recast the biblical story of Lot's wife.

Recent debates around body discourse, feminist criticism, and postmodernism inform both Nadya Peterson's study—which challenges the "erotic" label attached to Narbikova's texts—and my own essay, which sifts through the rhetorical elements of body inscriptions in Petrushevskaia, Tolstaia, and Narbikova. The paradoxical consequences of Russia's recent liberalization emerge clearly in the two entries that compare early and later (*glasnost'/perestroika*) phases of two authors' professional development: Richard Chapple surveys the career of Viktoriia Tokareva, one of Russia's most popular and successful women writers, in the process evaluating the effect of *glasnost'* on her authorial strategies. Similarly, Thomas Lahusen assesses the treatment of gendered temporality in the two large-scale narratives that frame the career of Natal'ia Baranskaia, doyenne of contemporary Russian women's fiction. Jerzy Kolodziej scrutinizes gendered features in the quasi-novel of Iuliia Voznesenskaia, expelled from Russia in mid-1980 for her activities as a member of the Maria feminist group, while Darra Goldstein dissects the sophisticated revision by Elena Shvarts of a female "tell-tale heart" in the poet's cycle of verses about a heretical nun. John Givens's essay completes the circle, in that its close reading of "Peters," the story that propelled Tolstaia to international fame, relies on Bakhtin's theory of discourse.

Scope of subject matter and specificity of address determined my ordering of the essays. Their sequence follows a centripetal or telescopic movement: from the broad theoretical sweep of Emerson's contribution through narrower purviews to Givens's detailed explication of a single story. I deviated from this principle of organization only when more compelling considerations suggested alternatives; Ivanova's contribution, for example, struck me as more effectively placed after Emerson's, as an immediate response to it.

Although I did not elicit any group debate by circulating the essays among the contributors, our multiple approaches to women's issues and our varied concerns resulted, quite spontaneously, in a pregnant dialogue vital to any collection of this sort. On first reading, the differences among the pieces may strike the reader more dramatically than the parallels. Sandler's avowedly feminist position, for example, has little in common with the critical standpoint from which Chapple discusses Tokareva's writings and could not be more remote from Emerson's near-dismissal of the entire feminist enterprise. These postures yield very different critical discourses and modes of argumentation. The diversity in structure and tone is likewise striking: Boym's and my occasionally playful modulations contrast sharply with the unwavering sobriety of Goldstein and Žekulin; Holmgren proceeds through accretion, Lahusen through juxtaposition; Kolodziej adheres strictly to a commentary on Voznesenskaia's novel, whereas Peterson moves beyond Narbikova's texts to elucidate their appropriation of techniques from Conceptualist art; and so forth.

To some extent the absence of uniformity mirrors the pluralism that constitutes one of the most appealing features of women's creativity in Russia today. The heterogeneity is not fortuitous, however. My constitutional antipathy to monologism prompted me to seek out contributors with divergent opinions, interests, and methodologies. The wish to include readings of Tolstaia and Petrushevskaia that do not concur with mine was a major consideration when I came to enlist participants in this enterprise. Hence I am happier about the clashes than about the overlaps in the volume. It was inevitable, I think, that Tolstaia,

Petrushevskaia, and Narbikova, as well as Bakhtin, should function as Goethe's red thread, loosely binding the essays together. My reluctance to pull that thread tighter in this Introduction stems from principle, not turpitude.

Notes

1. For a thorough and balanced summary of the conflicting principles that have fueled the heated debate between the French feminists and their Anglo-American counterparts, see the excellent review essay by Betsy Draine, "Refusing the Wisdom of Solomon: Some Recent Feminist Literary Theory," *Signs: Journal of Women in Culture and Society* 15, no. 1 (Autumn 1989): 144–70. See also Toril Moi's Introduction to *French Feminist Thought: A Reader*, ed. Toril Moi (Oxford and New York: Basil Blackwell, 1987), 1–13.

2. See in particular the early study by Juliet Mitchell, *Psychoanalysis and Feminism* (New York: Pantheon, 1974), and her *Women: The Longest Revolution* (New York: Pantheon, 1984), as well as the frequently cited study by Jane Gallop, *The Daughter's Seduction* (Ithaca, NY: Cornell University Press, 1982). Also Laura Mulvey, "Visual Pleasure and Narrative Cinema," *Screen* (1975), vol. 16, no. 3:6–18; Carolyn G. Heilbrun, *Toward a Recognition of Androgyny* (New York: W.W. Norton & Co., 1975/1982); John Berger, *Ways of Seeing* (Harmondsworth: Penguin, 1972).

3. Robyn R. Warhol and Diane Price Herndl, eds., *Feminisms* (New Brunswick, NJ: Rutgers University Press, 1991); Janet Todd, *Feminist Literary History* (New York: Routledge, 1988); Janet Wolff, *Feminine Sentences* (Berkeley: University of California Press, 1990).

4. See, e.g., William M. Mandel, *Soviet Women* (New York: Doubleday/Anchor, 1975); Richard Stites, *The Women's Liberation Movement in Russia* (Princeton: Princeton University Press, 1978/1990); Gail Lapidus, *Women in Soviet Society* (Berkeley: University of California Press, 1978); Barbara Alpern Engel, *Mothers and Daughters* (Cambridge: Cambridge University Press, 1983); Barbara Holland, ed., *Soviet Sisterhood* (Bloomington: Indiana University Press, 1985); Chanie Rosenberg, *Women and Perestroika* (London: Bookmarks, 1989); Mary Buckley, *Women and Ideology in the Soviet Union* (Ann Arbor: University of Michigan Press, 1989); Lynne Attwood, *The New Soviet Man and Woman* (Bloomington: Indiana University Press, 1990); Barbara Evans Clements, Barbara Alpern Engel, and Christine D. Worobec, eds., *Russia's Women: Accommodation, Resistance, Transformation* (Berkeley: University of California Press, 1991); Mary Buckley, ed., *Perestroika and Soviet Women* (Cambridge: Cambridge University Press, 1992).

5. During my trips to Moscow in 1990 and 1991, Russians of both sexes repeatedly singled out Petrushevskaia and Muratova (especially on the basis of her film *The Asthenic Syndrome*) as the most interesting of current artists.

6. Studies analogous to this volume are scheduled for publication in the near future and possibly will appear before *Fruits of Her Plume,* e.g., Jane Costlow, Stephanie Sandler, and Judith Vowles, eds., *Sexuality and the Body in Russian Culture* (Stanford: Stanford University Press); Toby Clyman and Diana Greene, *History of Russian Women's Literature* (Westport, CT: Greenwood). A major bibliography of Russian women writers from the Kievan period to the present also is scheduled to be published in 1993: Marina Ledkovsky, Mary Zirin, Charlotte Rosenthal, eds., *Biobibliography of Russian and Soviet Women Writers* (Westport, CT: Greenwood) (title tentative).

7. I enclose the term in quotation marks not to impugn Mandel'shtam's virtues as a poet but to underscore the fact that Nadezhda Mandel'shtam here was operating within the cultural genre of "great poet's widow."

Fruits of Her Plume

1

BAKHTIN AND WOMEN
A Nontopic with Immense Implications

Caryl Emerson

I should begin by explaining the irreverent and sassy title. Why a *non*topic? Because Bakhtin himself, in his voluminous writings stretching over half a century, had almost nothing to say about the currently fashionable liberationist triad: race, class, gender. This fact has greatly reassured Bakhtin's demarxified disciples in the former Soviet Union, who are bitterly aware that "thinking in group categories" has brought their country to the brink of moral and economic disaster. To that issue I shall return, for in general one of the most peculiar aspects of recent years has been the spectacle of literary scholars in the formerly communist East emulating what is conservative in the West, while Western academic critics lap up what has been thoroughly discredited in the East. It is sufficient to note that "gender consciousness" is not part of Bakhtin's legacy.

How might this absence be explained? The matter has puzzled many feminists. One critic admits: "It is a paradox indeed that the great thinker of alterity, whose whole philosophical project argues for respect for the Other, seems to have removed from sight (and mind) the Other par excellence: woman and the feminine" (Hajdukowski-Ahmed 153). Is it possible that Mikhail Bakhtin, apostle of difference, passed over in silence what many people today consider to be the most fundamental difference of all between one person and another? There are, it seems, several ways one might account for this perceived lack in Bakhtin, and let me run through them quickly.

First, there is always the Freudian possibility of repression—
the argument that *not* seeing something is in fact the clearest
evidence that it really exists, deeply matters, and for that reason
has been stowed away out of sight, where it does its dangerous
work out of the reach of consciousness. But somehow Bakhtin
does not lend himself to psychoanalytic manipulation. He is too
genial, too sloppy and generous in his thought; he carries too
much around on his sleeve, and he gives no indication, in his life
or in his works, of any special investment in guilt.

Second, there is the argument of tact and good taste. With the
exception of a few passages dealing with the body in the early
writings[1] and many matter-of-fact discussions of body processes
in the Rabelais book (in both places the tone is stultifyingly
academic), Bakhtin fully partakes of the Russian critical tradition
of bashfulness and reticence in print toward intimate matters,
such as sexuality and private life. As anyone who has translated
Bakhtin knows, much inspiration is to be had in those pages—but
"the pleasure of the text" is not. This well-developed sense of
propriety and privacy in written discourse is borne out by the
scant evidence we have of Bakhtin's behavior with others: he
was formal, correct, somewhat aloof even with devoted students
of long standing, such as the Mirkina sister; he avoided the telephone and wrote almost no letters, and those letters that do survive are largely businesslike appeals for work or reports on his
health. And he never turned—one cannot imagine him turning—
his own close and indispensable half-century of marriage into a
memoir.[2]

Then there is the argument of indifference. The gender issue
might not have been visible to Bakhtin because he took it so
totally for granted: equal rights for women had been, after all, a
major rallying cry of the Russian intelligentsia ever since the
1850s, and subsequently became an important platform in the
Bolshevik program. To be sure, Russian women enjoy the double
burden of women the world over—that is, childbearing frequently combined with work outside the home, domestic indis-
pensability combined with political invisibility, psychological

and biological needs often not satisfied in institutions created with men in power. Nevertheless, the case could be made that whatever her inferior status, Russian woman culturally has a superiority complex: a self-image rooted in shapeless, immortal Mother Earth, a sense of herself as a person who presumes strength and autonomy even under the most adverse conditions, who does not expect help, who is willing to endure; in short, an image of Russian woman as savior, survivor, and arbiter of the mess left by generations of "superfluous men." Something like this argument was made by Tat´iana Tolstaia in her defense of the recent controversial bestseller on Russian women by Francine du Plessix Gray (Tolstaya 3–7).

There is a fourth possible reason for the absence of gender consciousness in Bakhtin's work. In Bakhtin's world, things are either *dan,* "given" to us ready-made, or *zadan,* "posited" by us as a project requiring time and work. Writing a novel, learning a language, and getting through the day are examples of projects. Codes, dialectics, Aristotelian poetics, and one's class origins are givens. Gender identity, I am afraid, is also a given. And for Bakhtin, it was the differences that you worked at, not the differences you were born with or born into, that mattered most. It follows that you can best work at difference, at becoming what only you can become, not by stressing solidarity with others with the same givens as you but by doing quite the opposite, by continually differentiating your own ever-changing and radically individual potential. These convictions, so central to Bakhtin's passionately centrifugal thought, would seem to argue against any a priori assumptions of superiority by a group on the grounds of its subjection (or, for that matter, on any other grounds) and against "liberation movements" on behalf of women *as* women.[3]

There are two more possible approaches to the question. The first would dismiss the above options of repression, tact, indifference, and the given/posited distinction, claiming that there *is* gender bias in Bakhtin's writings, and it is directed against women. Often this argument is mounted on little but the thin ground of translation convention.[4] The translators of the volume titled *The Dialogic Imagination,* for instance, chose to use the male referent throughout, although Russian (like French and German) has a more or less unmarked third-person pronoun that implies no gendered image at all—as indeed English did not before the new sensitivities conquered the field. But more substantial complaints of sexist content have been raised as well. Most have to do with Bakhtin's treatment of carnival laughter, his broad tolerance of its promiscuous imagery, and his seeming indifference to sexually offensive behavior in print. The most famous objection along these lines is by Wayne Booth, who back in 1982 took Rabelais to task for sexism and Bakhtin to task for his "antifeminist" position toward it.[5] But for all the troubled sincerity of Booth's confession, and for all the manifest unattractiveness of Rabelais's bad taste and old-boy tone, a close look at Bakhtin's book suggests that the charge is unfair. According to Bakhtin, the popular tradition that inspired Rabelais was not at all hostile toward women. Quite the contrary: woman was seen as the source of all flow and change, the bodily grave of the unbendingly severe medieval Gallic man. Only when that image was impoverished and trivialized in later eras did it become sensual and base; it was, as Bakhtin argued (rightly or wrongly), "the new, narrow conception" of sexuality, described with the "moralizing and scholastic humanist philosophy" of the sixteenth century, that reduced women to a negative image (*Rabelais* 240–41).

Best, then, that we agree with the feminist critic Nancy Glazener, who opens her essay on Bakhtin and Gertrude Stein with the admission that "Bakhtin's work is not markedly feminist: he wrote mainly about canonical male authors, flirted with *auteur* theories of literary creation, and was conspicuously silent about feminism and the social effects of gender difference" (109). Except for the downputting aside about Bakhtin's "flirting with *auteur* theories of literary creation"—theories of the creative process being perhaps the single greatest contribution of Bakhtin's lifework—Glazener is absolutely correct. Although Bakhtin spoke quite eloquently against other -isms (Marxism,

Freudianism, Formalism, structuralism), he was indeed conspicuously silent about feminism.

But then Glazener goes on to say that Bakhtin's work "appears to be hospitable to the inclusion of gender as an additional significant social and discursive category" (109). Here is our sixth and final approach to the problem, and one that seems to open the door. Bakhtin overtly opposed most of the "group thinking" that characterized his desperately overly politicized age, but he is not, at least, on record as an opponent of gendered thinking (that isn't much of an endorsement, but it's a start). And many people would argue that in any case strong and original thinkers do not and should not control the use that others make of their thoughts. If Bakhtin's categories now appeal to new generations in different ways, this can only be cause for rejoicing.

To a certain point I agree with that reasoning. A bold and imaginative extension of someone else's thought is fully appropriate if it is acknowledged as such. But transforming a theoretician's ideas in the process of applying them does not release critics from the obligation to read texts carefully, nor does it empower them to draw any inferences whatsoever from any imaginable source. Nor should the new reading go violently against the grain of the original in whose spirit it claims to be cast. And it is my feeling that some feminist readings inspired by Bakhtin do overstep these boundaries, even as others have opened up responsible dialogue.

In the remainder of this essay, then, I will address some of the strengths, weaknesses, and pitfalls—as I see them—of applying Bakhtin to gender criticism, using recent work known to me. (I hasten to add that I am not widely or well versed in feminist theory or practice; my interest is that of an amateur, and my expertise comes entirely on the Bakhtin end of things.) I shall then offer a few comments on why it is so difficult and dangerous to politicize and radicalize Bakhtin—as is widely done in the West, and is rapidly being *und*one in Bakhtin's homeland.

The sample essays upon which I draw come from three collections published between 1989 and 1990: one is an anthology edited by American and British leftists, *Bakhtin and Cultural Theory;* the other two are special Bakhtin issues of the Amsterdam journal *Critical Studies.* As one of the contributors points out in a helpful survey of the literature, feminist readings take almost all of their Bakhtin from a few works of the middle period: the long essay "Discourse in the Novel," the much shorter "Epic and the Novel," and the reworked dissertation, *Rabelais and His World* (Thomson 143–44). The most "decentered" texts in the Bakhtin canon, these works do indeed lend themselves to theories of subversion, leakage, antitradition, collectivity, body talk, cycles of reproductivity, and the fertile life at the margins. Feminist readings also make occasional mention of the book on Dostoevskii, and of the Marxist and anti-Freudian works written by Bakhtin's associates. The early and late Bakhtin is almost never touched. This pattern of usage yields a somewhat skewed and pinched picture of Bakhtin—but the image is nevertheless there, and worth discussing.

Feminists who use Bakhtin's ideas tend to begin by celebrating his work. For much appeals intuitively: Bakhtin's obsession with open and receptive orifices, with the novel as an inherently subversive force, and his passion for undermining stable structures through the antics of such marginal figures as rogues, clowns, fools. The best among the feminists, however, celebrate these ideas with an increasingly uneasy conscience. For when they mobilize this subversive energy directly on behalf of a nominally oppressed group or "voice"—say, woman's voice—their readings end up with many more problems than celebrations. The stumbling blocks are two: first, the peculiarly apolitical, playful and impersonal utopianism of Bakhtin's carnival phase, and second, his inexhaustible good humor and benevolence. Bakhtin simply refuses to take offense. (It is for this reason, I note in passing, that Bakhtin, despite all his rhetoric about the lower bodily stratum, folk culture, and popular laughter, remains an aristocratically distanced stoic: he cannot be insulted.) The carnival he advocates really does go both ways, mocking all presumptions to privilege, holding no grudge. And we probably all agree that without some mechanism for gathering and retaining power, without some minimal investment in the individual's willingness to register an insult, it is difficult to get an effective politics out of all of Bakhtin's inversions, guffaws, decrownings, decenterings, and heteroglossia.

A good example of the problems this can cause is Dale Bauer's book *Feminist Dialogics: A Theory of Failed Community* (1988). "My first reaction to Bakhtin was to become seduced by his theory of dialogism," Bauer writes (5). But she soon realized that "Bakhtin's blind spot is the battle." To be used at all for liberationist goals, he had to be radically revised. The revision is a hair's-breadth away from rejection. In her Preface, Bauer correctly notes that "Bakhtin's model [of an active dialogic community] relies on a positive space, a community he celebrates because of its activity, its engagement of others. By adding a feminist turn to it, the dialogic community becomes a much more ambivalent territory. . . often the site of repression, subversion, marginalization, and suicide" (xiv).

Here the "feminist turn" must come face to face with the maddeningly imprecise politics of Bakhtin's carnival world—a world governed not by politics at all, but rather by a utopian antipolitics, a world where "repression, subversion, marginalization, and suicide" are simply laughed away. This disappearing act can happen, of course, because carnival doesn't contain any real bodies that hurt. Seeking some accommodation for the hurting female body, Bauer tries to "intersect [Bakhtin's] celebration of carnivalized language with the language of sexual difference." But she is honest enough to admit that in doing so, one sacrifices most of the spirit of carnival. She searches for ways to turn Bakhtin's heteroglossia and double-voicedness into responsible political dissent, but is left with such ultimately unsatisfactory, nonproductive categories as women's "inarticulation" and "silence." Bakhtin himself, we might note, rarely worried about people's not being able to talk—although he occasionally did worry that people would not be able to hear.

A more recent account of Bakhtin's contributions to feminism, by Myriam Diaz-Diocaretz, takes a more philosophical approach to the subject. But it too founders, albeit on the shoals of a different problem. The problem here comes not with the absence of a serious politics in Bakhtin—although that is a genuine problem—but rather with the logic of her feminist analogies. Diaz-Diocaretz notes, and properly, that Bakhtin and his associates were against Saussurean binaries and linguistic determinism. But then she makes the altogether arbitrary and sexist assumption that "Saussurean binaries, linguistic determinism and the fetishism of rationality" are "patriarchal structures," an assumption that permits her, as the final leg of her argument, to conclude that "these 'flaws' [are] quite attuned, although from a very different angle, to some of the patriarchal blemishes uncovered by feminist critique" (127). Much can be said against Saussure, determinism, and excessive rationality, but surely one need not invoke gender to say it.

This impulse to "engender" the most gender-neutral matters gets badly in the way of more than one appropriation of Bakhtin. Nancy Glazener, for example, opens her essay on Bakhtin and Gertrude Stein by referring to "individual literary creation" as "patriarchal" (109). She is poorly served by the presumption, and is understandably upset by its inevitable corollary: that many feminist Bakhtinians are left with no nonpatriarchal explanation of women's creativity, except that cache of slippery carnivalesque images gathered together under the label of the "anarchically disruptive, diffusely subversive Other." Such a carnivalized concept of self so neatly annihilates individual personality and its rights to create that it is, as Glazener correctly concludes, "more mystifying than enlightening" (111).

Additional complications arise when the depersonalized, predetermined ideology of gender feminism intersects with some of the more impersonal and predetermined fantasy-constructs of Marxism. Mary O'Connor's "Chronotopes for Women under Capitalism" illustrates some of the theoretical difficulties. O'Connor applauds Bakhtin for uncovering the ideological nature of discourse and for his "insistence on the historical nature of literary texts," which "makes his work valuable for feminist literary scholars" (146); but then she dehistoricizes Bakhtin's quite specifically historical insights in the process of applying them to "woman in Bourgeois time."

She opens with a long excerpt from the chronotope essay, where Bakhtin specifically credits Renaissance writers with freeing the world from transcendental medieval consciousness: "It was necessary to destroy and rebuild the entire false picture of the world"; a "new picture of the world will open up" on the resulting "new matrix of objects," "a world permeated with an internal and authentic necessity." In Bakhtin, these pages are a gloss on Rabelaisian carnival. In O'Connor's decontextualized use of them, they take on the Marxist overtones of a campaign against false consciousness and bourgeois object fetishism, all on behalf of a "necessity" guaranteed—it is assumed—by the proper consciousness. Marx's distinction between use value and exchange value becomes the subtext for Bakhtin's monstrous juxtapositions of Rabelaisian body imagery. There follows an analysis of woman-as-silenced-victim in two contemporary texts of fiction.

This reading is a possible one, although anachronistic and— for those alert to Bakhtin's relative unconcern with economic markers of difference—somewhat counterintuitive. A much sadder aspect of O'Connor's thesis is its predictable slide from the loosest and least responsible Marxist categories (retrofitted here to carnival) into the least creative, Procrustean slotting of woman —where all she can do is despair, destroy, resist. O'Connor claims that to know material objects *not* as fetishes but (much more desirably) as disruptive agents in the present means to struggle against the sort of language "that has organized the world into false relations of hierarchy, domination, repression, exclusion and silencing" (138). To defetishize the world, it appears, can only mean to de-form it. And then that naive giveaway sign of gender feminism, the reflex to insert one's own special, monstrously privileged form into the doughy mass that remains: "A materialist analysis of the world of objects conducted today must have a reading of what is usually repressed: the world of women" (139).

O'Connor acknowledges that Bakhtin ignores "the specificity of women's position in the chronotopes" (139). To her this is not a principled position worthy of investigation, however, but simply a lack that must be made good. And thus the saddest sentence of all in her essay, which bravely makes explicit what so many people merely presume: "Contemporary theory has ruled out the possibility of establishing a new humanist subject that would simply be male and female, and nicely satisfy the requirements of equality and specificity" (146). The degree of helpless conformism and collapse of common sense in that statement makes Bakhtin's early polemics against "theoretism" seem even more urgently relevant.

One final application of Bakhtin will be discussed, an essay in equal parts celebratory and problematic: Clair Wills on carnival, hysteria, and women's texts. Wills begins by expanding on an important idea extracted from a manifestly weak link in Bakhtin's theory of carnival, one that has received considerable attention from Peter Stallybrass and Allon White in *The Politics and Poetics of Transgression*. If popular festive forms are to become "self-conscious" and thus politically effective, Wills notes, they must gain "footlights" and "enter the institution of literature." But such an enabling entry into literature inevitably enfeebles, privatizes, and reduces the carnival impulse. Wills sees one such example of "domesticated carnival" in female hysteria, which she reads as a staged, condensed, reduced remnant of the carnivalesque. Trapped in a single body, hysterical display (along with its sister phenomenon, sorcery) might *aspire* to protest, but in fact triggers only disgust or desire (140). How does a feminist critic seeking in Bakhtin's constructs some affirmation of the creative self break out of this paradox? Wills really has no idea, except to say that Bakhtin's texts provide little help. She complains that Julia Kristeva and other popularizers of Bakhtin's carnival ideas have misled the public on this score.

The frustration that many feminists are now feeling with the concept of carnival is nicely reinforced by a parallel cooling off toward the carnival idea in the former Soviet Union. There, for

obvious reasons, the more anarchic, utopian, and jubilantly collective aspects of Bakhtin's teachings have long since fallen out
of favor. Russian intellectuals, confronted by a political and spiritual void, are currently reading Bakhtin as a rather conservative
thinker. For some time interest has been reviving in prerevolutionary philosophers—especially in religious humanists
such as Vladimir Solov'ev and Nikolai Berdiaev, who by the turn
of the century had tasted Marxism and rejected it. At first gin-
gerly, and then more boldly, Bakhtin has been assimilated to this
neohumanist, non-Bolshevik group.

Thus we arrive at a contrary movement noted at the beginning
of this essay. The "new liberal humanist subject" that Mary
O'Connor claims contemporary theory in the West has "ruled
out" has become the most fervent dream of Russian thinkers
reclaiming their Bakhtin for the postcommunist era. Today, judging from the increasing number of anthologies and lecture series
in Russia devoted to Bakhtin's early writings on ethics, serious
work with Bakhtin's ideas has come to mean applying his philosophical humanism to recuperate, in Russia's stubbornly class-
bound and collective society, the individual human being. As one
contributor to a recent anthology has observed, Bakhtin is valuable today primarily for his emphasis on human singularity over
class interests, for his affirmation of the priority of the individual
human being as the "measure of all things" (Brandt 24). On the
politically correct American campus of the 1990s, where group
identity is rampant, this vision of Bakhtin has an undeniably
musty and cranky feel to it.

Let me close with an illustration of women and carnival as the
topic is now being treated by Russian Bakhtinians. In 1990 the
first issue of a new periodical, *Bakhtinskii sbornik,* or the
Bakhtinian Anthology, was published in Moscow (Kujundzic and
Makhlin, 127 pp.). Among the issue's most probing essays is one
titled "Bodies of Terror," which takes as its starting point
Bakhtin's ostensibly joyous book on Rabelaisian carnival.[6] Its
author, Mikhail Ryklin, reads Bakhtin's whole folklore-carnival
idea as the product of a complex trauma. In writing about

Rabelais during the Stalinist terror, Bakhtin, Ryklin argues, was writing a liturgy and a "requiem" for the individual body. Your body, my body became incidental, replaceable, invisible, synthetic, mute—and in its place the collective body of the people was granted all the reproductive and rhetorical rights. *It* became the collective guardian of the word. But what is this "body of the people" in Bakhtin? You cannot actually see it, says Ryklin; "so brilliant and threatening is it in its primeval simplicity that it strikes blind anyone who dares glance at it" (63).

This eerie intimation of Medusa is then extended to the iconography of Stalinism—which was quite aggressively visible, and which did its share of ritual (and other) blinding. Ryklin analyzes the heroic and degraded image of "the people" as portrayed on the extravagantly kitsch marble-and-gold murals of Moscow subway stations built in the 1930s: ahistorical panoramas of victorious battles and buxom peasants feasting or bringing in the harvest (66–71). He treats the Moscow subway as a sort of folkloric pornography—pornography because, in transferring a rural myth to an urban setting during a time of famine, it portrays *collective* fantasy in such a way that live individual bodies in the basements of the city are deprived of actual everyday potential and made hopelessly ineffective in the real world.[7] The Russian folk pours into the cities and sacrifices itself. Intellectuals might have been "town criers" and guides in this process, but they had lost the independence necessary for the task; thus the only organizing principle left to society was utopia (64). The people's invisibility and faith in utopia were essential for the "ecstasy of Terror" to work. In this chilling piece of literary criticism—which may or may not have uncovered Bakhtin's real intention in writing on Rabelais—we see a very different side of Bakhtin's carnival mystique.[8]

The Bakhtin one increasingly sees in Russian contexts, then, is no apostle of carnival and certainly not of trend-setting literary theory. He is being read, rather, as an old-fashioned "philosopher of life" with roots in the pre-Romantics, a disputant with Kant and Henri Bergson rather than a Marxist or semiotician in any twentieth-century sense of the word. To contemporary Russians, Bakhtin now seems to matter not as a revolutionary or radical destabilizer but as a bridge to their own deeply felt but long-suppressed religious humanism.

Let me now summarize my impressions of the problems that come with attempts to "engender" and politicize Bakhtin. First, it is well-nigh impossible to get anything like a responsible politics out of Bakhtinian carnival. To the extent that feminist critics desire to mobilize the literary and everyday consciousness of their readers toward purposeful, collective political activity, Bakhtin is an extraordinarily poor guide. Second, in attempting to tie Bakhtin to protest literature and criticism, in spirit they're all wrong. The genial, anaesthetized, destabilizing impulse that Bakhtin celebrates in carnival tolerates almost everything except a rhetoric of victimization and the reflex of taking offense—and for most forms of contemporary protest, being offended is the first step.

A third and final problem has to do with the larger confusion over what Bakhtin believed literature should do. What was its proper relationship to power and to societal change? How do novels—Bakhtin's favorite genre—contribute to consolidating (or perhaps to undermining) the cultures and languages within which they are written? In short, does Bakhtin's thought have anything like a politics? I suggest that it does—but of a rather unusual sort.

A good place to start is with a comment Bakhtin made near the end of his life, in an open letter on the future of literary studies that was commissioned by the editorial staff of a leading Soviet journal.[9] "Authors and their contemporaries see, recognize and evaluate primarily that which is close to their own day," Bakhtin wrote. "The author is a captive of his epoch, of his own present. Subsequent times liberate him from this captivity, and literary scholarship is called upon to assist in this liberation" ("Reply" 5). Now, liberation is a fighting word, and currently much in vogue. But I propose that Bakhtin's intent of the word is quite different from the radical uses to which it has been put. In fact, it might be the exact opposite. For Bakhtin, "liberation" meant a *suspicion* of the impulse to measure all of past culture by the social or political standards of the present day. To reduce the products of world culture to what we happen to feel or believe at the present moment, then, would be to submit (and voluntarily) to become, in Bakhtin's words, "a captive of our own epoch." Releasing us from this captivity is perhaps the most important service that other times—the past, the future—can render us. That, in fact, is what makes novels so precious to Bakhtin: they are devoted to representing the otherness of other times in all its richness and detail. As Gary Saul Morson has argued:

> The novel, unlike the romance [or the epic], eschews all forms of temporal flattening and all types of social abstractness. For Bakhtin, the novel's appeal derives in great measure from its ability to let us experience how other people in quite different circumstances live and think. . . . It follows that forms of reading that impose our own values, that judge people and situations according to the standards of the critics' own time, necessarily "de-novelize" novels, which by their very generic nature implicitly treat current standards as tested, contested, and contestable. But critics of this sort recognize only one temporality, their own. (Morson)[10]

Paradoxically, then, to "liberate authors from their own epochs" need not at all mean to make them immediately politically relevant: much more likely for Bakhtin, it means to liberate them for and into a long tradition that is spread over what he calls "great time." Its standards of measurement are always multiple. Any other treatment of authors and their novels, Bakhtin states in his essay "Epic and Novel," works "as a force modernizing and distorting the uniqueness of that past."[11]

This precaution makes sense if we note the type of novels that Bakhtin really likes. They are indeed "centrifugal"—skeptical, experimental, full of disparate languages in uneasy balance—but equally basic to their genre identity is the continuity they embody and the debates between speaking people that they refuse to conflate, outdate, or close down. As many critics have observed,

Bakhtin's favorite novels are pretty old-fashioned, pre–twentieth-century things. And what makes them old-fashioned, surely, is their insistence upon a locus of experience and point of view in the radically individual human being. *Not,* note, in the "text," and not in the individual as a member of a particular gender, race, or class. These are categories, I repeat, in which Bakhtin evinced almost no interest.

In fact, Bakhtin's greatest contribution in his homeland will be, I predict, to get Russian literature out of its socially insistent, politically saturated space. This task will be accomplished, of course, in quite the opposite spirit and direction from current Western pieties. Bakhtin—and increasingly his fellow literary scholars—simply *know too much* to give credence to such claims as: the ultimate purpose of knowledge is power; imaginative literature is a sort of passive by-product of power relations; group identity is a substitute for individual voice and responsibility. For too long Russian literary critics have felt too keenly, on their own conscience and careers, the results of such a politicizing of culture.

To that familiar, reductive politicization Bakhtin offers a happy and almost simple-minded alternative: Do not be afraid to read a thing in its own time; let it be separate from yourself; put yourself in a learning and not a preaching posture before a cultural artifact. For he never tired of demonstrating that ethical and aesthetic value, to be durable, had to be generated *not* in political programs or calls to immediate action, and not in a reductive judging of past lives by present values, but in those rich, indeterminate contexts that most resemble the plots of great big novels.

Notes

1. See, for example, in Bakhtin's early essay "Author and Hero in Aesthetic Activity" (1919–23), this highly interesting—but hardly erotic—discussion of the sex act (considered as one category of self-other relations, but one that cannot give rise to aesthetic form because of its poorly developed exteriority): "The sexual approach to the body is an absolutely special one. It is incapable of developing on its own any form-shaping, plastic, or pictorial energies; that is, it is incapable of creating a body as an external, finalized, and self-contained artistic definitiveness. Under these conditions the external body of the

other disintegrates, becoming merely one aspect of my inner body; it becomes valuable only in connection with those inner-bodily possibilities—carnal desire, physical pleasure, gratification—that it promises me, and these inner possibilities flood and overwhelm the other's body's stubborn external finalizedness. During a sexual approach to another person's body, my body and the other's body fuse into one flesh, but this single flesh can only be internal" ("Avtor i geroi v esteticheskoi deiatel'nosti," in *Estetika slovesnogo tvorchestva*, 47–48).

2. The absolute solidarity and silence of Bakhtin's marriage has not gone unnoticed. Hajdukowski-Ahmed, for one, has criticized the Clark/Holquist biography for its insufficient, merely derivative attention to Elena Aleksandrovna's contribution to her husband's writing style, themes and very survival (154–56).

3. Thus I hazard the guess that Bakhtin would have welcomed the distinction made by Christina Sommers in her debate with orthodox feminists: "I distinguish between the classical liberal feminism to which I and most American women adhere, and the newer feminism whose matron saint is Simone de Beauvoir, and whose contemporary adherents are committed to the doctrine that women are a subjugated class living in an oppressive 'sex/gender system,'" Sommers writes. "The main objective of classical liberals such as Mary Wollstonecraft, Harriet Taylor and John Stuart Mill was: equity for women. The classical feminists are more liberal than feminist: they want for women what they want for everyone—freedom from bias, fair treatment, economic justice, civil right." Sommers then notes that "gender feminism," drawing on the nineteenth-century Marxist feminist Friedrich Engels, invented the concept of Woman as *class:* "By substituting 'gender' for 'class,' feminists shifted the moral focus of feminism from the individual and a devotion to her rights, to Woman subjugated within the system of male power, which opened up the present gap between academic feminism and the classical liberal feminism of most American women" (5).

4. When in thrall to sufficiently rigid gender determinism, the faultfinding can become quite ornate. See, for example, Hajdukowski-Ahmed (159–61), who in several pages of astonishing silliness takes to task Bakhtin's Russian-to-French translators (most of them women) for failing to accentuate what she perceives as the "maternal feminine" in his work, a quality that she nevertheless claims "permeates . . . [the] translations" (158). She hints darkly that the translations tend to be done by women, whereas men provide the introductions and forewords.

5. The essay was first published in *Critical Inquiry* 9 (September 1982).

6. For a translation of this essay by the daughter-and-father team of Molly W. Wesling and Donald Wesling, with a preface by Emerson, see *New Literary History*, 24 (1992): 51–74, 45–49.

7. As regards the image of women's bodies in the Moscow subway, Ryklin gives us one paragraph that, in the context of the present essay, is worth quoting in full: "In the Metro we see radically incomplete bodies, which need many metaphorical ligatures to keep them alive. One of the most productive of these visual ligatures on the metaphorical plane is Woman, who is always

located at the very epicenter of rejoicing and on the periphery of Terror. A metaphor for the intuitive, natural principle, she celebrates a modest triumph both in a world of total intuition and simultaneously in the most derealized of all possible industrial worlds. The infantilized male falls under her maternal care. He senses a deficit of the natural, is constantly refilled by Woman, and thus over and over again is revealed in all his emptiness. (It is no accident that in the Metro the very rare instance of a panoramic, distanced field of vision is linked precisely with Woman. I have in mind the mosaic panel at Avtozavod- skaia station, where Woman occupies the position of panoptic observation: the objects she beholds are males, working in a smelting shop.) In general, what is linked with Woman is the hope for a synthesis of fertility, which evokes rejoicing, with labor, which inflicts a joyless death" (69).

8. In an incisive piece of literary commentary, Ryklin analyzes the short stories of Iurii Mamleev, master of the sexual and necrophiliac grotesque, as exemplars of "the impossibility of collective bodies." "In Mamleev's world there is no 'glance' at all," Ryklin writes. "People 'look' there with any organ you like (primarily with their backsides), only not with their eyes; what we get is the remarkable phenomenon of 'anal vision' " (73).

9. The actual question put to Bakhtin was: "How do I evaluate the present state of literary studies?"

10. The anthology in which the essay appears will be published later this year by Northwestern University Press.

11. The phrase in context is as follows: "The depiction of a past in the novel in no sense presumes the modernization of this past. . . . On the contrary, only in the novel have we the possibility of an authentically objective portrayal of the past as the past. Contemporary reality with its new experiences is re- tained as a way of seeing, it has the depth, sharpness, breadth and vividness peculiar to that way of seeing, but it should not in any way penetrate into the already portrayed content of the past, as a force modernizing and distorting the uniqueness of that past. After all, every great and serious contemporaneity requires an authentic profile of the past, an authentic other language from another time" (29–30). Read against current attempts to expose sexism in Shakespeare and racism in Melville, this advice is sobering. Bakhtin would find oddly self-defeating the idea that wisdom in our time could be benefited by a confusion and conflation of our transitory, present-day values with the rich variety of values and times offered us by the past.

References

Bakhtin, Mikhail. "Epic and Novel." In *The Dialogic Imagination,* ed. Michael Holquist, trans. Caryl Emerson and Michael Holquist. Austin: University of Texas Press, 1981.

———. *Estetika slovesnogo tvorchestva.* Moscow: Iskusstvo, 1979.

———. *Rabelais and His World.* Bloomington, IN: Indiana University Press, 1986.

————. "Reply to a Question from the *Novyi mir* Editorial Staff." (1970.) In *Speech Genres and Other Late Essays*, trans. Vern W. McGee, 5. Austin, TX: University of Texas Press, 1986.

Bauer, Dale M. *Feminist Dialogics: A Theory of Failed Community.* Albany, NY: State University of New York Press, 1988.

Booth, Wayne C. "Freedom of Interpretation: Bakhtin and the Challenge of Feminist Criticism." In *Bakhtin: Essays and Dialogues on His Work*, ed. Gary Saul Morson, 145–76. Chicago, IL: University of Chicago Press, 1986.

Brandt, G.A. (Sverdlovsk). "Eticheskaia dominanta kul'tury v filosofii M. Bakhtina." In *Estetika M.M. Bakhtina i sovremennost'.* Saransk: Mordovskii gosudarstvennyi universitet, 1989.

Diaz-Diocaretz, Myriam. "Bakhtin, Discourse, and Feminist Theories." In *The Bakhtin Circle Today*, ed. Myriam Diaz-Diocaretz. *Critical Studies* 1, no. 2 (1989): 122–39.

Glazener, Nancy. "Dialogic Subversion: Bakhtin, the Novel and Gertrude Stein." In *Bakhtin and Cultural Theory*, ed. Ken Hirschkop and David Shepherd, 109–29. New York: St. Martin's Press, 1989.

Hajdukowski-Ahmed, Maroussia. "Bakhtin and Feminism: Two Solitudes?" *Critical Studies* 2, nos. 1/2 (1990): 153–63.

Kujundzic, D., and Makhlin, V.L., eds. *Bakhtinskii sbornik* 1. Moscow: Moskovskii gosudarstvennyi pedagogicheskii institut im. Lenina, 1990.

Morson, Gary Saul. "For the Time Being: Sideshadowing, Criticism, and the Russian Counter-Tradition." In *After Poststructuralism: Interdisciplinary and Literary Studies*, ed. Nancy Easterlin and Barbara Riebling. Evanston, IL: Northwestern University Press, 1993.

O'Connor, Mary. "Chronotopes for Women under Capitalism: An Investigation into the Relation of Women to Objects." In *Mikhail Bakhtin and the Epistemology of Discourse*, ed. Myriam Diaz-Diocaretz. *Critical Studies* 2, nos. 1/2 (1990): 137–51.

Ryklin, Mikhail. "Tela terrora (Tezisy k logike nasiliia)." In *Bakhtinskii sbornik* 1 (1990): 60–76.

Sommers, Christina. "Argumentum ad Feminam." *Journal of Social Philosophy* 22 (Spring 1991): 5–20.

Thomson, Olive. "Mikhail Bakhtin and Contemporary Anglo-American Feminist Theory." In *The Bakhtin Circle Today*, ed. Myriam Diaz-Diocaretz. *Critical Studies* 1, no. 2 (1989): 141–61.

Tolstaya, Tatyana. "Notes from Underground." Review of Francine Du Plessix Gray, *Soviet Women: Walking the Tightrope. New York Review of Books*, May 31, 1990, 3–7.

Wills, Clair. "Upsetting the Public: Carnival, Hysteria, and Women's Texts." In *Bakhtin and Cultural Theory*, ed. Ken Hirschkop and David Shepherd, 131–51. New York: St. Martin's Press, 1989.

2

BAKHTIN'S CONCEPT OF THE GROTESQUE AND THE ART OF PETRUSHEVSKAIA AND TOLSTAIA

Natal'ia Ivanova

Exaggeration, excess, and surplus are generally regarded as characteristic of the grotesque. According to Mikhail Bakhtin, a basic feature of the authentic grotesque is ambivalence, which expresses the two-sided fullness of life, embracing negation and destruction (the death of the old) as an essential component inseparable from affirmation (the birth of the new). What constitutes the grotesque is metaphorically summed up in two passages from Liudmila Petrushevskaia's story "Poetry in Life": "Help me, girl, my mother had an operation today for breast cancer, take a walk with me" (Devushka, pomogite mne, moei mame segodnia sdelali operatsiiu rak grudi, poguliaite so mnoi).[1] The next thing we know, that very mother after the operation and the same girl are spending the night in the same room: "Bed to bed, one could say, that stubborn battle of two loving hearts was taking place" (26). Death and copulation, the end of one life and the beginning of another, fear and laughter all coexist in the grotesque.

According to Bakhtin, the internal logic of the grotesque is that of "fertility, growth, and a brimming-over abundance."[2] The grotesque preserves the special celebratory character of the material bodily principle. No abstract tendency penetrates its imagery. Laughter within the grotesque has not an entertaining but a metaphysical significance; it is one of the most fundamental forms of truth about the world as a whole.

In Russian literature of the Soviet period the grotesque developed outside of official ideology and literature. Totalitarian ideology proscribed the grotesque, the hyperbolic, and the fantastic. All forms of laughter were persecuted except those that degraded. The writings of Mikhail Zoshchenko, for example, were subjected to devastating ideological attack. The publication of Mikhail Bulgakov's and Andrei Platonov's best works was prohibited. Excluded wholesale from officially sanctioned literature, the fantastic and grotesque went underground. It is no coincidence that Andrei Siniavskii and Iulii Daniel' were tried and sentenced to imprisonment for precisely their fantastic and grotesque works.

In the sociocentric view of man and his place in society and history that was imposed upon Soviet literati, a literary character was a function of impersonal processes. Literature was subject to legal formulas that ignored the distinctive features of artistic concepts. In response to a criticism of his excessive allegories, Siniavskii at his trial said: "As a writer I find fantastic realism, with its hyperbole and grotesque, congenial. I'd say some of the works of Gogol', Chagall, Maiakovskii, and Hoffmann belong to fantastic realism." Among the names cited by Siniavskii one should include that of their great predecessor, François Rabelais.

The drama of the Siniavskii-Daniel' trial took place in February 1966. They were arrested in 1965—by an ironic stroke of history, the same year that witnessed the publication of Mikhail Bakhtin's fundamental work on Rabelais, which elaborated his theory of laughter and in particular of the grotesque. It so happens that Liudmila Petrushevskaia's artistic method also took shape in the mid-1960s—a method whose salient features are the grotesque, hyperbole, and the fantastic. In 1988 Siniavskii would call that mode of writing "exaggerated prose."

Socialist realism calls above all for rigid hierarchical thinking. In practice, it requires a fundamentally immovable vertical line directed into the future, the primacy of a goal, the focus on a positive hero with the correct professional markings, and the complete exclusion of the female principle as such. Female characters are castrated, their "femininity" reduced to a minimum. Within the canon, pronounced femininity in a heroine, in fact, signaled her identity as a "negative" character.

Works with more lifelike women, less wooden and masculinized, made their appearance only toward the end of the Khrushchev era. A vast body of uncensored realistic literature could not be published at that time, and became accessible to the general Russian reader only at the end of the 1980s. Documentary "camp" prose by women, which for two decades was suppressed for obvious ideological reasons, occupies a special place in this backlog of texts.

Liudmila Petrushevskaia's works belong to this "unprintable" category. Her first story to be published, "The Overlook," came out in *Friendship of Nations* (*Druzhba narodov*) only in 1980.[3] Collections of her prose circulated, unpublished, among various editorial boards in Moscow for fifteen years. A similar fate met her plays, now so widely produced but for almost two decades rejected by one Moscow theater after another. Only amateur studio theaters dared to stage her drama in the 1970s.

Tat'iana Tolstaia fared better solely because she belonged to a different generation. Having embarked on a writing career in the early 1980s, she succeeded in getting her first collection published by 1987.

The two writers have much in common as regards their artistic method: what unites them, I believe, is precisely the grotesque, which official Soviet censorship found unacceptable less for ideological than for aesthetic reasons.

By the middle of the 1960s literature produced by women occupied a recognizable generic slot—that of the physiological sketch. The most significant text in this corpus was Natal'ia Baranskaia's *A Week Like Any Other* (*Nedelia kak nedelia*) (discussed by Thomas Lahusen in Chapter 10 of this volume). The author described a week in the life of a typical urban woman— day by day, hour by hour. Baranskaia's novella popularized the term "everyday life" (*byt*), while the author was accused of presenting a humbly low view of Soviet life. Petrushevskaia took the same material as Baranskaia but viewed it from an existentialist perspective.

Quotidian Soviet life viewed through an existentialist lens gives birth to what Bakhtin called "the subjective grotesque." The author's attention is concentrated not on the depressing, endless aspects of everyday life, which include housework and raising children (this is only the background of events), but on the intersection of the dreary daily routine with love, sickness, pregnancy, and death. The subjective grotesque yokes ultimate despair with existentialist hope. At the same time, it is organically linked to a sense of the joyousness of life, its inexhaustible bounties, its fabulous, fairy-tale magic. It is no wonder that Petrushevskaia called one of her best scenarios "The Fairy Tale of Fairy Tales," and her first volume of prose "Immortal Love." Or that in Tolstaia's story "Sleepwalker in a Fog" the hero is locked overnight in a restaurant called Fairy Tale, where all kinds of fantastic plots figure in his dreams. The boots with gold cuffs that belong to Lora, the story's heroine (elsewhere their cuffs are called "pale toadstools"),[4] are obviously of fairy-tale origin. The old woman in the hut to which Lora brings her father derives from the sorceress of fairy tales and, moreover, tries to heal him with incantations.

Likewise originating in the fairy-tale genre is the symbiosis of human and animal in the story's personae. Lora, for instance, wishes for a "thick fluffy tail, possibly striped." Her mad father is a zoologist, preoccupied with the problem of birds' kinship to reptiles and crocodiles, toads, cocks, and elephants. Denisov, the story's protagonist, yearns to be transformed into a bear: "Oh, to crawl into a cave like a bear, to burrow into the snow, close your eyes tight, grow deaf, depart into sleep, pass through the dead city along the fortress wall." Ladies' legs turn into "silver tails and patent-leather hoofs."[5] Everything, in other words, comes from a fairy-tale or has connections with it.

According to Bakhtin, the chief features of the grotesque are a limitless freedom based on carnival "truth"—a special kind of freedom of thought and imagination; the destruction of official

solemnity and official bans. Death thus becomes an indispensable part of life, as a prerequisite for its constant renewal and
rejuvenation: "Death [. . .] is always related to birth; the grave,
to the life-giving womb of the earth." In Bakhtin's scheme of
things, "there is never a corpse" at the height of grotesque realism, for new life always sprouts from it. By contrast, official
Soviet literature—the most solemn in the world—feared,
shunned, and avoided death. The grotesque in Petrushevskaia's
and Tolstaia's fiction destroys this solemnly pompous, bombastic
depiction of the world. And destruction begins with alienation,
with the ability to look at this world, as Gogol' put it, "with fresh
eyes."

In her story "Fakir," Tolstaia presents a surrealistic, grotesque
visual model of the concept of totalitarian art. Its symbol is the
high-rise apartment building in Insurrection Square.

> Filin's tower nestled in the middle of the capital, a pink mountain,
> ornamented here and there in the most varied way—with all sorts of
> architectural doodads, thingamajigs, and whatnots: there were towers
> on the socles, crenels on the towers, and ribbons and wreaths be-
> tween the crenellations, and out of the laurel garlands peeked a book,
> the source of knowledge, or a compass stuck out its pedagogic leg;
> or, if you looked, you'd see a puffy obelisk in the middle, and stand-
> ing firmly on it, embracing a sheaf, a firm plaster woman with a
> clear gaze that rebuffs storms and night, with flawless braids and an
> innocent chin. . . . You kept expecting trumpets to sound any mo-
> ment and drums to play something governmental and heroic.[6]

This frozen hierarchic structure is hardly sound—it is no accident that Tolstaia notes here the "black holes" of its ground floor
and the "abyss of darkness" encircling Moscow, on whose outskirts live the poor protagonists, beguiled by the bright lights of
the false facade, false comfort, and false "owner" (*khoziain*) of
the apartment in the building.

From the height of the high-rise apartment house windows the
city "glowed in wreaths of golden street lamps, frosty rainbow
rings, multicolored crunchy snow" (165), while in the apartment

presides the pseudo-owner in a raspberry robe and Oriental slippers, a dwarf king who is clearly a carnival figure. Later we see him in a completely different guise, fallen from the false heights to the underground of the Moscow subway, where he, whose unusualness had so appealed to the heroine, now "walked like an ordinary man; his small feet, accustomed to polished parquet, spoiled by velvet slippers, stepped on the spittle-covered bathroom tiles of the passageway" (174).

Tolstaia inverts the situation, the hero, and the surroundings, reversing top and bottom, so that the hero's image is degraded from that of an inaccessible romantic heartbreaker and ladies' man to the most common ordinary fellow. Now she emphasizes the insignificance of his physical appearance: "[His] small fist rummaged in pockets, located a handkerchief, hit his nose—boof! boof!—and back in the pocket; then he shook himself like a dog, adjusted his scarf" (174). The hero and his surroundings are directly subjected to the divestment (decrowning) characteristic of the grotesque. The mysterious archway of the apartment is parodied in the "archway with faded gold mosaics" under which he disappears from the heroine's view in the metro. The description of his evening party likewise parodies the Last Supper: we have the breaking of bread, unusual drinks, a clean tablecloth, lit candles, and the "chosen" guests, specially invited so that the "fool-king" can preach his sermon to them (that is, tell his jokes and grotesquely fantastic tales).

The hero's surname, Filin, denotes a bird (eagle owl), and one of his stories tells of a ballerina named Sobakina (dog) whose two marriages changed her name first to Koshkina (cat) and then to Myshkina (mouse). Valtasarov (Balthazar), one of the occasional guests, knows how to imitate animal calls, and the wolf on the city's periphery emerges on a hill just like a human being, "in a rough wool coat," its "teeth gritted in sadness, and a cold tear hangs like a stinking bead on his furry cheek" (167). The grotesque symbiosis of human and animal reticulates throughout the story, which travesties the sacred vertical axis, with its immutable top and bottom, combining it with the grotesque circular horizontal axis ("the boundary road, an abyss of darkness marked by doubled red lights," even "the invisible sky slipped down, resting its heavy edge on a beet field," "the thick darkness extended farther, over the fields that blended into a wild roar," "over trees pressed into the cold earth" [166–67]).

Each of the protagonists in the story may legitimately be called, in Bakhtin's term, "carnival effigies," whose distinguishing features are "comic pretentiousness" and a liking for "degrading junk," which clutter their carnival "paradise" and their carnival "hell." The pseudo-paradise of Filin's high-rise tower proves in fact to be a utopian kingdom of material-bodily abundance and excess (the incredibly flaky *pirozhki*—the last on earth, for the recipe disappears forever; the Wedgwood china, which literally descends from the sky, etc.). That kingdom vanishes without a trace in the grim light of reality. The grotesque here is Tolstaia's bitter mockery of the instilled hierarchical model of Soviet life, which purportedly extends from the gloomy, impoverished earth of "according to your work" to the utopian riches of the "skies." That model is completely illusory, "just fireworks in the night, a moment's run of colored zephyrs, the hysteria of fiery roses in the dark over our hair" (178). In sum, as Tolstaia phrases it, "our god is dead and his temple is empty" (178). The dead god turns out to be a "fool-king," a faker who for a while replaced the real God in a deluded mind, and the "empty temple" is the apartment in which the pseudo–Last Supper took place.

Tolstaia's grotesque, then, captures the collapse of the constructed Soviet universe and its corresponding world view, in which a fakir has taken the place of God.[7]

The grotesque in Petrushevskaia's works is of cosmic dimensions. In her short story "Through the Fields" ("Cherez polia"), which I believe serves as a philosophical epigraph to her entire oeuvre, Petrushevskaia turns directly to the cosmic elements as manifest in her characters' bodies and souls. The everyday plot of the story is simple: two young people walk from the railway station to a house where their friends await them. "We had to

walk about four kilometers through a forest and then through a
bare field."[8] The open natural-historical space is analogized with
the path of humankind through life: they walk through "the bare,
absolutely bare, broken earth, the downpour and the lightning"
(235). At one time something had been planted in this earth, but
"as yet nothing had grown" (235). The encounter with nature and
history, with life-death (as Bakhtin puts it), subjects humankind
to the ultimate test. This test reveals the individual's true nature
(essence), about which the civilized twentieth-century person is
highly self-conscious ("at that time any manifestations of my
natural state [essence] embarrassed me and most of all my bare
feet" [236]). The image of the body in Petrushevskaia is dual: it
embraces both woman and man, placed by God in equality vis-à-vis
life and death. At the story's end what awaits them is the "warm
home," with friends seated at the table (the image of the "feast" that
runs throughout Petrushevskaia's oeuvre). The warmth of the food
and drink, of the house and the friends "warms the soul after the
long and difficult path of [. . .] life" (237). The first-person narra-
tor/protagonist realizes that "tomorrow and even today I will be torn
away from the warmth and the light and thrust out again to walk
alone through the clay field in the rain" (237).

Petrushevskaia's heroes and heroines constantly attempt to
enter a house or an apartment, to settle there and "obtain a residence permit." For them a house, an apartment, and a room are
synonyms for salvation, survival. Their life for the most part is
lived on the threshold.[9] A house or home protects them from the
active dangers of open space, fraught with illness, contamination,
and death, a space that threatens one's life and freedom. A house
or apartment in Petrushevskaia is analogous to the human body,
to all the functions, temperature, secretions, ailments, and "orifices" to which Petrushevskaia is especially attentive. A
house/apartment opens up like a human body. This existential
entrance-and-exit aperture is the door that opens onto a staircase
landing, where the protagonist of "Our Crowd" ("Svoi krug")
forces her small son to wait and where the entire action of the play
Staircase Landing (*Lestnichnaia kletka*) takes place. The perso-

nae inhabiting the house/apartment and bumping into each other on the landing are making their journey through life-death.

Petrushevskaia deflates and parodies the euphemism of Soviet literature by depicting the human body and its needs grotesquely and minutely, in every conceivable detail. Soviet literature carefully avoided anything of the sort by portraying disease and death not in physiological but in abstract terms, as the sacrifice of human life in the name of an exalted goal.

The structural principle of Petrushevskaia's grotesque is the ambivalence ("two in one") associated with its formation, the integrated, unified depiction simultaneously of both poles of phenomena and processes: the old and the new, death and birth. In "Our Crowd," for instance, the protagonist, who is gradually growing blind from a kidney disease (only she knows that she will soon die), cruelly beats her little son during the Easter celebration (when all the couples have switched, and her ex-husband has married the former wife of one of the company), saving him by her apparent rejection, for his father, shocked by her violence, takes the boy into his care. The feast of the Last Supper takes place on Easter Sunday, and the protagonist prepares the meal with special care after visiting her mother's grave with her son. The image of death, pregnant with life, reticulates throughout the story: "Alyosha, I think, will visit me [once I am dead—N.I.] on the first day of Easter, that's what I mentally agreed to with him, showing him the way and the day. I think he'll figure it out, he's a very perceptive boy, and there among the painted eggs, among the plastic wreaths and the rumpled, drunken, kind crowd he'll forgive me for not having let him say good-bye, and for hitting him on the face instead of giving him my blessing."[10] A slap in the face instead of a blessing is indeed a carnival gesture in the grotesque world of the story, where a faithful friend, a traitor, an adulteress, a representative of official power (the policeman), and its violator come together to celebrate Easter.

The story's grotesque carnivalization of the world accounts for the constant chain (the circle of the title)[11] of copulation, body secretions (saliva, vomit, mucus, blood, urine, excrement, semen), references to D-cup breasts, a plastic penis, incest, loss of front teeth, baldness, as well as cosmic forces, flying saucers, human values, complete freedom, and the like.

In the story "A Girl Like That" ("Takaia devochka") the focal character is described as "the world's conscience" and "a professional prostitute"—in the same sentence. "To teach the girl how to wipe herself" is virtually tantamount to saving the human race ("Hygiene" ["Gigiena"]). The juxtaposition of the elevated with the grotesque bodily lower stratum ridicules the former and sanctifies the latter.

The middle-aged Pania in the story "Pania's Poor Heart" ("Bednoe serdtse Pani") is sick, is married to an invalid, and has three children. The story's action takes place in a maternity hospital, in the pathology ward for abnormal pregnancies. All of the social, intellectual, and cultural barriers in this world of "moaning women with swollen bellies" are eliminated;[12] there is no hierarchy, all are equal. Pania, who because of her heart could die in childbirth and orphan her three children, wants only one thing—an abortion. Yet the doctor evidently extracts from her old, sick womb a premature angel-faced baby girl the size of an apple. This scene exemplifies Petrushevskaia's dialectic of "the world in reverse," where sickness and death (Pania is called a "murderess") bring forth life.

Petrushevskaia's special mode of depicting the human body differs radically from the "classical" and "naturalistic" method. The grotesque body in her prose is never completed: it is always in the process of formation and it creates other bodies: "it swallows up the world and in turn is swallowed up by it" (Bakhtin). A key role in the grotesque body depicted by Petrushevskaia is played by those parts "that grow and expand beyond their limits," such as the womb, male genitals, breasts, hips, mouth (the intake of food and drink), and the bottom (excrement and urine in "Hygiene"), which eliminate the boundary between the body and the world. In a similar vein is the combination of praise and curses in the dialogue of her plays, as is Petrushevskaia's characteristic device of having men dress in women's clothes and vice versa ("Columbine's Apartment" ["Kvartira Kolombiny"]).

Petrushevskaia's grotesque language deserves special attention. Drawing on the devices of comic folk genres, she creates deliberately nonsensical verbal utterances that grotesquely expand various sounds into words and words into phrases. This re-creation of sounds and the ideas they represent (deduced by us), which are free from any constraints of sense, logic, and linguistic hierarchy, constitutes verbal play in the form of riddles. With the fundamental breakdown in a hierarchical world view and a renewed sense of words and concepts long rendered meaningless in our language, this carnivalization of speech frees us from one-sided gloomy solemnity.

In discussing the affinity between Tolstaia's and Petrushevskaia's works, on the one hand, and Bakhtin's ideas of the grotesque and of laughter, on the other, I am certainly not making a case for Bakhtin's "influence" on them. My point is that we have entered a new era of the liberation of humankind. It may ultimately prove politically unsuccessful, usher in new ideological and economic freezes, and even lead to collapse. Literature, too, has started liberating itself from fear, singing tragic dirges to the shades of those who perished in the most ominous, dreadful catastrophe of the twentieth century—the Soviet experience. But authentic liberation comes only with the flowering of those cultural buds that seemed to have been frozen forever not only by political but also by aesthetic frosts. Bakhtin realized this better than anyone. That is why in his theory of the grotesque he predicted the emergence of such talents as Petrushevskaia and Tolstaia.

Translated by Helena Goscilo

Notes

This chapter was translated from the manuscript version of Ivanova's talk at the conference "Glasnost in Two Cultures," hosted in March 1991 by the Humanities Center, New York University. Since Ivanova follows "Soviet" conventions of criticism—that is, she omits documentation of sources and quoted passages—I have exercised my editorial prerogative by inserting that information wherever I consider it useful. Ivanova is therefore not responsible for any of the notes.

1. L. Petrushevskaia, "Poeziia v zhizni," *Ogonek*, 1990, no. 28, 26. Here and elsewhere, unless another translator is named, the translations are by Helena Goscilo.

2. Mikhail Bakhtin, *Rabelais and His World*, trans. Hélène Iswolsky (Bloomington, IN: Indiana University Press, 1984), 19.

3. This is an error on Ivanova's part, which she did not authorize me to correct in the text. By 1980 five of the many stories Petrushevskaia kept submitting for publication had been printed in journals: "The Storyteller" ("Rasskazchitsa") and "Clarissa's Story" ("Istoriia Klarissy") in *Avrora* (1972); "The Violin" ("Skripka") and "Mania" ("Mania") in *Druzhba narodov* (1973); and "Nets and Traps" ("Seti i lovushki") in *Avrora* (1974).

4. The word in Russian is *poganka*, which means not only "toadstool" but also "heathen" and "unclean," both of which hint at connections with dark, irrational, primal powers.

5. Tatyana Tolstaya, *Sleepwalker in a Fog*, trans. Jamey Gambrell (New York: Knopf, 1991), 14.

6. Tatyana Tolstaya, *On the Golden Porch*, trans. Antonina W. Bouis (New York: Knopf, 1989), 165–66, slightly emended for greater accuracy.

7. For a reading of "Fakir" that coincides with Ivanova's in many specifics, but arrives at markedly different conclusions, see Helena Goscilo, "Perspective in T. Tolstaia's Wonderland of Art," *World Literature Today*, 67, no. 1 (Winter 1993), 80–90.

8. Lyudmila Petrushevskaya, "Through the Fields," trans. Stefani Hoffman, in *The New Soviet Fiction*, ed. Sergei Zalygin (New York: Abbeville, 1989), 235. The translation is emended where necessary for greater accuracy.

9. This is one of the many parallels between Dostoevskii and Petrushevskaia.

10. Lyudmila Petrushevskaya, "Our Crowd," trans. Helena Goscilo, in *Glasnost: An Anthology of Russian Literature under Gorbachev*, ed. Helena Goscilo and Byron Lindsey (Ann Arbor, MI: Ardis, 1990), 24.

11. The Russian title, "Svoi krug," means literally "One's Own Circle."

12. Liudmila Petrushevskaia, "Bednoe serdtse Pani," *Ogonek*, 1990, no. 28, 29.

3

SOVIET RUSSIAN WOMEN'S LITERATURE IN THE EARLY 1980s

Nicholas Žekulin

In the early 1980s the careful reader of *Novye knigi*, the Soviet guide to forthcoming books, might well have remarked on a curious phenomenon: several publishing houses, conspicuously Sovremennik and Sovetskii pisatel', announced plans to issue an unusual number of volumes of collected stories by women. Moreover, in the blurbs that accompanied the announcements (many of them later reappeared as the blurbs in their respective books—every Soviet book had one) several telling phrases recurred with pointed regularity: at the center of the author's concern was the heroine, "our contemporary"; the issues broached in these works "raise the problem of the search by the contemporary woman for her place in life"; furthermore, the "problems that the author raises are very acute, very pertinent."[1]

The appearance of these books was probably not accidental. In the first place, 1979 saw the *samizdat* appearance of a collection put together by a group of Leningrad women under the title *Women and Russia* (*Zhenshchina i Rossiia*) and subtitled *A Miscellany for Women about Women* (*Al'manakh zhenshchinam o zhenshchinakh*). This miscellany was produced by an uneasy alliance of "orthodox" feminists on the one hand and a group of women whose inspiration was primarily religious, and specifically Marian, on the other. The authors of the miscellany came under immediate attack and several were exiled.[2] A number of essays in *Women and Russia* systematically criticized the entire social network that is supposed to help women, on the grounds that it was totally inadequate and frequently downright criminal and dangerous to their health and welfare. The criticism spared neither maternity homes, day care, nor kindergarten, neither pensions nor medical services, and was particularly harsh in regard to abortion clinics, called "slaughterhouses" (Golubeva 58). The central essay, Natal'ia Malakhovskaia's "Maternal Family" ("Materiinskaia sem'ia"), analyzes the history of the division of labor between the sexes and suggests that what was once an equal division based on mortal danger is, with the degeneration of man-the-hunter, now so entirely one-sided that "we see the rise, indeed there has already arisen, a maternal family" (39), a society of women whose only support comes from other women. Certainly Tat'iana Mamonova is convinced of the impact of this small underground publication by a group that the authorities repressed with such alacrity. In exile some years later she wrote:

> The Almanach [sic] *Woman and Russia* forced our authorities to move. . . . There was also a transformation of the official press. Within a year of the emergence of the feminist movement in the Soviet Union, many articles on the question appeared in the official press. Often the articles were purely rhetorical, but the questions were nevertheless raised, and that is the main point. People are now talking about these questions and are forced to think about them. (xxiii)

In all likelihood, a second factor also helped these women writers obtain approval for publication of their collections. There is a striking coincidence between the themes they treat and the official concerns of the day. The appearance of these collections was thus in part a function of their ability to be parasitic, in the sense that they were able to graft themselves onto a mandate that was actively being promoted by Soviet literary policy, charged yet again at the Twenty-sixth Congress of the Communist Party of the Soviet Union (CPSU) in 1981 with fulfilling its function as a moral and ideological educator (Vykhodets 393). At the beginning of the 1980s the major concern was alcoholism; the authors' concern with the impact of drunken husbands on the domestic lives of Soviet women thus coincided with the new campaign against alcoholism as a major disruptive factor in the Soviet economy.[3]

Despite the phenomenon represented by these collections, the question whether one can or ought to speak of "women's literature" as a distinct category has inevitably been raised. In what was the Soviet Union there is a pronounced reluctance to establish such a category, and many prominent Russian women writers, such as Tat'iana Tolstaia, are vociferously opposed to it. Ruth Zernova, an émigrée author, quotes a skeptical Lidiia Chukovskaia: "What does 'women's literature' mean? You can have a women's sauna, but literature?" Zernova herself, however, has no hesitation in arguing for the concept of women's literature and in adopting the most simple definition: "a literature created by women about women" (5). She recalls the legacy of a generation of women, including Nadezhda Mandel'shtam and Evgeniia Ginzburg, who preserved the memory of the bitter experience of the Stalinist period. If their function was to record "the spiritual experience of women" of that difficult age (Zernova 6), more recently other women have taken it upon themselves to transmit a more contemporary but in some instances scarcely less bitter experience.

Philosophical differences of this nature are, of course, a different issue from the neglect that this phenomenon receives. A perusal of the most recent books concerning Soviet literature of the 1980s in general, including authoritative surveys intended for both teachers and postsecondary students, such as *History of Soviet Russian Literature (Istoriia russkoi sovetskoi literatury)*, edited by P.S. Vykhodets, and the two-volume *Contemporary Soviet Russian Literature (Sovremennaia russkaia sovetskaia literatura)*, edited by A.G. Bocharov and G.A. Belaia, shows not only that women authors are not treated as a distinct group (which is at least an arguable proposition) but that individual woman authors are seldom treated at all.[4] There has been no roundtable discussion of women writers, or even a major article in the journal *Problems of Literature* (*Voprosy literatury*). Leading critics have also largely ignored the question, but as Galina Skvortsova has pointed out, the psychological and social positions of the woman in the man-woman relationship is in fact a touchstone issue of contemporary society and the subject of much public discussion by sociologists, psychologists, philosophers, doctors, and, to a degree, writers and therefore critics (106). Critical interest has indeed been displayed in a few instances, but the occasionally caustic titles, such as Iu.I. Sokhriakov's "Feminism, Antifeminism, or 'Courtly' Emancipation" ("Feminizm, antifeminizm ili 'galantereinaia' emansipatsiia") and Leonid Zhukovskii's "Where Have the Real Men Disappeared To?" ("Kuda ischezli nastoiashchie muzhchiny?"), clearly reflect their authors' perception of the dangers, both moral and social, inherent in any radical change in the relationship between the sexes.[5]

Given a commitment to describing the specific experience of Soviet women, it is not surprising that at this stage women's literature should have developed within the phenomenon called *literatura byta,* literature of daily reality. This generally small-scale literature, with its focus on the everyday and the mundane (especially the domestic), carved out a niche for itself within the mainstream of Soviet literature while declining to link the individual with the universal, to resolve personal as well as more general problems, or to comment on ideological or philosophical matters.[6] Consequently, although the short story genre does predominate and first-person (female) narrative is a notable, indeed a dominant, feature, this "women's literature" is characterized or identified more by theme than by style or literary method. It concentrates on the stark reality of the domestic life of the ordinary, primarily urban Soviet woman. The recurring themes, which ultimately come as no surprise, are a reflection of those factors that in practice distinguish the everyday life of Soviet women from that of Soviet men. They are the factors that define, to extend André Malraux's famous phrase, the Soviet *condition féminine* as a specific and distinct category of the *condition humaine,* or, to use a different literary metaphor, that define the species *femina sovietica* within the genus *homo sovieticus*. What is perhaps more surprising is the forthrightness with which these Soviet women writers discuss the reality of their existence. The difference between official and unofficial literature, between fiction and the exposé of *Women and Russia,* is one of degree, not of substance.

I

Any comprehensive history of Russian women's literature in the latter part of the twentieth century will undoubtedly identify Natal'ia Baranskaia's story "A Week Like Any Other" ("Nedelia kak nedelia"), published in November 1969 in the journal *New World* (*Novyi mir*), as one of the principal sources of women's *literatura byta*. Significantly and appropriately, "A Week Like Any Other" was included in Baranskaia's first collection of stories, *The Woman with an Umbrella* (*Zhenshchina s zontikom*), among the first of the collections of stories by women to be published in the early 1980s.[7]

Perhaps the most striking feature of the works in these collections is the extraordinary concentration on domestic chores, a graphic manifestation of the discrepancy in the number of hours worked by men and women as a simple factor of the domestic burden borne by women.[8] A sardonic example is provided by the heroine of "A Week Like Any Other" when she is faced with a questionnaire that requires her to specify her "cultural activities":

> Personally, I'm into sport: running. I run here, I run there, with a bag in each hand and—up and down, from trolley to bus—down the metro—up out of the metro. There are no shops out where we are; we've lived there for over a year and they still haven't finished them. (8)

A woman's frustration over this situation not infrequently leads to a spirited exchange between husband and wife, as in Valentina Sakovets's story "Mushroom Picking" ("Poezdka za gribami"):

"You suggest we go to the movies or to the park, and I have a tub full of laundry or the apartment to tidy. . . ."

"You've always got something, it never stops. . . ."

"So why don't you stop what you're doing when I suggest something? It's always either soccer, or hockey, or 'I got a great schematic, I've got to figure it out.' " (9)

Of course there is no need to go into detail about the daily chasing after essential food items or the fact that up to three hours a day can be spent traveling to and from work on overcrowded public transport.

As might again be expected, inordinate amounts of attention and energy are devoted to the question of an apartment. The variations on this theme are almost endless. Since most of the stories are set in a large city (as often as not, Moscow), one rarely encounters the fervent wish for indoor plumbing expressed by the heroine of Ol'ga Reviakina's "Desdemona's Day" ("Den' Dezdemony" [81]), and even communal apartments with their perennial problems are becoming less and less common. But the new apartments are no guarantee of bliss. The amount of space allotted is always an issue. Many of these apartments are on the periphery of the city, where there are no services, indeed, where there is nothing but "empty streets and bleak, long apartment blocks" (Bashkirova 17). Tat'iana Nabatnikova describes one such modern apartment where the walls are so thin that as the heroine lies in bed she hears her neighbors' alarm clocks, their radios, their showers, and even their breathing (141–42). Besides, it is always difficult to get an apartment unless you have pull. In "That's How They Lived" ("Tak oni i zhili") Sakovets recounts how, after many years of waiting and being passed over, a family consisting of a widowed grandmother, her son and daughter-in-law, and their two daughters is finally assigned a new three-room apartment. Joy and anticipation turn to outrage and dismay when one of the three rooms is then assigned to somebody else. The bureaucrat in charge explains to the elderly woman, equably and in beautiful, logical, and apparently universal bureaucratese:

"We have examined all the optimally operative variants in the allocation of apartments. . . . You can judge for yourself; you have a family that doesn't quarrel, your son doesn't drink, the children" (he glanced at the paper on his desk) "are unisexual, I'm sorry, both girls. Four females in the same family. That's why Smirnova was assigned in with you." (27)

Another constant theme is the upbringing of children in a society where it is not only the norm for both parents to work but in most instances an economic necessity. Problems occur whether or not one has children. What the sociologists who put together the questionnaire in "A Week Like Any Other" refer to as the problem of "insufficient population accretion" is immediately translated into ordinary language by the women in the story as "why women don't want to give birth" (9). The possible reasons suggested in the questionnaire itself are surprisingly straightforward and candid: "medical exigencies, socioeconomic conditions, marital status, personal considerations, etc." (19). The heroine, Olia, personally favors the "etc.," but a quick consideration translates the neutral terminology of the questionnaire into a rather harsh reality. One of her co-workers, for example, is a single mother. Her child is looked after by her mother while she works to support all three of them. The father, an army captain who came to Moscow to study at a military academy, neglected to mention that he already had a wife and children. This woman always wanted to be a dressmaker, not the research scientist she has become, but she was afraid to pursue her interest because, as she says, "Who marries dressmakers these days?" (24). Olia herself is exceptional in two ways. Not only does she have two children rather than just one, but she also has a husband who will occasionally help with both the children and the housework—within reason, of course. But Olia realizes that over the winter she has already missed nearly a third of her working days because of the children's illnesses, and that she is not infrequently late because of other problems with them. Her absenteeism has not gone unnoticed, although so far there have been only gentle warnings. In Reviakina's "Desdemona's Day" the heroine faces the problem of a child with a fever who has already been examined three times by the staff of the medical center. They refuse to make another trip. Finally, leaving the child in the care of a retired neighbor and borrowing from her the five rubles she needs until she gets her pay, she goes to a retired doctor with a sizable private practice who agrees to make a house call that day. Even when a child is well, there are constant problems with the day-care center, including the difficulty of actually getting your child into one; nor do conditions there inspire great confidence. The search for someone to look after preschool children is endless, and the obvious solution of bringing in Granny (when there is a granny) can present its own problems. The potential for conflict is ever present and exacerbated by cramped apartments. The day may well soon come when Granny will need as much looking after as an infant. And a new generation of grandparents, having struggled to bring up their own children, is not always willing to take on the task of bringing up yet another generation. Of course there are pensioners in desperate need of supplementing their meager allotments, but they are difficult to find, for a significant segment of the national economy relies on them.[9]

There can be no doubt, however, that the most critical problem is the drunken husband. This theme is such a constant thread running through this literature that the works come to seem part of the official campaign against alcoholism. This is not in any way to suggest that they were designed as official propaganda; Rather, they are tragic cries of despair at the misery that drinking creates. The extent to which alcoholism, with its concomitant physical abuse, is ingrained in the national consciousness is demonstrated again by Baranskaia in "A Week Like Any Other": exhausted and frustrated at the end of a long hard week, Olia slaps her wriggling daughter while giving her a bath and then bursts into tears at her husband's reproach. At that moment, without the slightest justification from past practice, her small son screams from the next room: "Daddy, don't beat Mummy, don't beat Mummy" (46). Nowhere is the full tragedy of alcoholism seen so graphically as in Sakovets's story "After the Bonus"

("Posle trinadtsatoi zarplaty"), which depicts the development of an alcoholic, his wife's reluctance to use a court order to have him sent to a detoxification center, and her eventual desperate recourse to a remedy popular among women, Teturan tablets, which, when dissolved in alcohol, are believed to make it unpalatable in the future. In this case, seeing that one tablet seems to have no effect, the wife slips two more into his drink, only to find him in the middle of the night—dead (49).

After encountering so many male characters described as "a drunkard and a womanizer," occasionally with "good-for-nothing" thrown in for good measure (Nabatnikova 130), we are not surprised to find that this literature is full of single-mother families, extended whenever possible into a new "nuclear" family consisting of mother, child, and grandmother, or if there is no grandmother, a female friend and confidante: the "maternal" family described by Natal'ia Malakhovskaia. Some of these single mothers have been left by their husbands or by apparently steady boyfriends (many of whom have another family elsewhere), but not infrequently the women leave their husbands either because the husbands drink and beat them or because they have had an affair. The new maternal family with its single, usually low-paid wage earner, her income perhaps supplemented by the grandmother's inadequate pension, is constantly plagued by money worries.

Given this extraordinarily depressing picture of bitter marriages, single mothers, sickly only children, and interfering mothers-in-law, one inevitably wonders why these women ever marry and have children. That they are under social and cultural pressures to do so cannot be denied, any more than can the unstated but clearly evident inadequacy of birth control measures. Another constant, fundamental, and dominant factor, however, lies at the very center of this literaure: the loneliness that so many of these heroines experience and their essential need for affection and companionship.[10] A poignant instance of this need is found in the title story of Sakovets's collection *Expectation* (*Ozhidanie*). The heroine, crippled by a bomb during the war, is brought to the verge of suicide after the last of four pathetic dates when she experiences her first, and last, kisses: "She had not mastered the art of love, she had no experience in it, but sincerity and a desire for love lived ineradicably in her, she wanted to love and to be loved at least a tiny bit" (69). Tragedy is averted only because she finds and looks after a lost puppy that provides her with a purpose in life and an outlet for the affection for which she has such an enormous capacity. This need is so great that it is commonly assumed that any man of any age or character can always find some woman to marry. In "Widowed" ("Vdovye") by Larisa Fedorova, whose special theme is the plight of elderly women, a widower proposes marriage to a neighboring widow. Without compunction he indicates that his primary concern is to have help in selling his garden produce, and he lays down restrictive conditions. She rejects his proposal, but he does not see her refusal as a major setback: "There's plenty of widows around. The war, booze, and tobacco, there are your main destroyers of the male species" (154).

Baranskaia, once again, provides the most striking and unusual illustration of this theme in "The Kiss" ("Potselui"). The heroine, Nadezhda Mikhailovna, a well-adjusted professional woman, has lived what cannot be described as an unusual life:

> first love and separation by the war, the joys and tribulations of family life, discord and divorce, single motherhood, and work, work, work: a trial and a joy. And just off to one side, apart from work, from her daughter, there were deceptive infatuations, love that was not love, jealousy, farewells . . . and, finally, stable equilibrium. . . . (263)

Nonetheless, her ultimate analysis of her own position is neither self-assured nor flattering; she sees herself as "left, abandoned, ditched, or, as the slang expression has it (how absolutely horrible!), dumped" (264). Now, however, a totally unexpected kiss in an elevator from an embarrassingly young man who is but the most casual of acquaintances throws her off completely. Before she knows it, he has made a date with her for the next evening, at her apartment. The next day she leaves work early to do all the necessary shopping and arrives home to a phone call from her daughter, who asks her to come and keep her and her baby company. Nadezhda Mikhailovna reluctantly declines, but as she is primping for the date, her nerve fails her. She grabs the food she has bought and sets out for the outlying district where her daughter lives. She could say simply that she changed her mind. "Except for the wine; she would have to explain the wine to Natasha somehow and she couldn't explain anything" (266).

The early 1980s thus witnessed a flurry of works written by women with a woman as the central character, works that revealed the spiritual experience of women principally through first-person narrative. The subject matter is dominated by a concentration on urban *domestic* life, though almost all of the women in these works have full-time jobs. That situation, of course, reflects the fact that it is precisely the domestic aspect of life, with its inequitable distribution of labor, its family pressures, the inadequate social and economic services, and above all the necessity of living with alcoholism, that immediately and on a very basic level distinguishes women's lives from those of men. On another level these works focus on the problems of marriage and love or, given the realities, more often on the problems of a single-parent family. Despite the recurring common themes, however, each story clearly focuses on an individual woman and on the miserable quality of her individual life. Underlying this focus is a fundamental assumption that each woman is entitled to a degree of happiness—not the happiness of class or of society but personal happiness. Furthermore, although this is a literature that concentrates on female lives in which the physical presence of a man is secondary, peripheral, or totally lacking, men are far from irrelevant. We find the constant assumption that the happiness these women expect and indeed consider their innate right is a direct outgrowth of the equilibrium of an intimate personal relationship—that is, mutual affection and stable love—with a man. This is what is absent in so many of these works, and consequently all the criticism is ultimately directed at those elements that destroy this equilibrium, whether these elements are external (society, societal conditions, other individuals, and especially the partner) or internal (the woman herself). At the same time, *literatura byta* offers no analysis of the specific causes of the distinctive *condition féminine;* even the particular and specific conflicts in these stories are usually not resolved. But through constant repetition these works clearly document the rift between the reality of the maternal family and the perceived need for a stable intimate relationship between a woman and a man. The absence of such a relationship is seen to stem particularly from the male predilection for vodka, from inherent male sloth, or from an apparently innate male proclivity for infidelity. And although individual stories actually appeared over several years, this focus in Soviet women's literature became concentrated through the publication of a significant number of volumes of collected stories by women writers concerned with these issues in the first years of the 1980s.

II

After an issue has been identified and its parameters defined through a multitude of examples, one might expect a subsequent stage in which longer and more complex works attend to the difficult psychological and philosophical questions that emerge out of the situation identified in the initial stage. Furthermore, if Soviet women's literature is indeed parasitic in the sense suggested earlier, one might expect such questions to be raised again in the context of more orthodox themes. Galina Bashkirova's novel *Yesterday and Tomorrow (Vchera i zavtra)* and I. Grekova's long story "The University Department" ("Kafedra") exemplify this second stage of development. Both works are more substantial and more complex than the earlier stories. While still concentrating on the inner emotional life of the heroine, they consider her not only in her domestic environment but also in the workplace. The number of characters treated in some detail is expanded, and they now include men. If men served principally as the villains of the earlier works, the time has come to consider why men are the way they are. The more difficult questions concerning the nature of love are raised in the context of personal morality. It is therefore perhaps no surprise that a perusal of the press reveals that official corruption had become a major concern and that writers were being urged to deal with moral issues.[11] Here once again was an officially promoted theme that women authors could exploit in order to make their own particular concerns palatable to the literary establishment.

Ironically, the centrality of the love theme in both Bashkirova's and Grekova's works is most clearly evident in the incredible complexity of the love relationships they depict. In Bashkirova's *Yesterday and Tomorrow,* Olia, who lives alone with her largely neglected young son, is being persuaded by her mother and her ex-husband (who, of course, now has a second family) to move in with his dying mother so that at the old woman's death Olia can lay claim to her apartment. This scheme does not sit particularly well with Olia's current lover. He goes off to Leningrad to "punish" Olia for paying him less attention. While he is away, Olia falls in love with an older gentleman, a descendant of one of the Decembrists. He falls in love with her, too, and would propose marriage if only he could find a way of persuading the young woman who lives with him in Vladivostok to move out of his apartment. This maze of emotional interrelationships (and the list is far from complete) is set against the background of the Decembrists, a tangible presence through their museum, of which Olia is the much-embattled director. In this novel, however, the Decembrists are a vivid symbol not of political activism but of idealism, steadfastness, and morality. They provide a historical contrast to modern Soviet society, in which young people are constantly being criticized for selfishness by their parents, when in fact it is they who are repeatedly shown to be morally bankrupt. In a complaint that clearly applies as much to himself as to anyone else, Olia's cynical ex-husband laments: "These days people come into the world to get something out of it, not to reform it" (25). The instability of personal relationships is attributed to selfishness, itself the result of amorality.

I. Grekova

Olia senses, if only vaguely, that her own inability to establish the stable relationship of mutual love for which she instinctively strives will have to be resolved in the context of the antiquated concepts of good and evil, that is, of a system of personal morality. What is needed is a conscience that can create the kind of life in which "it is assumed that justice will triumph, good defeat evil, and even if it doesn't, then at least evil is called by its real name and only a person who performs good deeds is esteemed as a good person" (105-6).

The love relationships in I. Grekova's "University Department" are no less complicated on the surface, and the whole question of love and ethics is even more complex. Nina Astashova is divorced and lives with three boys: an older son by her ex-husband, the son of her closest friend (who died in a traffic accident), and Astashova's younger son by Valentin, who has a wife and daughter as well as several other mistresses. Astashova has a strong affection for N.N., her mentor and the head of her department, who is poignantly faithful to the memory of his dead wife despite the possessiveness of his housekeeper, attempts by the departmental secretary to mother him, and a platonic infatuation with a young lab assistant. In addition Astashova suffers from the attentions of a lovelorn colleague. He eventually gives up and marries one of his students, a young woman who has a child as a result of a brief fling with an ambitious, careerist fellow student. As if to justify this complexity, Grekova from the first emphasizes the irrationality of love, an idea curiously overlooked in most of the works under discussion. As Astashova laments about Valentin: "What can you do? That's the kind of man I love; he's not noble, not faithful, not a knight of the round table. Him and only him" (23). Irrationality, however, cannot obscure the need for a moral base in life. This is the message of N.N., who, it is emphasized, had a prerevolutionary education and upbringing. When he dies, Astashova is charged with sorting his papers, which are curiously lacking in scientific material but full of considerations that lead her to conclude that "above all he was a human being. More than that: he was a good human being, warm, attentive, kind, conscientious" (110). N.N. himself did not examine the nature of this moral base. Instead, he likened it to the tuning fork occasionally used by a piano tuner to check "his relative perceptions against an absolute scale. Every person needs such a tuning fork in his soul, helping him in the search for justice. The sign of a correct decision is a perfect accord with the tuning fork" (110).

The fundamental unselfishness of this morality is apparent in the one question N.N. always asks of himself: "Have I been fair? Have I learned that in the course of my long life?" (141). It is this lesson that Nina Astashova tries to learn and apply both in her private life and at work, with mixed success. At the university her newfound zeal unmasks a plagiarist but severely wounds the man designated to be the next department head, whose apparent insensitivity and dictatorial manner in fact disguise an inferiority complex and an inability to show his emotions. And when Valentin, in the wake of a heart attack, proposes that they bring up their children together, Astashova realizes that her relationship with him, based until then on a mutual "for the moment, I love you forever" (220),[12] is not a sufficient foundation, that some more fundamental moral principle is required for a stable relationship.

As these two works show, the belief in personal happiness has not been abandoned, but the onus for its achievement has shifted from external factors to internal, personal behavior and standards.

III

In view of the fact that these books attracted little serious critical attention and that their impact on the reading public has been questioned,[13] it is interesting and important to note the appearance of other works by women with detectable elements of a dialogue, symptomatic of evolution and reaction to the works of their predecessors. A striking collection in this respect is *A Woman in a One-Room Apartment* (*Zhenshchina v odnokomnatnoi kvartire*), by Liubov' Iunina, published in 1985. Throughout these stories Iunina seems to be challenging the axiom that a woman needs a mutual stable love with a man—the axiom that was so prominent a feature of the earlier works—only to finish by proclaiming it anew. In the title story (which can be seen as a deliberate elaboration of Baranskaia's "The Kiss"), the heroine declares herself to be a successful single career woman:

> Dar'ia Pavlovna was well satisfied with herself, with life, with her station in that life. (80)

"But I don't live just for my work. Although a large part of my interests are in fact in the area of work. . . . And now I have a one-room bachelor apartment, where I live in complete independence." (85)

It was just that she didn't need a husband any more than she needed that status of being a married woman. Therefore, speaking crudely, she had no intention of enticing anyone with her beauty. It was just that a mousy woman on her own was one thing. . . . And a beautiful, elegant woman on her own was something quite different. On her own, because what did she need a husband for? She was fine just the way she was. (87)

But "things were not quite so simple as Dar'ia Pavlovna explained them" (86). By the end of the story Dar'ia Pavlovna's brave words are made to seem like bravado; she abandons her rationalism for the emotion of a genuine, if rather naïve, love with a younger subordinate in the research institute of which she is the deputy director.

In "The Director" ("Direktor") Iunina seems to challenge another accepted idea, only to back down once more before the final irrevocable step. "The Director" highlights rampant consumerism and arrogant egoism among young people, thus yet again reflecting official concern about the moral and social degeneration of the new "golden youth." The problem is seen, at least in part, as a result of increasing affluence in certain strata of Soviet society, in which two career-oriented parents ignore their children and then try to compensate for their neglect by extravagant spending on them.[14] In addition Iunina takes on another popular cause: the perennial Soviet issues of quality control and plan fulfillment. Against this background, stamped with an official seal of approval, the story poses questions that have resurfaced in Soviet sociology concerning the conflict between work and home.[15] Zoia Vasil'evna, the heroine of "The Director," is the only woman among all the factory directors in her ministry. She admits frankly that she is the exception and that she was given the job over strong opposition—opposition that derived precisely from the fact that she is a woman. While Zoia

Vasil'evna acknowledges the existence of such views, her daughter goes much further, arguing against the value of a higher education, since it is a man's world when it comes to getting jobs: " 'There were probably a hundred girls in your year, but you are the only one who has become a factory director' " (197). This attitude provokes Zoia Vasil'evna to begin to question the value of working mothers: "I am responsible for the factory, but it's not my child, I alone did not create it, whereas I *am* responsible for my daughter, with my whole life" (202). These doubts admittedly occur when Zoia Vasil'evna finds herself facing domestic and professional crises at the same time. The resolution is rather unconvincing: our heroine overcomes her doubts and determines both to devote more time to her neglected family and to persuade the entire Soviet bureaucratic apparatus to lower the quotas in order to achieve higher quality.

The fact that this ending is so unconvincing poignantly emphasizes the totally unrealistic demands that were being made of Soviet women as mothers, workers, and wives (the order depended on who was making the demand). Zoia Vasil'evna raised the issue only to dismiss it, but this was only the beginning. Other heroines, perhaps early signs of the changes permitted under *glasnost'*, illustrate the increasing questioning by Soviet women of the purpose of their lives and particularly of the roles that were set for them and that they had set for themselves. Olia, the heroine of Nadezhda Kozhevnikova's "Telepathy" ("Telepatiia"), is tempted by the excitement of an affair with a man whom she symbolically calls Gray Wolf. After a single lunch date, however, she quickly returns to the comfort of her admittedly dull husband, Tolia; he may be dull, but he is someone with whom she has so much in common that they are virtually telepathic. But if Olia is tempted only momentarily, Tamara Antonovna, the heroine of Kozhevnikova's "The Background" ("Vtoroi plan"), goes further. A silly quarrel over a dinner invitation with her husband, Oleg Dmitrievich (a model bourgeois Soviet husband who might well have been the envy of literary heroines in the books published at the beginning of the 1980s), pushes her to question the value of her role as the dutiful wife of a man whom she herself has carefully molded into a successful but hard and calculating creature:

> But after all, what was it that she had achieved? She had succeeded in molding her own husband, but she now held no sway over him. . . . And it wasn't even that. It wasn't the fact that her husband had ceased to be obedient that hurt, but the fact that she herself had lost her head. Somewhere a shift had occurred as she came to feel that there was *no point* in wanting anything any more, it was important simply not to lose *anything* of what she had. (278)

Even these initial doubts about fulfilling the role of the woman behind the successful man proved only an intermediate step as writers began to explore possible alternatives. In "Polina," in the 1986 collection *Color Postcards (Tsvetnye otkrytki)*, Nina Katerli presents two heroines, best friends and former classmates, who embrace radically different philosophies of life. The apparently successful Maiia berates her friend Polina for her wild gypsy-like existence: married and divorced several times and now involved with an eccentric impotent Bohemian poet, estranged from her mother and father, childless, and in many ways rootless. Maiia, by contrast, is a model neobourgeois Soviet woman. She snared the best boy in their class and now she is doing everything to help his progress up the ladder of success, apparently without compromising her own talents in any respect:

> Maiia Andreevna did not consider herself a housewife; it would have been ridiculous to do so. She had a graduate degree and over fifteen years of job experience in her field. . . . But ever since childhood Maiia Andreevna had had a hard and fast rule: to do everything properly, to commit herself totally, because that was the only way, as experience had shown, of achieving your goal. Maiia Andreevna owed a great deal to this principle of hers. (102)

Her prodigious energies create a perfect home environment for her husband and ensure the best for their daughter, including private music lessons and tutors. In the end, however, Maiia's "perfect" world collapses. From a passing bus she sees her husband smiling and laughing in the company of an unknown woman. A domestic scene, without satisfactory explanations, leads to a nervous breakdown and an attempted suicide; neither the solicitous attentions of her husband nor those of her best friend rescue her from the psychiatric hospital.

A similar contrast, in a work whose style could scarcely be more different, can be found at the heart of Tat'iana Tolstaia's "Fire and Dust" ("Ogon' i pyl'"), also first published in 1986 and then reprinted in Tolstaia's collection *"On the Golden Porch"* (*"Na zolotom kryl'tse sideli"*). Rimma, the heroine, sees a bright and rosy future in an orthodox and rather mundane existence centered on a husband, home and exemplary children. But that rosy future never dawns. Time, devastating in its ravages, marches on, until one day Rimma realizes that "it was all over; life had shown its vacuous visage: its collapsed coiffure and its sunken eye sockets" (108). From that moment Rimma's daydreams turn sour: "And the song of the sirens, deceitfully whispering sweet words of what could never be to the foolish mariner, fell silent forever" (108–9). The disappearance of these dreams coincides with the disappearance of Svetlana-Pipka, the mysterious woman who has floated in and out of Rimma's life from the fantasy world of impossibly exciting adventures in which Pipka seemed to live.

Whether or not either author is actively advocating an "alternative lifestyle," it is undeniable that major changes occurred in the depiction of the heroine of Soviet women's literature in the 1980s. If the fundamental assumption that a woman is entitled to personal happiness remained constant, the search for this goal underwent radical modifications. From decrying the absence of worthy men (perhaps not surprising in a generation that had experienced the demographic consequences of Stalin's camps and the war) by way of seeing stability as a function of personal morality (again perhaps not surprising in a period notorious for its cynicism and hypocrisy), women writers had come to question the very concepts that earlier had pointed to the desired goal, especially the concept of personal fulfillment in a happy bourgeois marriage. Such works as "Polina" and "Fire and Dust" seem to represent less a further stage of evolution than a substantively new phenomenon. Time will tell if they will come to be seen as reflections of *glasnost'* and *perestroika* or as harbingers of a new, post-Soviet Russian literature.

The issue of "women's literature" in the context of contemporary Russian literature is, like all such issues, both thematic and aesthetic. Even a sympathetic critic such as Alla Latynina has said:

> The real problem of women's prose, in my opinion, lies not at all in the fact that it contains too much about love and too little about production. . . . The real problem lies in the fact that there is no prose writer concerned with the "women's theme" who speaks with a uniquely distinctive voice. . . . Perhaps there will be? (295)

The breaking of the parasitic mold (and works such as Katerli's "Polina" and Tolstaia's "Fire and Dust" are certainly no longer parasitic in the same sense as the works published in the early 1980s), the appearance of works that engage in dialogue with earlier works, and the creation of works that provide distinctively different approaches to the old themes are obviously important steps in the emancipation of themes. Critics are increasingly commenting on the unique voices of such authors as Tat'iana Tolstaia, Liudmila Petrushevskaia, and Valeriia Narbikova (to mention just three). At the same time, however, one cannot help noticing that the most recent collections of prose by women writers echo the questions and the issues that resounded a decade earlier. The new announcements in *Novye knigi* differ only in being somewhat more forthright, as in the blurb for the first issue of *Eve: A Miscellany (Eva: Al'manakh)*:

> The miscellany recounts a woman's complex and mysterious world, her relation to family, to love, to a man, to children. Through the eyes of women authors the reader will see the universe of a

woman's feelings, thoughts, and psychology: the world of day-dreams and fantasies, the world of ecology and politics, the world of eros and love, the world of health and beauty, the earthly world with its concerns for "daily bread."[16]

The editors of *A Pure Life: Young Women's Prose* (*Chistenkaia zhizn': Molodaia zhenskaia proza*) suggest that much has already been accomplished:

> In recent times one can sense the surge of a new "women's" wave in literature. . . . These are works by women about themselves, about their problems, their spiritual highs and lows, their doubts and victories, about the philosophical and moral search for the self within the conditions of actual reality. (3)

Yet the authors of *She Who Remembers No Evil: New Women's Prose* (*Ne pomniashchaia zla: Novaia zhenskaia proza*), a collection described as consisting of the works "of ten women authors who could not have their works published during the years of stagnation" (3), affirm that much still remains to be done, and probably always will:

> Women's prose exists inasmuch as there is a world of women that is distinct from the world of men. . . . One must preserve one's dignity, if only through the fact of belonging to a particular gender (perhaps especially through belonging to it). (3)

Notes

1. I. Grekova, *Kafedra;* M. Ganina, *Sto zhiznei moikh,* published by Sovremennik in 1983 and announced in *Novye knigi SSSR,* 1982, no. 38, item 77. It should be noted that, at least to judge by the number of names identifiable as belonging to women in the category "Sovetskii period" of the section "Russkaia literatura" under the rubric "Khudozhestvennaia literatura" in the annual *Ezhegodnik knigi SSSR* for the years 1979 to 1981, the total number of books of fiction by woman authors did not change dramatically over this period, either in total numbers or as a percentage of all books published (around 12.5 percent).

2. See Alix Holt, "The First Soviet Feminists," in Holland, *Soviet Sisterhood,* 237–65. Although feminist groups did not occupy a highly visible place

in the Soviet social scene, some feminists did emerge to take the place of those who were exiled and some *samizdat* feminist materials continued to appear in the Soviet Union into the late 1980s. Since her exile, Tat'iana Mamonova, one of the leading forces behind *Women and Russia*, has achieved some prominence in Western feminist circles. The Marian group continued to exist independently and occasionally produced a small journal, *Mariia*, a number of issues of which were published in Frankfurt. One of its leading voices, Tat'iana Goricheva, has published an account of the movement: *Filles de Job: Les féministes de "Maria*," trans. (from German) Florence Quillet (Paris: Nouvelle Cité, 1989).

3. This campaign began with a major policy statement on the subject from the Central Committee of the CPSU, which was then disseminated widely in the Soviet media. See, e.g., *Pravda,* 11 September 1979, pp. 1, 3.

4. At least one Western study does include a chapter titled "Women Writers and Women's Problems": N.N. Shneidman, *Soviet Literature in the 1980s: Decade of Transition* (Toronto: University of Toronto Press, 1989), 169–90. There is now, of course, a considerable body of *specialized* literature by Western Slavists devoted to individual women authors or to groups of women authors, as well as translations of their works. In addition, in the late 1980s a number of volumes devoted to the neglected or forgotten works of women authors from the late eighteenth to the early twentieth century were published in the Soviet Union. For a more detailed account of these phenomena, see Helena Goscilo, "Paradigm Lost?: Contemporary Women's Fiction" (forthcoming).

5. One of the few critics to have taken up the challenge has been Alla Latynina. Her "Love, Family, and Career (The 'Ladies Story,' Women's Writing, and Naïve Suffrage)" ("Liubov', sem'ia i kar'era [O 'damskoi povesti,' zhenskoi proze i naivnom sufrazhisme]"), first published in *Literaturnaia gazeta,* 27 June 1984, 5, and reprinted in *Znaki vremeni,* picks up on the term *damskaia povest',* apparently introduced, or rather reintroduced, by Vladimir Lakshin. Latynina notes that, on the one hand, any critic who wishes to dismiss out of hand a work by a woman on the subject of " 'a broad living among broads,' with men completely out of the picture" (" 'zhitie baby sredi bab' pri polnom otsutsvii muzhchin" [288]) can simply dismiss it as a *damskaia povest'.* Latynina does not deny the existence of such a subliterature but notes that it is far from the exclusive province of women authors, and her rather acerbic definition makes clear that the true *damskaia povest'* is the Soviet equivalent of the Harlequin romance. One candidate for such a definition might be the title story of Ol'ga Reviakina's collection *Dva medovykh mesiatsa* (120–90).

6. *Literatura byta* is most commonly associated with the name of Iurii Trifonov. See, e.g., the chapter "Iurii Trifonov: City Prose," in N.N. Shneidman, *Soviet Literature in the 1970s: Artistic Diversity and Ideological Conformity,* 88–105 (Toronto: University of Toronto Press, 1979).

7. This bibliographical detail serves to emphasize the fact that, in view of the normal Soviet practice of publishing a work of fiction first in a journal and then in a collection of the author's works, it is extraordinary that so many

collections by women writers appeared at this time, each containing stories that had been published throughout the previous decade but few of which had ever been collected between the covers of a book before.

8. See, e.g., *Facts on File* 404, no. 41 (12 June 1981), 2117. More recent works hint at possible changes in this situation, at least in model bourgeois families. The heroine of Liubov' Iunina's "Captain Kuz'micheva" stories has a strict division of domestic labor with her husband (she cooks, he does the dishes; she delivers their child to kindergarten, he picks him up, etc.), although, as it turns out, the exigencies of daily life occasionally require them, however unwillingly, to make ad hoc changes in the chores they have assigned themselves. See Iunina, "Iz zhizni kapitana Kuz'michevoi," in *Zhenshchina v odnokomnatnoi kvartire*, 3–78, and the three Captain Kuz'micheva stories in her *Proisshestvie* (Moscow: Sovetskii pisatel', 1989), 6–190.

9. See, e.g., the description of the five pensioners who are the custodians at the Decembrist Museum in Bashkirova's *Vchera i sevogdnia* (51). Iunina describes the reverse phenomenon in "Chelovek na pensii," in which a grandmother is actively prevented from helping out because her children feel that she should take it easy now that she has retired. An emergency permits her to help and gives her the courage to tell her children that for her psychological well-being she needs to feel useful.

10. Ekaterina Alexandrova analyzes the diverse pressures on Soviet women to marry in "Why Soviet Women Want to Get Married," in Mamonova, *Women and Russia*. She goes so far as to say that "Soviet women need this stamp ['married' in the internal passport] for their own psychological sense of well-being, for their self-affirmation. . . . Without that stamp, the Soviet woman feels incomplete" (32). Buckley notes that in Soviet sociological studies "women are depicted as sensitive, delicate, thoughtful, gentle and emotional and physically in need of greater protection than men" (44). See also Attwood.

11. The members of Leonid Brezhnev's family made international headlines, but corruption was by no means confined to the topmost echelons. A. Rekunov, the Soviet procurator general, admitted as much in "Dictated by the Standards of Law: The Citizen, Society, and the Law" ("Prodiktovano normami prava: Grazhdanin, obshchestvo, zakon"), *Pravda*, 27 April 1982, 3. Soviet literature, of course, has always been expected to play an active role in the promotion of "correct" moral values, as is shown by the very existence of such books as *Problems of Individual Moral Education in Contemporary Soviet Literature* (*Problemy nravstvennogo vospitaniia lichnosti v sovremennoi sovetskoi literature*) (Moscow: Mysl', 1979), as well as by numerous official exhortations.

12. See also Grekova 22: "Right now I love you—forever."

13. In a 1988 interview with Helena Goscilo, Natal'ia Baranskaia, noting with some bitterness the difficulties she still encounters in having works published and the inadequate press runs of her works, commented on the antagonistic reaction of the male-dominated literary establishment to her "A Week Like Any Other" (one critic categorically stated that the work should never

have been allowed to see the light of day). Conversely, she said, women who normally read little or no literature at all continue to write to her to express their solidarity with the work's heroine. (I am grateful to Professor Goscilo for acquainting me with this interview before its publication.)

14. The moral and ideological education of young people was of increasing concern in the Soviet Union throughout the late 1970s and early 1980s. It was the principal issue raised at the plenum of the Central Committee in June 1983, at which Iurii Andropov demanded improvements in ideological upbringing through the combined efforts of the mass media and educational institutions, and was incorporated into the school reforms of 1985. See J. L. Black, "Perestroika and the Soviet General School: The CPSU Loses Control of Vospitanie," *Canadian Slavonic Papers* 33 (1991).

15. See, e.g., Buckley 40–46.

16. *Novye knigi,* 1990, no. 39, item 61.

References

Alexandrova, Ekaterina. "Why Soviet Women Want to Get Married." In *Women and Russia,* ed. Tatyana Mamonova, trans. Rebecca Park and Catherine A. Fitzpatrick, 31–50. Boston, MA: Beacon, 1984.

Attwood, Lynne. "The New Soviet Man and Woman—Soviet Views on Psychological Sex Differences." In *Soviet Sisterhood,* ed. Barbara Holland, 54–72. Bloomington, IN: Indiana University Press, 1985.

Baranskaia, Natal'ia. "Potselui." In *Zhenshchina s zontikom,* 261–66. Moscow: Sovremennik, 1981.

———. "Nedelia kak nedelia." In *Zhenshchina s zontikom,* 3–54. Moscow: Sovremennik, 1981.

Bashkirova, Galina. *Vchera i zavtra.* Moscow: Sovetskii pisatel', 1982.

Bocharov, A.G., and G.A. Belaia. *Sovremennaia russkaia sovetskaia literatura.* Moscow: Prosveshchenie, 1987.

Buckley, Mary. "Soviet Interpretations of the Woman Question." In *Soviet Sisterhood,* ed. Barbara Holland, 24–53. Bloomington, IN: Indiana University Press, 1985.

Fedorova, Larisa. "Vdovye." In *Vo dniakh Marii,* 142–56. Moscow: Sovremennik, 1982.

Golubeva, V. "Obratnaia storona medali." In *Zhenshchina i Rossiia,* 53–59. Paris: Editions des Femmes, 1980.

Grekova, I. [E.S. Ventsel']. *Kafedra.* Moscow: Sovetskii pisatel', 1983.

Holland, Barbara, ed. *Soviet Sisterhood.* Bloomington, IN: Indiana University Press, 1985.

Iunina, Liubov'. "Chelovek na pensii." In *Zhenshchina v odnokomnatnoi kvartire,* 106–30. Moscow: Sovremennik, 1985.

———. "Direktor." In *Zhenshchina v odnokomnatnoi kvartire,* 188–219. Moscow: Sovremennik, 1985.

———. "Zhenshchina v odnokomnatnoi kvartire." In *Zhenshchina v odnokomnatnoi kvartire,* 79–105. Moscow: Sovremennik, 1985.

Katerli, Nina. "Polina." In *Tsvetnye otkrytki*, 96–181. Leningrad: Sovetskii pisatel', 1986.

Kozhevnikova, Nadezhda. "Telepatiia." In *Vnutrennii dvor*, 250–62. Moscow: Sovetskii pisatel', 1986.

———. "Vtoroi plan." In *Vnutrennii dvor*, 263–80. Moscow: Sovetskii pisatel', 1986.

Latynina, Alla. "Liubov', sem'ia i kar'era (O 'damskoi povesti,' zhenskoi proze i naivnom sufrazhisme)." In *Znaki vremeni: Zametki o literaturnom protsesse, 1970–80-e gody*, 287–95. Moscow: Sovetskii pisatel', 1987.

Malakhovskaia, Natal'ia. "Materiinskaia sem'ia." In *Zhenshchina i Rossiia*, 31–40. Paris: Editions des Femmes, 1980.

Mamonova, Tatyana, ed. *Women and Russia: The First Soviet Anthology of Feminist Writing*, trans. Rebecca Park and Catherine A. Fitzpatrick. Boston, MA: Beacon, 1984.

Nabatnikova, Tat'iana. "Doch'." In *Domashnee vospitanie*, 85–254. Moscow: Sovremennik, 1984.

Ne pomniashchaia zla: Novaia zhenskaia proza. Moscow: Moskovskii rabochii, 1990.

Reviakina, Ol'ga. "Den' Dezdemony." In *Dva medovykh mesiatsa*, 81–94. Moscow: Sovremennik, 1981.

Sakovets, V. I. "Ozhidanie." In *Ozhidanie*, 64–73. Moscow: Sovremennik, 1981.

———. "Poezdka za gribami." In *Ozhidanie*, 3–16. Moscow: Sovremennik, 1981.

———. "Posle trinadtsatoi zarplaty." In *Ozhidanie*, 35–49. Moscow: Sovremennik, 1981.

———. "Tak oni i zhili." In *Ozhidanie*, 17–34. Moscow: Sovremennik, 1981.

Shavkuta, A.D., comp. *Chistenkaia zhizn': Molodaia zhenskaia proza*. Moscow: Molodaia gvardiia, 1990.

Skvortsova, Galina. "Sem'ia i lichnoe shchast'e (Muzhchina i zhenshchina na poroge XXI veka)." *Sever*, 1987, no. 10, 106–13.

Sokhriakov, Iu.I. "Feminizm, antifeminizm ili 'galantereinaia' emansipatsiia." *Literaturnaia ucheba*, 1984, no. 2, 164–70.

Tolstaia, Tat'iana. "Ogon' i pyl'." In *"Na zolotom kryl'tse sideli. . . ,"* 96–109. Moscow: Molodaia gvardia, 1987.

Vykhodets, P.S., ed. *Istoriia russkoi sovetskoi literatury*. 4th rev. and enl. ed. Moscow: Vysshaia shkola, 1986.

Zernova, Ruf'. "Predislovie." In *Zhenskie rasskazy*, 5–6. Ann Arbor, MI: Hermitage, 1981.

Zhenshchina i Rossiia. Paris: Editions des Femmes, 198.

Zhukovskii, Leonid. "Kuda ischezli nastoiashchie muzhchiny." *Literaturnaia gazeta*, 10 October 1984, 12.

4

THE POETICS OF BANALITY
Tat'iana Tolstaia, Lana Gogoberidze, and Larisa Zvezdochetova

Svetlana Boym

In response to a questionnaire on mass culture distributed among prominent Soviet writers, artists, and intellectuals, Tat'iana Tolstaia wrote that mass culture is "by definition not culture." "Mass culture," in other words, is a contradiction in terms, and Tolstaia dismisses its Soviet variant as "kitsch" (*Iskusstvo kino* 6 [1990]: 69–70). Yet elements of "mass culture" and of what at various moments in history has been considered kitsch, banality, bad taste, and petit-bourgeois *poshlost'* are woven into the artistic texture of many works and creatively reinterpreted in Tolstaia's own artistic works as well as in the works of many other contemporary women artists, filmmakers, and writers.

Vladimir Nabokov considered the Russian conception of banality (*poshlost'*) culturally untranslatable into other languages: it combines artistic triviality and spiritual deficiency, an attitude toward love as well as toward mass culture ("Philistines and Philistinism," 309–14). The untranslatable aspect of *poshlost'* has to do with the Russian conception of national culture echoed in Tat'iana Tolstaia's response, which is always culture in the singular, Culture with a capital *C*. The sphere of the everyday is not part of Russian culture in its heroic self-definition. *Poshlost'* has been frequently represented as a woman, an impertinent goddess of bad taste. Nabokov writes that the *o* of *poshlost'* is "as round as the bosom of a bathing beauty on a

German picture postcard" (*Nikolai Gogol*, 70). The history of *poshlost'*, which reveals many connections with the cultural myth of femininity and feminine writing, illuminates the relationship between aesthetics, politics, and everyday culture. The poetics of *poshlost'* is conceived here as a double movement between the historical metamorphosis of the concept and its transformation within a single contemporary work of art. Works by the writer Tat'iana Tolstaia, the film director Lana Gogoberidze, and the painter Larisa Zvezdochetova offer alternative framings of *poshlost'*, kitsch, and everyday culture. Rethinking kitsch and *poshlost'* and revisiting some theoretical commonplaces will give us new insight into shifting cultural hierarchies and conceptions of taste in contemporary Russian art.

Poshlost' comes from *poshlo*—something that has happened. In Vladimir Dal''s dictionary, the obsolete meaning of *poshlyi* is, in fact, "old, traditional, common, ancient, ancestral" (374). Initially *poshlyi* had no moral or aesthetic connotation.[1] The history of the use of the words *poshlyi* and "banal" demonstrates how a descriptive term can turn into a term of discrimination; it reflects a changing conception of communality and of artistic convention, a transformation of a "common good" into a commonplace. This transformation occurs with the advent of Romanticism and its aesthetics of originality, authenticity, and individual genius. At the core of the problem of *poshlost'* is the paradox of repetition, of communality, and of tradition. *Poshlost'* is repetition gone sour, a convention turned into a cliché, into an infinitely exploitable set of devices that preclude the critical aesthetic process. It closes off experimentation and experience. It is often difficult, however, to distinguish between "good" and "bad" repetition and to draw a line between a convention that is needed to reflect our cultural predicament and the triteness and trivialization that create culture's malign doubles.

The struggle against *poshlost'* plays a crucial role in Russian cultural history; it is linked to mythologies of social class (a perpetual war between the intelligentsia and the *meshchanstvo*, or bourgeoisie), attitudes toward material culture and the everyday, and conceptions of national identity and sexuality. The evolution of the concept of *poshlost'* reveals a remarkable metamorphosis. The Soviet Academy Dictionary lists the following meanings for *poshlost'*: "1. Lacking in spiritual qualities, ordinary, insignificant, worthless, paltry. 2. Not original, worn-out, banal. 3. Indecent, obscene, tasteless, vulgar" (*Akademicheskii,* 476). It is amazing that a single concept can embrace sexual indecency, artistic triviality, and lack of spirituality. In Russian culture the separation of the sexual, spiritual, and artistic spheres, or the split between the ethics of behavior, metaphysics, religion, and aesthetics, did not occur in the same way as it did in the West. Art never became completely autonomous; rather, the nineteenth-century Russian intelligentsia regarded Russian literature as always more or less than literature—a voice of national consciousness, the foundation of Russian identity.

In the Russian tradition *poshlost'* is also linked to the discourse of love, as we see in Anton Chekhov's short story "A Lady with a Dog." Here Chekhov turns a Western-style affair into a typical Russian love story complete with tears, gray dresses, autumnal landscapes, and yearning for a happy ending.[2] *Poshlost'* might refer both to sentimentality construed as tastelessness and to obscenity, often construed as any explicit expression of sexuality. The discourse on banality in the Russian context reveals a quasi-religious discourse on good and evil superimposed on the Romantic discourse on what is original or common, so that *poshlost'* becomes a peculiarly syncretic concept. It also has to do with the perpetual cultural opposition of *byt* (daily grind) and *bytie* (spiritual being)—the Russian symbolist version of the Orthodox Christian paradigm. The everyday is a modern secular concept. The opposition between *byt* and *bytie* fosters a peculiar cultural ostracism of diverse experiences associated with everyday culture, from "private life" to attitudes toward material objects.

While the Russian intelligentsia launched a war on *poshlost'*, Russian writers from Pushkin to Chekhov derived a great deal of pleasure from describing and savoring it.[3] In this respect they are not unique. Baudelaire wished to "create a cliché," and Flaubert from his very first letter at the age of ten claimed that his artistic impulse was to record banalities (Baudelaire 23). *Poshlost'* in Russia, like banality in France, has been conceived as opposed to the creative force of art, but in fact the relationship between the two is symbiotic and paradoxical. I am interested less in defining "banal" than in tracing its adventures through history and examining how an element of the habitual becomes defamiliarized and reclaimed by art, and then turns into an artistic cliché that in turn has to be reinvented. What is the relationship between banality and irony, banality both with and without quotation marks? How do we distinguish between artistic and self-conscious references to *poshlost'* and its involuntary uses? Where is the line between *poshlost'* with an aura and *poshlost'* without an aura, good "bad taste" and simply bad taste?

Poshlost', according to Nabokov, is "an unobvious sham"; it is "not only the obviously trashy but also the falsely important, the falsely beautiful, the falsely clever, the falsely attractive" (*Nikolai Gogol,* 70). In other words, *poshlost'* is false not only artistically but also morally; yet it is also very seductive. *Poshlost'* is an older sister of German kitsch. In Western Europe and the United States, the critique of kitsch reached its peak in the 1920s and 1930s in reaction to the commercialization of art and later to totalitarian fascist art.[4] What is fascinating and disturbing about kitsch is that it blurs the boundaries between art and life, denying autonomy to art. Kitsch is not merely bad art but also an unethical act, an act of mass manipulation. Kitsch is presented as "the debased and academic simulacra of genuine culture" (Greenberg 10), as "a parody on catharsis" (Adorno 340), and as a "sentimentalization of the finite ad infinitum" (Broch 75). Certain stylistic elements characterize kitsch—a propensity for ornamentation, eclecticism, and sentimentality. But, as Clement Greenberg points out, more important are the mechanisms by which kitsch imitates art's effects and not its inner processes (15). Yet the examples that critics cite betray their own cultural tastes and the climate of the time, and warn us against an uncritical reification of a single conception of kitsch. Milan Kundera, one of the great critics of totalitarian kitsch, has written that "none of us is superman enough to escape kitsch completely. No matter how we scorn it, kitsch is an integral part of the human condition" (256). So instead of trying to be supermen or rather superwomen fighting the empire of kitsch, we will examine kitsch and *poshlost'* as syntactic phenomena that depend on context and angle of vision. At the center of our attention will be neither the universal "structure of bad taste" that Umberto Eco began to discern (180–216) nor the "timeless beauty of *poshlost'* " that Nabokov ironically sought, but its historical and fictional transformations by three women—a writer, a filmmaker, and a painter—in works that reveal instances of cultural intolerance as well as of poetic generosity.

From the eighteenth century on (in Russia from the nineteenth), "bad taste" became increasingly feminized. In Sasha Chernyi's poem "Poshlost'" (1910), *poshlost'* is personified as a tacky salon goddess. She is presented as a middle-aged sexually loose woman, a nouveau riche who probably bought herself a title of nobility. Madame Poshlost' dresses in lilac and yellow, paints watercolors of roses, and sleeps with her cabby:

Lilac corset and yellow bow on her bosom;
Eyes like navels—eyeless eyes.
Someone else's curls cling thick to her temples
And greasily hang down her sides.

. . . In her salons *everyone,* the audacious crowd,
Having torn the skin off virginal ideas,
Clutch in their paws the unfeeling body
And zealously neigh like a herd of horses.

There they say eggs went up in price
And over the Neva a comet fell,—
Self-admiring, like mantelpiece Chinamen,
They nod to the beat of the gramophone's wail. . . .

She sings, and paints a watercolor rose.
She follows fashions of all sorts,
Saving up jokes and rumors, phrases, poses,
Corrupting the muse, corrupting love.

She's in kinship and in constant friendship
With effrontery, nonsense, talentlessness.
She's familiar with flattery, pathos, betrayal,
And, it seems, love affairs with dunces. . . .

The only ones not to know her are . . . who?
Of course: children, beasts, and common people .
The first when they don't look like grownups,
The last when away from their masters.

The portrait is ready. As I throw down my pens,
Please don't make a scene about my crassness:
When you paint a pig beside its shed—
No belle Hélène can appear on the canvas.

(Chernyi 27–29)

Cheap eroticism, infatuation with foreignness, and the vanity
of a nouveau riche in art and life happily merge in this grotesque
female figure who embodies all aspects of *poshlost'*—its relation
to sexuality, Western influences, and the mythology of social
class. She is a guardian of a pseudo-artistic salon and of a hearth
of hypocritical bourgeois domesticity, with its tacky attributes:
fashionable porcelain "Chinamen" on the fireplace, elaborate
satin comforters on the queen-size bed, the "howling" of gramophone records in the background. The proliferation of material
objects from the eclectic urban domestic culture at the turn of the
century goes hand in hand with the profanation of "ideals." The
major sin of Madame Poshlost' is her eclecticism; she mixes lilac
and yellow, the works of the erotic writer Ivan Barkov and
gramophone romances, watercolor roses and clichés about political "crises." But a close reading of the poem demonstrates the
ambiguous position of the poet himself and unintentional ironies

in the war against banality. In fact, the new Pygmalion of Madame Poshlost′ is implicated in her bestial salon scene, and does not completely escape the dated charms of the goddess of bad taste.

In the Russian tradition the figure of Madame Poshlost′ threatens any woman writer of prose or poetry.[5] What is important here is less the writer's gender than the use of gendered metaphors in aesthetics, and the ways in which femininity, effeminacy, decadence, excessive ornamentation, and cosmopolitanism become entangled with the idea of bad taste. "Feminine" writing has been described as excessive lyrical exaltation, perpetual lovesickness, an abusive use of metaphor, and a lack of a sense of history or historical responsibility. The woman writer has been conceived as a kind of nouveau riche who lacks the blue blood of literary aristocracy. She is an exalted weaver who by mistake picked up the wrong materials for her knitting, someone who can excel only in textiles, not in texts. All women writers and poets, including Tsvetaeva and Akhmatova, were accused of displaying various kinds of "feminine genetic deficiency," and each responded to the threats of Madame Poshlost′ in her own way.

In Russia in the 1920s a campaign was launched against "petit-bourgeois *poshlost′*," which encompassed everything associated with private life, love, and domesticity—everything that went against the virile ascetic spirit of the revolution. The poet Vladimir Maiakovskii decried the effeminate interiors of the new Soviet middle class, with their porcelain elephants on the mantelpiece, phonographic love songs (*romansy*), lace curtains, yellow canaries, and Marx in a crimson frame. By the late 1920s any art not sponsored by the state was prohibited and the heterogeneous culture of the early 1920s was displaced by the doctrine of socialist realism, coupled with a sanitized version of nineteenth-century Russian high culture, which in a cruel and paradoxical manner realized the old dream of the Russian intelligentsia, the dream of creating a unified "people's culture." Jeffrey Brooks has convincingly analyzed particularly hostile attitudes toward "popular literature" on the part of the state, the church, and the intelligentsia in the nineteenth century—attitudes that were perpetuated by the new Soviet state (295–99).

This process culminated in a peculiar pact between the Stalinist state and the new Soviet middle class and two decades of middlebrow art, which Milan Kundera defined as "totalitarian kitsch." The postwar Stalinist culture of the 1950s was marked by a return of the repressed: the despised coziness of the "bourgeois interior." The fashionable color of the Soviet 1950s was no longer red but pink: pink lampshades and postcards with exotic views substituted for Marx in a crimson frame (Dunham 41–48). The semiotics of color, and especially shades of red (from pink to crimson), played a crucial part in the construction of "good revolutionary taste" or "petit-bourgeois" effeminate taste. In the 1960s the intelligentsia of the thaw generation rebelled against the "bad taste" of the 1950s, which smacked of Stalinism and philistinism, and rediscovered in a somewhat distorted form the heritage of revolutionary modernism. In the eclectic age of Mikhail Gorbachev, "totalitarian kitsch" or the "high Stalinism" of the 1930s, old *poshlost'* from the time of NEP, 1950s middlebrow art, and the neomodernist euphoria of the 1960s all reappeared as aesthetic and political styles, occasions for nostalgia and laughter.

Contemporary Soviet women artists—both of the thaw generation and of the 1980s—have inherited and often internalized the conceptions of effeminate "bad taste" and are still haunted by the grotesque female figure of Madame Poshlost'. For Tat'iana Tolstaia "women's prose" is synonymous with superficiality, philistinism, commercial psychology, and excessive sentimentality—a "saccharine air" (McLaughlin 77–80). At the same time, in Tolstaia's short stories we easily find elements of what she describes as "women's prose"—a term that has to be reevaluated and considered without its deprecating quotation marks; here *poshlost'* mingles with poetry, and the boundaries between irony and banality are often blurred.

Everyday trivia, minor rituals, and tacky domestic objects with an aura of time past occupy a central place in Tolstaia's stories and provide a major writerly "pleasure of the text." As Helena Goscilo remarks, "the most striking effects of her prose issue precisely from the dramatic contrast between the seemingly lack-luster characters and events of her stories, on the one hand, and, on the other, the lush, colorful prism of multiple perspectives through which they are glimpsed and conveyed" (283). In this respect Tolstaia follows the tradition of Gogol', Flaubert, and Nabokov: she both decries *poshlost'* and takes a special writerly delight in describing it. Yet the flashes of "high culture" do not fully illuminate Tolstaia's fictional world; her central subtext is Soviet urban folklore, especially slightly outmoded urban romances and sentimental songs.

The word *poshlyi* actually occurs in Tolstaia's "Okkervil River," one of her most poetic stories, about a man's dream romance with a recorded singer in an imaginary land on the banks of the Okkervil River. The area bordering the Okkervil River is a peculiar margin, the folkloric "end of the world" and the limit of Simeonov's everyday existence, with its bachelor's feasts of pasteurized cheeses and bits of bacon served on yesterday's newspaper. But how does one imagine the limit of one's world, the marginal? The story offers us two equally hypo-thetical pictures—the ideal Okkervil valley as a land of "blue mists" and an imaginary Petrine landscape of clear waters, nas-turtiums on the windowsills, little bridges with towers and chains, on the one hand; and on the other the Okkervil as the edge of the city, a land of urban trash, pollution, excrement, and residue, "something else hopeless, provincial, and trite" (*chtonibud' eshche beznadezhnoe, okrainnoe, poshloe* [Tolstaya 21]). Thus the limit of the world poetically embodied in the "Okkervil River" (which actually exists in Leningrad/St. Peters-burg) can be seen as an ideal escape or as something inescapably banal and paltry, something inescapably of *this* world—its resi-due, its poisonous triviality. In other words, the euphonious Okkervil River has two banks—the bank of the blue misty ideal and the bank of *poshlost'*.

At first glance a similar duality is to be found in the images of two women: Vera Vasilievna, the heroine of Simeonov's heroic solitude, of sentimental songs about withering chrysanthemums, the ephemerality of being, and unrequited love; and Tamara, an ordinary woman, with domestic flowery curtains and home cooking. (Both women have their flowery attributes, but the flowers are of distinctly different styles: Vera Vasilievna's are pseudo-aristocratic chrysanthemums and nasturtiums, while Tamara's are standard Soviet flowers on homey curtains.) This opposition of ideal beauty and *poshlost'*, however, does not hold throughout the story. In fact, even the ideal Vera Vasilievna is depicted at the beginning as a queen of turn-of-the-century *poshlost'* (not a nouveau riche like Sasha Chernyi's Madame Poshlost' but a true queen of démodé). She is described as a "languorous naiad," which reminds us of turn-of-the-century soft-porn postcards and the German bathing beauty, the bosom of Nabokov's *poshlost'*. At the end of the story Vera Vasilievna is not even a queen of old-fashioned *poshlost'* bathing in the aura of past ideals, only the tacky and vulgar Soviet prima donna Verunchik, who ends up taking a bath in Simeonov's house—bathing, but not a beauty. (But then, the distinction between *poshlost'* with an aura and *poshlost'* without an aura is tenuous at best.)

The narrative both distances itself from and engages with the sentimental discourse of "romances"—those popular songs that Maiakovskii and the writers of the Left Front considered the embodiment of bad taste. Two that play a prominent part in the text are "The Chrysanthemums" and "No, It's Not You I Love So Passionately."[6] Here is the refrain from "The Chrysanthemums," which resounds throughout Tolstaia's story: "The chrysanthemums have withered in the garden long ago, / but love is still alive in my ailing heart." (Otsveli uzh davno, chrizantemy v sadu, / no liubov' vse zhivet v moem serdtse bol'nom). The other romance begins like this: "No, it's not you I love so passionately, / it's not for me the shining of your beauty, / I love in you my past suffering / and my perished youth." (Net, ne tebia tak pylko ia liubliu / ne dlia menia krasy tvoei blistan'e / liubliu v tebe ia proshloe stradan'e / i molodost' pogibshuiu moiu). The second song is in fact based on a Lermontov poem. The romance as a genre moved down from high culture to become a part of people's oral culture, an urban and middle-class folklore, and then turned into a *meshchanskii,* a petit-bourgeois artifact that the new high culture wished to suppress. At last it is recovered, now that it is completely outmoded, within the eclectic texture of a self-conscious artistic text.

The distinction between Tolstaia's defamiliarizing ironic narrative and the free indirect discourse that incorporates the perspective of Simeonov, the romance lover, is often difficult to trace. The story is a wistful meditation on the "hopelessness, the *poshlost'*" of existence, to the accompaniment of the powerful, larger-than-life voice of Vera Vasilievna on the phonograph. The last paragraph of "Okkervil River" incorporates some lines from old romance songs, and recycles and poetically rewrites clichés about rivers, lives, loves, and beautiful stories that can wither like chrysanthemums in autumn.

Tolstaia's "Sonia" is yet another meditation on romance and bad taste. Let us examine the first paragraph of the story:

> A person lived—a person died. Only the name remains—Sonya. "Remember, Sonya used to say . . . " "A dress like Sonya's . . . " "You keep blowing your nose all the time like Sonya. . . ." Then even the people who used to say that died, and there was only a trace of her voice in my head, incorporeal, seeming to come from the black jaws of the telephone receiver. Or all of a sudden there is a view of a sunny room, like a bright photograph come to life—laughter around a set table, like those hyacinths in a glass vase on the tablecloth, wreathed too with curly pink smiles. Look quickly before it goes out. Who is that? Is the one you need among them? But the bright room trembles and fades and now the backs of the seated people are translucent like gauze, and with frightening speed, their laughter falls to pieces, recedes in the distance—catch it if you can. (Tolstaya 144–45)

The first sentence of the story is a cliché, a trivial statement about life and death: "A person lived—a person died." It could be uttered by a *skaz*-narrator, a wisewoman storyteller in a communal apartment. In the first paragraph the narrator does not merely describe but acts out the difficulty of recovering the story and the characters from oblivion. The first cliché actually reveals to us what the story is about: about death and revival by fiction—what is poetically called "festively dressed-up immortality" (*nariadnoe bessmertie*). The disembodied voices, traces of overheard conversations, conjure up some visual memory: "All of a sudden there is a view of a sunny room, like a bright photograph come to life." The room emerges like a scene from an amateur home movie, and the characters appear as projections of light, fragile and semitransparent, "like gauze." The space of the story is presented to us not according to realist conventions as a three-dimensional space in perspective but rather as a space of memory that is fragile and on the verge of vanishing. But what this fragile representation brings us is a picture of an old-fashioned *meshchanskii byt*, a private banal scene with tacky objects. The little glass vase and the hyacinths with their curly pink smiles remind us of some evil flowers of *poshlost'*. It is difficult to say whether this *poshlost'* is with or without quotation marks. (The color pink figures prominently in Tolstaia's fiction. We find it, for instance, in the first paragraph of another story in the collection—"Sweet Shura.") The smiling curly hyacinths in a little vase function as the main triggers of memory. It is a memorable tacky object and some everyday clichés in overheard conversations that make the story possible.

Sonia, whom the female narrator of this story wishes to recover from the blurred background of an old photograph, is radically unphotogenic, like her fictional sisters in the world of Tolstaia stories—Shura, Zhenia, and others, all those old women from a different era who inhabit tiny rooms in godforsaken communal apartments in Leningrad. Sonia is a kind of blessed fool whom everyone considers unattractive, stupid, and always guilty of bad taste. The two main female characters are described in terms of their taste: Ada Adolfovna (the alliteration is hellish: *ad* means "hell" in Russian) is said to possess "a serpentine elegance," whereas Sonia is dressed very "unbecomingly" (*bezobrazno*).

One detail of Sonia's clothing becomes particularly important in the story—the little enamel brooch in the form of a dove, which she never takes off. In the context of the history of Soviet taste this little enamel dove is an emblem of bad taste and *poshlost'*. In the story it is ridiculed as an ultimate embodiment of Sonia's lack of style. Sonia falls victim to a party joke orchestrated by the powerful Ada Adolfovna, who invents a passionate epistolary lover for Sonia named Nikolai. The clichés of a tacky romance work for poor Sonia, who falls in love with Nikolai, a product of Ada Adolfovna's powerful "feminine prose." At the moment Ada is ready to "kill" Sonia's imaginary romantic lover, Sonia encloses her enamel dove, her most intimate and sacred object, in one of her letters. This gesture allows the epistolary romance to continue just a bit longer. At the end, the narrator, wishing to reconstruct Sonia's story from fragmentary tales and old blurred photographs, asks Ada for Sonia's letters. Considerable time has passed. There has been a war, a siege; Sonia and her mythical love have died their natural or unnatural deaths; and Sonia's letters may have been burned along with the books to heat the house during that impossible first winter of the siege of Leningrad. In the end the only thing that has survived, or at least is believed to have survived, is the enamel dove. The last line of the story—"After all, doves don't burn" (Ved', golubkov ogon' ne beret)—is introduced by the colloquial and affective Russian *ved* (after all, just, you know). The line also paraphrases the proverbial phrase in Bulgakov's *Master and Margarita,* "manuscripts don't burn" (rukopisi ne goriat), which perpetuates the myth that art survives all purges and repression. In Tolstaia's story, however, it is not a work of art that does not burn but a tacky enamel dove.

The adventures of the enamel dove parallel the adventures of *poshlost'* and the complex shifts in the narrative perspective on it. Not only does the dove make the epistolary romance more "physical," saving the lover from premature death; it also triggers both the romance and the narration of the story itself. From an emblem of ridiculed old-fashioned tackiness it turns into a sympathetic sentimental object, a souvenir, imbued by personal warmth. At the end it is reframed as a poetic thing par excellence, the last eccentric romantic survivor of the world of daily *poshlost'*. Sonia's little brooch suggests the infinite powers of poetic metamorphosis, of the metamorphosis of *poshlost'* into poetry and back. The dove can be regarded as a symbol of spirituality, but it is a mass-reproduced one and a clichéd element of decoration that has frequently been used in book illustrations, architectural bas-reliefs, and cheap women's jewelry since the late nineteenth century. It is associated with popular versions of the eclectic and art nouveau style in the applied arts and in crafts. Strongly disliked by the intellectual arbiters of taste, it is beloved by many people who are deprecated as having the tastes of the *meshchanstvo*.

That kind of trashy jewelry is not valuable, but it is priceless. Tolstaia has admitted to a particular affection for trash; she said that she found the inspiration for her story "Sweet Shura" in the discards thrown from a communal apartment into the trash in one of Leningrad's asphalt yards. Sonia's dove can be seen as this kind of trashy found object, with a special fictional charisma. The dove becomes a metaphor for the protean powers of fiction. From a spiritual symbol the dove is transformed into a romantic cliché, embodied in a tacky artifact that suddenly reveals itself as pregnant poetic metaphor. The narrative adornment and the meaning the enamel dove acquires depend on the context; it defies a clear-cut opposition between *byt* and *bytie* (everyday existence and spiritual being, the opposition particularly promoted by the Russian symbolists in their reinterpretation of traditional Russian spirituality). The dove appears as an ideal narrative gift that ensures the imaginary exchange between the fictional lovers of the story and between the writer and her readers. But gifts should not be overinterpreted. The enamel dove will "burn" and disappear the moment we attempt to reduce its poetic suggestiveness and rich textuality to any kind of universal symbolism.

Through its narrative perspectives the story invites us to rethink any one-sided mockery of sentimental kitsch. Tolstaia's own writing, full of ornamental excesses and artistic density, vacillates between poetic clichés and poetic discoveries, and the clear distinction between the two tends to evaporate in the "blue mist" of the narrative streams.

We observe that most of the kitschy items in Tolstaia's stories are not contemporary; they belong to another time and are colored by the aura of memory. In Walter Benjamin's conception, the experience of an aura is the experience of distance, of involuntary memory and historical temporality. It is that element of uniqueness which art objects preserve.[7] Yet in Benjamin's own thought, an aura escapes a single critical framework. Photography, which is an example of art in the age of mechanical reproduction, may seem to be antithetical to traditional oil painting, which possesses an artistic aura. But the photographs of Atget, a professional photographer and a poet of emptied domestic interiors, a pioneer of modern nostalgia, are, in Benjamin's view, suffused with an aura, and so are the tacky objects of the old communal apartments that Tolstaia describes. Susan Sontag characterizes this particular attitude of eroticization, or in Tolstaia's case poeticization, of daily life and tacky trivia as a "campy sensibility." Camp is described as anything outrageously inappropriate, old-fashioned, out of date, *démodé,* all those things that, "from a 'serious' point of view, are either bad art or kitsch." Camp sensibility is based on the conception of "Being-as-Playing-a-Role," of the metaphor of life as theater. It is also "a triumph of the epicene style," of playful reversals of gender and sexual impersonations, often associated with gay sensibility (Sontag 280–81). Sontag remarks that "camp taste is by nature possible only in affluent societies, in societies or circles capable of experiencing the psychopathology of affluence" (291). Affluence is hardly a feature of Soviet life even among the privileged circles of the intellectual elite. Although Tolstaia's framing of trivial objects and her affection for artifice may coincide with Sontag's description, *theatrum mundi* is hardly her metaphor. Sexual playfulness is not her forte either. In Tolstaia's fictional world sympathy and morality are as important as literary artifice (Goscilo 281). Perhaps one should not simply ally Tolstaia with camp, since she has expressed her strong dislike for any kind of "group activities," however theatrical they may be. Rather, we can reread her stories and examine her particular way of poeticizing the everyday, her playful transformation of some stereotypes and unplayful preservation of others.[8]

Lana Gogoberidze's film *Turnover* (1987) also pays tribute to the ordinary marvelous; it shifts the relationship between cultural categories, between public and private spheres, between history and the everyday. The title of Gogoberidze's film may be seen as a rewriting of the *perestroika* metaphor; rather than a directed linear movement—from destruction to reconstruction or vice versa—"turnover" suggests an unpredictable dynamic force in human life that is played out in a series of fragmented narratives, intertwined and entangled like lines of fate. At the center of the film are a pair of "unphotogenic women," the aging actress Manana and the spinster and would-be playwright Rusudan. Although Gogoberidze confessed that she never saw *Sunset Boulevard,* her *Turnover* can be viewed as a peculiar remake of that famous film presented from a woman's perspective.

At the beginning Manana, with all her tacky clothes—fake furs, black lace, scarves—seems to be a parody of idealized femininity. She is perpetually "too much"—overdressed, over-made-up, and hysterical. In another film these two women might have been caricatures, parodies, and embarrassments. Yet in Gogoberidze's film they emerge as sympathetic and problematic characters who can laugh at themselves and at their absurd, unfortunate turns of fate. In this respect the two explosive scenes of women's laughter are of great importance. After one of them, Manana and Rusudan turn into would-be authors and write a play about "two mature women." Hence "feminine excess" is played out with humor throughout the film and turned into potential creativity.

Turnover was released at a time when films denouncing Stalin and Stalinism were flooding the Soviet screen after the unshelving of *Repentance*. In a scene in which Manana, after an unsuccessful audition for a film, stops in at a shoemaker's shop, a photograph of Stalin appears—briefly, in the background. Here we see a new, interesting way of using cinematic depth of field for a peculiar subversion of high political discourse. A tacky collage in the shoeshine booth, made up of a jumble of found objects and outmoded images, includes a picture of the young Manana—the superstar of the 1950s—and the portrait of Stalin, perpetually young and smiling through his handsome mustaches.

After a showing of the film at Boston University, when Gogoberidze was asked about the political meaning of her use of Stalin's picture, she replied that it is simply a "documentary element" of the film, something one sees in Tbilisi in most shoeshine booths, and as a decoration in trucks and cars. Gogoberidze pointed out that she did not intend to make a straightforward political statement. The picture of Stalin hanging in the background in the mid-1980s reveals the persuasiveness of the Stalin myth (and of the cult of personality in general) and shows how "unreconstructed" Soviet daily experiences really were. Gogoberidze commented that for her "cultural liberation" does not consist exclusively of the opportunity to make more openly political films; it also represents a chance to make films that resist the overpoliticization of culture. In many ways the film is about women's invention of the everyday, the famous prosaic *byt,* the site of *poshlost'* par excellence. Whereas the film's male characters escape to search for truth away from home (the cliché of the male quest for abstract truth), women learn ironically and sympathetically to reestablish the everyday. Ultimately the film is not simply about the turnover of a series of fragmentary narratives, which has become a mark of the new Georgian school of cinema, but also about the possibility of recovering alternative forms of communication and sympathy that badly need recovery.

Larisa Zvezdochetova also takes part in a magic turnover of everyday kitsch objects, childhood memories, and high art clichés. She has said that she wants to recover in her work everything that art history has ignored: amateur embroidery by provincial women on collective farms, 1950s postcards, "deer" carpets from communal apartments, matchbox labels showing the battleship Aurora, chocolate foil wrappers (*fantiki*) bearing Ivan Shishkin's classic painting *Three Bears,* badges with the logo

"Be Ready for Labor and Defense" and a gilded athlete covered with rust, black-and-white reproductions of Nefertiti, the beauty queen of ancient Egypt, who became the most popular Soviet pinup after Ernest Hemingway. All of these found objects disclose the minor aesthetic delights of bleak Soviet everyday culture and were doubly censored, by high art and high politics.[9] Just as Tolstaia found inspiration for "Sweet Shura" in Leningrad trash, Zvezdochetova affectionately excavates Soviet dumps—and finds there not only all those *poshlye* objects, the petit-bourgeois "domestic trash" scorned from the 1920s to the 1960s, but also reproductions of high art torn out of popular magazines. In her works "the feminine" and "bad taste" are placed within quotation marks and creatively reinterpreted.

A dialogue with the avant-garde—and, between the lines, with some Soviet conceptualists of the older generation—is played out in some of her key works. Her installation with fragile paper angels hanging from trees, programmatically titled *The End of the Avant-Garde,* was presented at the exhibition "Aptart—Beyond the Fence" in 1983. The angels, cut out of white paper like the ready-made snowflakes familiar to all Russian schoolchildren, evoke both children's art and turn-of-the-century mass culture, which was populated by angels, "fat flirtatious cupids," and the other whimsical winged creatures against which the avant-gardists fought so ferociously (Malevich 123). The flimsy angels in the natural setting signal the end of the seriousness and stylistic purity of the newly fetishized historical avant-garde. In her work Zvezdochetova wants to confront high avant-garde culture, predicated on originality, with everyday culture—the mass—reproduced and repetitive female arts and crafts, the communal apartment decorations, the Soviet wallpaper designs that frame one's memories of childhood.

Zvezdochetova's artistic work can be placed in the context of the younger generation of conceptual artists that includes Konstantin Zvezdochetov and Mariia Serebriakova, but she also has cross-cultural references of other kinds. Zvezdochetova remembers an amateur "aesthetic therapist," a woman she got to know during her work with craftsmen in the small towns near Odessa. With her followers the woman made large embroideries patterned on reproductions of paintings that had become Russian and Soviet classics—from the nineteenth-century *End of Pompeii* by Aleksandr Briullov to the portrait of Lenin in his study. When Zvezdochetova asked why she embroidered portraits of Lenin rather than her own designs, the woman explained that this was the true way to bring art to the masses: when the embroiderers followed the lines and brush strokes of the great artists, they were both propagating art and raising the prestige of the embroidery. Zvezdochetova wants to do exactly the opposite—to copy embroidery into art and challenge cultural hierarchies. Moreover, unlike constructivists of the 1920s such as Varvara Stepanova, she is trying not to impose her pure, nonobjective patterns upon mass design but rather to learn from women's unofficial mass culture itself.

In a recent work Zvezdochetova touches—and invites us to touch, literally sense—one of Russia's main avant-garde icons, Kazimir Malevich's *Black Square.* Imagine the *Black Square,* which was supposed to be an ultimate pure nonobjective painting, "zero degree of form," as an attractive object of soft velour in a gilded frame—an avant-garde antique. Zvezdochetova goes further, however—what she offers us is zero degree of painting; the Suprematist surface is nothing but a folding velour curtain that invites us not to search for avant-garde absolutes but to look right behind the cover—only to find an enlarged reproduction of a common embroidery. Moreover, the black squares themselves are reproduced and repeated three times. The work, called *Classical Genres of Art: Portrait, Landscape, Still Life,* is a kind of trompe-l'oeuil or trompe genre. It appears at first as a perfect classical ensemble: a gray monumental pedestal in the center and three black squares. On three sides of the pedestal are three little embroideries—a portrait of a girl, a landscape, and a still life. The embroideries are actual found objects: one was found on an old pillowcase; the others were rescued from the trash or bought at a cheap store. They are the products of craftswomen, collective and anonymous. Moreover, they are incomplete, nothing but fragments, unfinished because of lack of time and the burden of domestic chores or simply badly preserved, ruined, unvalued. The three black-square velour curtains cover up, like the most precious museum artifacts, the enlarged photographic projections of the embroideries, merely mechanical reproductions, even less original than their anonymous originals.

The work has many tricks, devices and levels of irony. It plays with and humorously and creatively borrows not only from Malevich, the suprematist master, but also from the master of embroidery, the amateur "aesthetic therapist" from a small town near Odessa. Moreover, it is the embroidery that is given the most prestigious place and cherished as a found masterpiece, while the black square, the icon of high avant-garde art, serves only as the frame and cover. The most unoriginal collective craft is positioned as unique, while the avant-garde art is reproduced. The space also creates a trompe l'oeil museum space, because what is covered by the rich velour is in fact reproductions or projections of the originals. And the frame, which appears to be of sumptuous gold, is actually made of a gold tablecloth that Zvezdochetova found at a Turkish flea market in Germany. In a museum, a painting is untouchable; its aesthetic distance is carefully patrolled and protected by watchful guards. Zvezdochetova's installation is supposed to be touched. But many viewers have internalized the conventions of museum behavior and are too embarrassed to play erotic games with a work of art—the status that Zvezdochetova's installation, composed of many found objects, has certainly acquired. The work is a clash of tactile experiences—the embroidery, a very tactile art, is turned into a flat photograph that is covered by the luxurious velour. So one is invited to touch the curtain, while the photograph itself is immaterial.

According to Zvezdochetova, she was attempting to make what she calls "erotic art," but art with a particular kind of tactile female eroticism. It is not sexually explicit at the level of visual representation—the obligatory nude scene of any recent Soviet or post-Soviet film. Nor is it eroticism in quotation marks, a kind of intertextual eroticism. Her erotic art is not violent but playful; it consists of a variety of tactile experiences, including tactile trompe l'oeil, the games of revealing and concealing the "body of work." The installation plays not only with arts and crafts, high and low styles, but with aesthetic distance itself. Zvezdochetova's is the art of tactile conceptualism. Of course, it is up to the viewer to decide whether to touch or not.

Classical Genres of Art is one of Zvezdochetova's more explicitly conceptual works. It is also more of an ensemble than a fragmented souvenir, the lost memory that some of her other works resemble. The silhouettes, cut out of paper covered by a lace curtain, offer us again a clash between the immateriality of the silhouette and the ostensibly tactile quality of the lace. The work reminds us of a child walking through the streets of her native city, peeking through the brightly lit windows and eavesdropping on the lives of strangers, and never resolving the plots of their dramas. Not kitsch but something prior to it—a childhood surprise, a gust of curiosity, naive admiration, wonder and bewilderment, before the categories and hierarchies of art and culture, the distinctions between high and low, original and common, are irrevocably ingrained in the mind.

One of Zvezdochetova's mottos is a proverb that may have come from prison jargon: "candy out of shit" *(iz govna konfetku),* which means to make something out of nothing. While reading *The Encyclopedia of Bad Taste,* which is based exclusively on American mass culture, I discovered that making "treasures from trash" is a common occupation of lower-class suburban American housewives, an activity that has moved from hippy art and the counterculture into suburban mass culture (Stern and Stern 293–94). In the United States this is a kind of popular recycling program, a reaction against a culture of wasteful overabundance of commercial goods. In Russia, by contrast, the idea of making something out of nothing is a result of material scarcity, not a countercultural gesture but an expression of a need—and not simply a material need, but also an assertion of minimal aesthetic necessity and self-affirmation. Zvezdochetova associates it not with housewives' culture but with "prison art and the prison mentality——[. . .] a kind of all-Soviet aesthetic therapy—making something out of nothing, 'candy out of shit.' "

In Zvezdochetova's artistic quilt two cultural levels are absent—the official socialist realism of high Soviet political icons and the media culture and Western mass culture with which Zvezdochetova has become increasingly familiar. "Mickey Mouse is uninteresting," she said in an interview. "He's just too cold." Instead of working with major political events or major historical figures in the manner of the artists of the *sots art* movement, who play ironically with socialist realist icons, she recovers another level of culture—the everyday, forgotten and yet familiar. At this level of culture there are no heroes or antiheroes, only endless tacky ornaments of communal apartments, standardized Soviet children's books, women's needlework, icons of official commemoration (Tupitsyn 35–53). The everyday represents resistance to artistic defamiliarization; it is both too familiar and too uncanny. Yet, unlike Il'ia Kabakov, a founding father of Soviet conceptual art and producer of stark works, Zvezdochetova enjoys the banal ornaments of the old-fashioned Soviet communal carpet and the material details of standard Soviet furniture and mass-produced objects. It is not Kabakov's metaphysical "emptiness" but the material particularity of detail, with its aura of outmoded ordinariness from the totalitarian past, that motivates her work. Her creative recuperation of the everyday is not totalizing but an invitation to a forgotten children's game, a childhood secret framed by the artificially aged golden foil.

Zvezdochetova's art, as well as that of the other conceptual artists, reminds one of American art of the 1960s and 1980s that incorporates and reinterprets many elements of American mass culture. The cross-cultural artistic comparison, however, makes clear the striking difference between the two mass cultures. Whereas the American cultural text is heavily televisual, full of references to commercial and consumer culture, Soviet mass culture has plenty of high art and high politics; it includes Pushkin and Stalin, political slogans, school manuals, and bureaucratic clichés. The commonplace of Soviet mass culture is not the shopping mall but the communal apartment.

The works of women artists of the former Soviet Union demonstrate that the relationship between irony and sympathy, distancing and engagement, material and conceptual, is far from simple. *Poshlost'*, like beauty, is in the eye of the beholder. Beauty is often embodied in the female figure, and so is *poshlost'*. In the women's artistic works that we have examined *poshlost'* no longer appears as a reified goddess of bad taste. Rather, its effects and affects are paradoxically interwoven in the artistic texture. If, as Clement Greenberg claims, kitsch can be defined as a mere mechanical reproduction of the effects of art, here we observe how women's artistic works meditate upon the effects of kitsch and *poshlost'*, challenge cultural hierarchies, and creatively reinvent that illegitimate and untranslatable Russian and Soviet everyday which is so often a blurred background to a larger historical tableau.

Notes

1. The French and then English word "banal" underwent a similar shift in meaning. In medieval French *banal* referred to something shared and common in the feudal jurisdiction; thus one spoke of banal fields, mills, and ovens.

2. After the mid-nineteenth century the word *poshlyi* developed many derivatives—*poshliak, poshliatina,* etc.—all linked to sexual indecency and obscenity. *Poshlost'* determines attitudes toward sexuality and femininity. The fear of *poshlost'* reflects less a fear of sex per se than fear of sexuality as an autonomous sphere of existence, independent of love and social concerns—in other words, fear of sexuality as a Western cultural construct. For more on this topic, see "Loving in Bad Taste: Eroticism and Literary Excess in Marina Tsvetaeva's 'The Tale of Sonechka,' " in Costlow et al.

3. Pushkin was one of the first to use *poshlyi* to refer to conventional poems of high society and to epigones of the Romantics who fancied themselves as Russian Mephistopheleses or Russian Napoleons of German descent, such as Herman in *The Queen of Spades* (Pushkin, ch. 5, XLIV, 99). To Gogol', *poshlost'* and banality are connected to the idea of realism, and Belinskii, in his discussion of *Dead Souls,* rewrote Gogol''s *poshlyi* as "realistic" (293). So Russian realism could have been called *poshlizm.* Chekhov is also a powerful explorer of *poshlost'* and banality in love, art, and boredom. Late in the nineteenth century, with the emergence of commercial culture, *poshlost'* was used in reference to popular artistic genres—sentimental romances, books by women, English drawing room stories.

4. In contemporary Russian, *poshlost'* and "kitsch" are occasionally used as synonyms, although kitsch can be seen as only one instance of *poshlost'*, referring to pseudo-artistic phenomena as well as to the elements of Western popular culture that have begun to make their way into Russia. "Kitsch" comes from the jargon of Munich art dealers of the 1870s, to whom it signified cheap artistic stuff.

5. In the essay "Literary Moscow," Mandel'shtam poetically synthesizes the attributes of the cultural mask of the "poetess." She is described as a parody of the poet, a conglomeration of lack and excess—lack of true genius, hence suffering from a perpetual "genetic deficiency," and an emotional and sentimental excess. This notion actually goes back to the Romantic concept of genius as a virile spirit, and the Kantian description of the beautiful (not to be confused with the agreeable, with its languid appeal to the senses and its propensity for decoration). See Svetlana Boym, "Loving in Bad Taste," in Costlow et al.

6. Several versions of these romances are still known by heart and sung in Russia. I quote the texts from the 1989 edition of *Russkie pesni i romansy*, 200, 390.

7. For Benjamin's shifting concept of aura, compare "Some Motifs in Baudelaire" (188–89) and "The Work of Art in the Age of Mechanical Reproduction" (222–23).

8. Occasionally Tolstaia's journalism, once she abandons narrative and other subtleties, appears as a reiteration of clichés about "Russia and the West," the intelligentsia, and the *meshchanstvo*. One would like to think that perhaps Tolstaia the journalist is only one of the writer's stylized personae, whose straightforwardness counteracts the ambiguities of her fictional narrators.

9. Interest in everyday culture is not exclusive to women artists. In fact, this movement in Soviet conceptualism was pioneered by Il'ia Kabakov. In *The Communal Apartment* Kabakov uses a female character—his mother, a long-time victim of the housing shortage—as his invisible guide to the communal labyrinths. The walls of the corridors in Kabakov's communal apartment are covered by his mother's autobiography, awkwardly typed on an old manual typewriter. Yet Kabakov's communal apartment is a realm of Soviet uniformity and of badly executed socialist realist paintings produced by an "untalented artist." It is an overcrowded place from which the artist escapes into the white emptiness of the canvas, and there is no place in it for the decorative tacky and old-fashioned objects that come from the "feminine" culture of the communal apartment.

References

Adorno, Teodor. *Aesthetic Theory*. Trans. C. Lenhardt. London and New York: Routledge & Kegan Paul, 1984.
Akademicheskii slovar' russkogo iazyka. Moscow, 1957.
Baudelaire, Charles. "Fusées." In *Oeuvres complètes*. Paris, 1965.
Belinskii, Vissarion. *Polnoe sobranie sochinenii*. Moscow, 1953.
Benjamin, Walter. *Illuminations*. New York: Schocken, 1985.

Boym, Svetlana. *Death in Quotation Marks: Cultural Myths of the Modern Poet.* Cambridge, MA: Harvard University Press, 1991.

Broch, Hermann. *Kitsch: The Anthology of Bad Taste.* Ed. Gillo Dorfles. London: Studio Vista, 1969.

Brooks, Jeffrey. *When Russians Learned to Read.* Princeton, NJ: Princeton University Press, 1985.

Chernyi, Sasha. *Stikhotvoreniia.* Moscow, 1991.

Costlow, Jane, Stephanie Sandler, and Judith Vowles, eds. *Sexuality and the Body in Russian Culture.* Stanford, CA: Stanford University Press, 1993.

Dal', Vladimir. *Tolkovyi slovar' zhivago velikorusskogo iazyka.* St. Petersburg: Volf, 1882.

Dunham, Vera. *In Stalin's Time.* Cambridge: Cambridge University Press, 1976.

Eco, Umberto. *The Open Work.* Trans. Anna Cancogni. Cambridge, MA: Harvard University Press, 1989.

Flaubert, Gustave. *Correspondances.* Paris, 1942.

Goscilo, Helena. "Tat'iana Tolstaia's 'Dome of Many-Coloured Glass': The World Refracted through Multiple Perspectives." *Slavic Review* 47, no. 2 (Winter 1988): 280–90.

Greenberg, Clement. *On Art and Culture.* Boston, MA: Beacon, 1965.

Kundera, Milan. *The Unbearable Lightness of Being.* Trans. Michael Heim. New York: Harper & Row, 1984.

McLaughlin, Sigrid. "Contemporary Soviet Women Writers." *Canadian Woman Studies* 10, no. 4 (Winter 1989): 77–80.

Malevich, Kazimir. "From Cubism and Futurism to Suprematism." In *Russian Art of the Avant-Garde,* ed. John Bowlt. New York: Thames & Hudson, 1991.

Mandel'shtam, Osip. *Sobranie sochinenii,* vol. 2. New York: Inter-Language Literary Associates, 1971.

Nabokov, Vladimir. "Philistines and Philistinism." In *Lectures on Russian Literature.* New York: Harcourt Brace Jovanovich, 1981.

———. *Nikolai Gogol.* Norfolk: New Directions, 1944.

Pushkin, Aleksandr. *Sochineniia,* vol. 3. Moscow, 1955.

Russkie pesni i romansy. Moscow, 1989.

Sontag, Susan. *Against Interpretation.* (1961.) New York: Dell, 1969.

Stern, Jane, and Michael Stern. *The Encyclopedia of Bad Taste.* New York: Harper Perennial, 1991.

Tolstaya, Tatyana. *On the Golden Porch.* Trans. Antonina W. Bouis. New York: Knopf, 1989.

Tupitsyn, Margarita. *Between Spring and Summer: Soviet Conceptual Art in the Era of Late Communism.* Ed. David Ross. Cambridge, MA: MIT Press, 1991.

5

THE CREATION OF
NADEZHDA IAKOVLEVNA MANDEL'SHTAM

Beth Holmgren

> Surely it is rare to find such a marriage, such understanding,
> such spiritual kinship. Nadezhda Iakovlevna was equal to her
> husband in intelligence, education, and her enormous spiritual
> strength. I never heard her complain, I never saw her irritated
> or depressed. She was always even-tempered, outwardly calm.
> Without a doubt she was Osip Emil'evich's moral support. Their
> life depended on her. His difficult, tragic fate became hers. She
> took this cross on herself as if there was no other way.
>
> —Natasha Shtempel'

> With her long hooked nose, large mouth, and jutting teeth,
> bow-legged Nadia was a celebrity in that club of worldly
> people. How did she manage this? With her glib tongue? Of
> course. With the self-assuredness of a girl who tosses out the
> paradoxes she has picked up from smart people?
> Undoubtedly. With the daredevil tricks of a mischief-maker
> *(ozornitsa)* who knows how to drink and not get drunk? That,
> too. But when her loud shameless laughter died down, the
> tender watercolors of her face became more noticeable: soft
> ashen hair, bright blue eyes (slanted, don't forget) with
> bird-like pupils, rosy delicate skin, prominent white forehead.
>
> —Emma Gershtein

In his 1974 review of Nadezhda Iakovlevna Mandel'shtam's second volume of memoirs (*Hope Abandoned*), Joseph Brodsky solemnly recognized the emergence of a "unique phenomenon: the
widow of a great poet turned out to be a great writer" (13).

Notwithstanding the controversy provoked by her plain-speaking texts, Brodsky's claim has been echoed by an impressive array of literary scholars and historians. In his survey of postrevolutionary Russian literature, Edward Brown lauds Nadezhda Iakovlevna's memoirs as "a work of art" (47); Barbara Heldt equates them with the documentary feats of Aleksandr Solzhenitsyn (145). Both Robert Conquest and Robert Tucker, renowned historians of the Stalinist era, use her texts as important references and sources of pungent epigraphs.[1] Indeed, even when her first volume of memoirs was still circulating as a *samizdat* manuscript in the 1960s, no less an authority than Aleksandr Tvardovskii praised its "exceptional strength and talent."[2]

Yet this extraordinary recognition—so uncommonly *un*qualified for a Russian woman writer (and especially the mere wife of a greatq Russian poet)—has not generated the kind of critical investment conferred on other "unofficial" Soviet artists. Nadezhda Iakovlevna's achievement has been commended in book reviews and the summary passages of survey works, but, as Charles Isenberg observes, "not much attention has been paid to her qualities as a writer" (1990, 193). There are several plausible reasons for our neglect: an implied hierarchy of recovery, according to which scholars labor first to canonize the work of Osip and not Nadezhda Mandel'shtam; the complexities of analyzing "boundary genres" (memoirs, documentary prose); the related predisposition of critics to focus on fiction writers. Perhaps Nadezhda Iakovlevna's "canonization" is only a matter of time; certainly Isenberg's essays (1987, 1990) have contributed substantially to this end. But I also suspect a more systemic obstacle. We in Russian studies are just beginning to discern possible models for the creative biographies of Russian women writers— that is, the often circuitous and duplicitous routes women have had to improvise in their assumption of authorship and a subject position. And Nadezhda Iakovlevna's biography presents an especially problematic (as well as dramatic) case, for she came to write, as it were, by way of the service entrance, producing her own texts from her position as Osip Mandel'shtam's caretaker and conservator. How can we account for the "unique phenomenon" of Nadezhda Iakovlevna, the transformation of a great poet's widow into a "great writer"?

Nadezhda Iakovlevna herself does not make our task any easier, because she never presumed that she had become a writer. It is only in *Hope Abandoned* that she at least conceives of the possibility of her own value as subject. Here she says that she excluded herself from the first volume because she "still did not exist" (11); although she announces that she "will write about [her]self alone," her narrative projects an extraordinarily diffuse, other-oriented "I" that is regularly distorted by the moral-political schema she imposes.[3] On the one hand, Nadezhda Iakovlevna's concept of selfhood seems to echo that of many women writers, with its figuring of an "I" always situated among and responsive to others.[4] On the other hand, for her (as for so many memoirists of the Stalin period) political context inexorably dominates and to some extent restricts her analysis. In her effort to foreground the poet's moral resistance to a destructive state, Nadezhda Iakovlevna tends to devalue those stages of her development—childhood, adolescence—that lie outside of the marriage relationship (*Hope Abandoned*, 13, 181).[5] As a result, her general conclusions seem drastically reductive: Nadezhda Iakovlevna defines the first, formative period of her life as her twenty-year marital relationship with Mandel'shtam (181–82) and actually describes herself as "the work of his own hands" (218).

Throughout her writing Nadezhda Iakovlevna repeatedly invokes the life story her husband imagined for her. She appears on the scene as a spoiled, silly young girl—a Europa whom her husband abducts, tames, and trains to share his tragic destiny as Leah, the faithful Jewish wife.[6] In effect, she imposes this ready, manmade plot on doubly uncharted territory—on the life of a woman spent in inconceivable conditions.[7] Yet even though she seems to endorse this plot, Nadezhda Iakovlevna gradually reveals a far more capacious, ambiguous, and boisterous self-image—a self-image that she seems to relish and even indulge, despite her retrospective criticism of the "silly girl." Over the

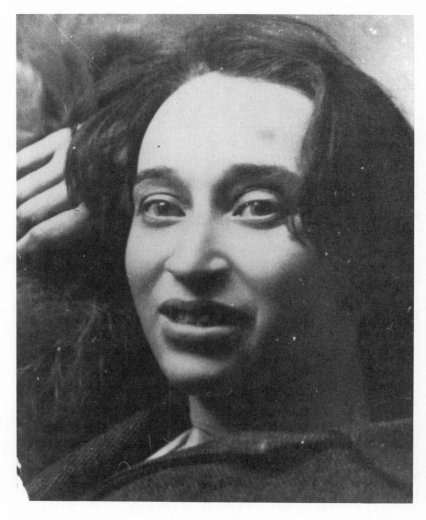

Nadezhda Iakovlevna Mandel'shtam   Photo courtesy of Ardis Publishers

course of two volumes of memoirs and sketches for a third, and after public recognition of her own writing achievement (however self-deprecated), she actually discloses what *she* brought to this "formative" relationship with Mandel'shtam and demonstrates that their marriage, while dedicated to her husband's artis-

tic genius, represented a true collaboration of talent and temperament that sustained both partners, preserved Mandel'shtam's poetry, and ultimately engendered her own distinctive authorship.

Family Life

In order to appreciate her development both within and outside of
her relationship with Mandel'shtam, I propose to reconstruct the
narrative of Nadezhda Iakovlevna's premarital life—to compile
and reorder the information she sporadically divulged and, whenever possible, corroborate these data with the testimony of her
friends and associates.[8] I do so not to discount Nadezhda
Iakovlevna's own projection of self and autobiography but to
analyze what I consider to be the productive paradoxes in her
self-conception and role playing. It seems most appropriate to
proceed from the end of her oeuvre; in her last years Nadezhda
Iakovlevna composed three sketches—"Father," "Family," "Girls
and a Boy"—which assay her reconstruction of childhood and
family life.[9] Written under the double constraints of poor health
and a persistent self-disregard, restlessly shifting in focus and
time sequence (from childhood to revolution to Stalin era), these
fragments nevertheless intimate the specific importance of her
girlhood. Nadezhda Iakovlevna offers no systematic analysis of
her early years—her religious training, schooling, routine family
life. Yet we can recover certain facts and features from her desul-
tory comments: that she was the youngest of four children, the
baby of the family and the object of her brothers' merciless teas-
ing; that her family was materially comfortable, able to travel in
Europe and inclined to eat too well; that her household was not
religious, but observed Orthodox fasts out of respect for their
devout cook; that, after a series of English governesses, she eventually attended a girls' gymnasium with a "male" (that is, implicitly more difficult) curriculum that required such impressive
subjects as Latin.

While these sketches stylistically reflect her lack of reverence
for certain autobiographical conventions, they register mainly the

constant interference of political context. Nadezhda Iakovlevna's venture back into childhood is precarious, overshadowed by memories of its destruction. Describing a family portrait or an inventory of household goods, she flashes forward to scenes of confiscation and bereavement—her father's calm acceptance of his ruin (82), the terrible deaths of her older brother and sister. She filters the habits and appurtenances of her middle-class life through the purifying, sharp-eyed lens of loss; she itemizes individual objects and episodes as if they were the few remaining artifacts of an extinct culture, a destroyed paradise. In her narrative, militant outside forces (most often Soviet) lay constant siege to this childhood world—stealing the family's money and furniture, carrying off her brothers, threatening them all (a Jewish family converted to Christianity) with pogroms.

In "Girls and a Boy" she most pointedly illustrates the danger and undesirability of the political world (and public life in general) with an anecdote about the tsar's visit to her school. She remembers being moved by the sight of the tsar's children—"the very handsome boy and four sad girls"—and eventually she ponders their tragic murder, but first she detects a more insidious hazard:

> I suddenly understood that I was much happier than these unfortunate girls: after all, I could run around with the dogs on the street, make friends with the boys, not learn my lessons, make mischief, go to bed late, read all kinds of junk and fight—with my brothers and anybody else. . . . I and my governesses had a very simple arrangement: we'd leave the house together, purposefully, and then go our separate ways—they to their rendezvous and I to my boys—I didn't make friends with girls—you can only really fight with boys! But these poor princesses were bound in everything: they were polite, affectionate, friendly, attentive. . . . They weren't even allowed to fight. . . . Poor girls! (90–91)

In juxtaposing herself with the tsar's daughters—prisoners of decorum and victims of political intrigue—Nadezhda Iakovlevna indicates her own private advantage. She discovers real freedom and pleasure in informal play, an unscrutinized life. She depicts herself as conniving her life free from the restrictions of class and gender—escaping the supervision of parents and teachers, taking to the plebeian streets, and behaving as ladylike etiquette would never permit.

In focus and content, then, Nadezhda Iakovlevna's childhood recollections gradually describe an idiosyncratic set of values derived from family practice and her own temperament, and dismissive of certain institutions and conventions in her society.[10] She highlights her parents' practice of materially indulging themselves and their children, their basic attitude of tolerance and respect for others. She quotes her mother's theory of child rearing—that "you had to spoil children silly—otherwise they wouldn't survive this unbearable life . . . you had to anticipate every wish so that your children could think up nothing more . . . " (87). She emulates both father and mother in savoring good food and commending their cook, Dar'ia, for her remarkable culinary talent (80).[11] She remembers, too, how her father, a confirmed atheist, taught her to respect the Christian scriptures. Within this protected universe, material comfort, domestic art, mutual respect, and high culture are named as equal values; her narrative simply deflects signs of "proper" political or domestic behavior.

This at once indulgent and privileged universe also seemed to exempt Nadezhda Iakovlevna from traditional gender roles and activities; she gives no evidence of a "girlish" education, of training to become a good housewife and mother. Although her mother is a positive presence in her text, Nadezhda Iakovlevna highlights her father, Iakov Arkad'evich, as the larger, more distinct influence.[12] In the opening scene of "Father" she frames him from her adoring childish vantage point, describing his enormous height and heavy step and remembering her sudden conviction that "he was a *barin*" (79). In effect, Nadezhda Iakovlevna *entitles* her father as her intellectual mentor, her link with an urbane, cultured world. (She is markedly silent about her mother's professional achievement, despite the fact that Vera Iakovlevna was in one of the first groups of Russian women to train successfully as physicians.)[13] Nadezhda Iakovlevna writes that after her father completed a degree in mathematics, he finished law school in several months and staggered his professors with his brilliance (81). It was her father who moved them from provincial Saratov to the cultural center of Kiev in a successful search for a job. Interestingly enough, her father also presented her with an example of informal yet serious scholarship. She reports that in his leisure time he read Greek tragedies in the original; he quietly encouraged his daughter to buy good books and read important authors (85).

Perhaps most important, her father equipped her with a peculiar kind of public persona, a provocative speaking part. In contrast to her father's kindly "meek" image at home, Nadezhda Iakovlevna documents episodes of his fiery public behavior—his outspoken protest against what he perceived to be immoral or illegal acts. She tells us that her father repelled a pogrom of their household with "choice swear words"; that he attempted to sue the Cheka for evicting them from their apartment; that he failed to get work as a defense attorney under the new regime because he told his interviewers just what he thought of Soviet law. In relating this last outburst, Nadezhda Iakovlevna identifies her father's basic stance—his defiant urge to snap out the "whole truth" (*pravda-matka*) and to counter indecent action with indecent language. And in a later sketch she intimates that she took him as her model at an early age. She remembers that when her older brothers abandoned her on top of a tall wardrobe and her giant father had to rescue her, she assumed her father's speaking part:

> [. . .] and I howled and learned how to swear: "Idiots, blockheads!" [. . .] I've had great success with this all my long life. Father said, "Why do they hurt the little one?" and comforted me as best he could. . . . And I kissed him and said, "You tell them, those blockheads." (89)

Whereas Iakov Arkad'evich cannot raise his voice against his sons, his daughter adopts his image to defend herself. She not only matches him in verbal scrappiness but forms a kind of partnership with him in which she plays the role of the unabashed belligerent, the profane truthteller.[14] Through this kind of testimony Nadezhda Iakovlevna reveals an empowering father-daughter connection: although her father still occupies the position of family patriarch, he shelters and indulges his daughter and even arouses an unorthodox fighting spirit in her.

Unfortunately, Nadezhda Iakovlevna tells us little about the years when she reached sexual maturity and made the important transition from family life to participation in the wider world. Once the barely adult Nadezhda Iakovlevna does appear in her work, what we learn mainly is that she is changed for the worse:

> I am not proud of my early youth. The image that comes back to me is of a great herd of cattle stampeding over a field of ripe corn and trampling it underfoot in vast swaths. In those days I ran around as one of a small herd of painters. (*Hope Abandoned,* 13)

Her account distorts her accomplishment, degrading her experience as bestial and denying her capacity for independent thought and action. Yet during her "stampeding" youth, Nadezhda Iakovlevna was working in the studio of Aleksandra Ekster, one of the most renowned theatrical artists of the Russian avant-garde.[15] Although she later relegated herself to the status of "dabbler" (218), her connection with this teacher was impressive and her descriptions of her experience with the "herd," even as she judges it here, convey some of the heady excitement she must have felt at the time. In particular, she describes the curtain call she shared after her performance in the 1919 production of Lope de Vega's *Fuenteovejuna* in Kiev; she recalls the artists in their "hectic round of pleasure"—painting, frequenting night clubs, buying "mountains of pastries," and charging about the streets after curfew. For a brief time after the October Revolution, Nadezhda Iakovlevna's irreverent, free-spirited tendencies seem to be officially encouraged and she has no need to distinguish between her private and her public life.[16]

It is intriguing, however, that her one flirtation with worldly success incurs such strong retrospective condemnation. On the one hand, her response is marked by a sort of ascetic pride: she disdains her foolishness in accepting the world's opinion of her and joining the establishment. On the other, she dismisses her own talent as a creator, for she represents herself as an undifferentiated member of a falsely self-important collective of artists, a group that unwittingly serves its new "masters." Her iconoclasm and self-criticism combine to cast her as a deluded sinner, a young woman who must renounce her prideful claims of importance in order to save her immortal soul. And these notions of excess and conversion may strike a resonant chord because they partially evoke her relationship with her father. He was the one who quietly, effectively rebuked her when she ridiculed the Christian scriptures; her escape from the mocking "herd" is facilitated by similar paternal mentors. The first such instruction takes place in Ekster's studio. Nadezhda Iakovlevna has the weakness to laugh at a cruel verse about killing tsarist officers, and the writer Il'ia Èrenburg, already disaffected by the bloody carnival, is on hand to scold her:

> He gave me such a talking-to that I still respect him for it, and I am proud that, silly as I was at the time, I had the sense to listen to him and remember his words forever afterward. This happened before my meeting with M., so that he did not have to cure me of the head-hunting mentality. . . . (*Hope against Hope*, 107).

Sporadically noted, the pattern is nonetheless important. Her father, it seems, prepared the way for Èrenburg and Èrenburg prepared the way for Osip Mandel'shtam. Nadezhda Iakovlevna's life story is not so much subsumed as reiterated by her husband's Europa-Leah plot. Reviewed from the beginning, her "wildness" is not an early expendable stage but a permanent condition periodically tempered and redirected by an older, seemingly wiser male authority.

In their carnival surroundings, then, Osip Mandel'shtam happened on a ready listener in Nadezhda Iakovlevna. They met in a nightclub and entered into a casual liaison, but the effect of their union was instantly significant. The collective singled out Mandel'shtam as an undesirable influence: "Our sudden friendship annoyed everybody for some reason" (*Hope Abandoned*, 16). His improvidence was distinct from the frivolity of the herd; his attitude, she realizes, implied "a serene acceptance of life" (21). Yet while arguing his singularity, she also indicates that she was "different" enough to heed it. Brought together by chance, the established poet and the apprentice painter already shared the qualities of "lightheadedness and a sense of doom." Among her thoughtless companions, Nadezhda Iakovlevna alone seemed predisposed to absorb Mandel'shtam's unusual reflections, to be entranced by the cautious glimpses he granted her of his inner world.

Even given Mandel'shtam's singularity, Nadezhda Iakovlevna's decision to go with him seems driven mainly by external dangers: the civil war waylaid any plans for a career or a stable family life. When Osip Emil'evich abruptly left for the Crimea, Nadezhda Iakovlevna had plans to join him, but could not move "with all the bloodshed in the streets" (21). By the time Mandel'shtam came for her, her family had been evicted twice from their home. A novelist could not have staged their reunion more suspensefully: against the backdrop of an emptied apartment, in counterpoint to a vulgar chorus of female criminals who have been commandeered to clean the place, Mandel'shtam reads his poetry to his beloved and announces that he will take her away (22). The young woman (she is twenty-one) thus leaves her ruined family and invaded home for the makeshift refuge of life with an artist. As Nadezhda Iakovlevna interprets it, their casual relationship was renewed and truly forged by luck, a strange coincidence of temperament, and just such extenuating dramatic circumstances.

The Marriage Relationship

I have attempted to review Nadezhda Iakovlevna's autobiography *without* Mandel'shtam up to the period she deems formative in her life, the period that functions as the centripetal core of almost all her writing. She herself designates three further stages in her relationship with her husband, each stage advancing them toward a more complete union. The first phase encompassed their life in the early 1920s, when the poet stubbornly secluded his wife from social contact and trained her to appreciate poetry.

The second phase took shape in the aftermath of Mandel'shtam's affair with another woman, Ol'ga Vaksel: Nadezhda Iakovlevna threatened to leave, he struggled to keep her, and their relationship was mended and renewed. The "third and final stage" was prompted by "his journey to Armenia and return to writing verse" (*Hope Abandoned,* 263); despite their physical persecution, they were happy with each other and the poetry Mandel'shtam could now produce. Each stage presumed Mandel'shtam's larger importance; his creative success was a key factor in their good relations. Each stage also depended on the determining role he played in their marriage. Nadezhda Iakovlevna may have rebelled against his control, but she was inevitably the one who responded, adapted, and made compensation.

But why did Nadezhda Iakovlevna submit? She is painfully frank about her degradation, at least in the early phase of their relationship. She admits that she then "felt like a horse in the hands of a trainer," "a compliant and easy charge" (260). In later years Mandel'shtam's domineering role was softened somewhat: he behaved "much more like a protector and friend than as an overseer and trainer" (260). Nevertheless, Nadezhda Iakovlevna lived with the hard fact that she was important, loved, and kept in large part because Mandel'shtam had invested so much in her "creation." She accepted this unflattering truth and stayed with him, but, as she herself seems to sense, love cannot adequately explain her attachment. In order to understand her "submission," therefore, I offer the following analysis of their relationship—its distribution and revision of various conventional gender roles and plots, its obvious costs and subtle benefits—as Nadezhda Iakovlevna reveals it in her writing.

Once again, political context is depicted as the most overwhelming influence. In her narrative the Soviet regime fundamentally, inexorably shapes their relationship; the "sense of doom" that Nadezhda Iakovlevna shared with Mandel'shtam was confirmed over the years. Unlike so many other witnesses to Soviet history, she views the first postrevolutionary decades as a steady downward slide into totalitarian control. The harassment of Mandel'shtam began in the 1920s, in tandem with the movement toward a conformist society. Nadezhda Iakovlevna experiences and reports this decade so often termed "liberal" as a time of desperate confusion, uncertain work, and grinding poverty. The 1930s then ushered in true political terror, and Mandel'shtam—arrested, exiled, and arrested once again—was virtually sentenced to death. Facing such horrific physical and psychological conditions, husband and wife were both compelled and inspired to remain together. They joined in a single unit of support as their only means of physical and moral survival. Of the two, Nadezhda Iakovlevna seemed to have the better chance for escape; she might have spared herself much grief if she had divorced Mandel'shtam and recanted her association. But she chose, again and again, the noble, tragic role of sharing his life and persecution, of working for him and even begging with him as they staved off his inevitable doom.

Along with pain and suffering, then, the Stalinist context also imposed an unforeseen benefit. It redefined both the terms and the nature of their relationship. In his reading of Nadezhda Iakovlevna's work, Charles Isenberg has astutely observed that the Stalinist terror allayed her other great terror—a conventional marriage (1990, 198). Just as it disrupted careers and lives, the regime undermined the possibility of a "bourgeois family romance." Isenberg draws a fascinating parallel between the Mandel'shtam's marriage and the relationship of Jean-Paul Sartre and Simone de Beauvoir. For both couples, he asserts,

> it is the writings of the female partner that create the relationship as a literary phenomenon, and both the Russian and the Frenchwoman represent their primary relationships as a critique of, and counter-example to, the ideology of marriage in its Stalinist-bourgeois and French-bourgeois forms. And both women portray couples that are morally exemplary in their determination to live their values. (195)

Isenberg tends to trace Nadezhda Iakovlevna's distaste for the "family romance" to a fear of being abandoned (197–98). Certainly she herself "is quite prepared to admit" that, given a normal life, Mandel'shtam might have left her for another woman

(*Hope Abandoned,* 264); it is perhaps a matter of strategy as well as analysis that she dates the second, improved phase of their relationship from her husband's break with Ol'ga Vaksel. But, as we have learned from her childhood narrative, her distaste also reflects her long-standing aversion to convention and institutionalized practice. Mandel'shtam attracted an already confirmed iconoclast and free spirit with the prospect of a "countermarriage"—what seemed to be an adult version of her family refuge.

Within this countermarriage Nadezhda Iakovlevna did not need to play the conventional wife, but she embraced other roles that, I maintain, still reflect women's secondary position in a patriarchal system.[17] Nadezhda Iakovlevna explicitly subscribes to the gender assignments her husband first suggested in his poetry collection *Tristia:* "M. had a peculiar way of dividing humanity into 'men' and 'wives.' The 'men' bore all responsibility for worldly matters, while the 'wives' were mourners, fortune-tellers, and gatherers of 'the light ashes that remain'. . . ." (61). The poet devised for his wife a conserving, interpreting, passive role based on his own recodifying of European culture. Therefore, when Nadezhda Iakovlevna serves as his loving widow and biographer, she is empowered through Mandel'shtam's composite archetype of a woman in the traditionally female roles of mourner and seer. Although the Soviet authorities prevented her from gathering up his ashes, she commemorates her husband as best she can, and she is largely heeded and commended (and Mandel'shtam's poetry hailed as prophetic) because she enacts his vision.

By enacting this vision, moreover, Nadezhda Iakovlevna is included in another sanctioning and signifying tradition of Russian women who deliberately share their loved ones' persecution. In her voluntary and extreme devotion, she recalls the wives of the seventeenth-century schismatic Avvakum and the nineteenth-century Decembrists.[18] In fact, it is the poet Anna Akhmatova—that emblematic authority on bereavement and self-renunciation—who pronounces her a Decembrist wife (Chukovskaia 438). Through her sacrifice Nadezhda Iakovlevna achieves not only a ready public image but an approved public voice. She benefits from perhaps the most powerful and productive variant within the flourishing genre of Russian women's memoirs: the memoir of the female political martyr.[19] The writers of these texts are not all innocent casualties—they range from Princess Dolgorukaia (1714–71), who virtually married into banishment, to Vera Figner (1852–1943), who helped plot the assassination of the tsar—but they are linked in their justification for writing.[20] Silenced and limited by a patriarchal society, these women assumed the right to speak because their private experience had been rendered public and political by a repressive state. Their lives, in themselves deemed unrepresentative and unworthy of attention, thus offer valuable documents of "greater" political campaigns and injustices.[21] Paradoxically, by suffering and submitting, Nadezhda Iakovlevna has appropriated the *traditional* role of a *writing* Russian woman.

While their "marriage made co-martyrdom" transformed Nadezhda Iakovlevna into beloved wife, noble archetype, and sanctioned female writer (again, roles that convey a secondary, complementary status), it also enabled her to adopt a very different mode of being and (eventually) writing. Fortunately for Nadezhda Iakovlevna, her husband's authoritative example, curbed by their hard life, accommodated and fostered certain extant features of her character. On the most urgent level, Mandel'shtam elicited the sturdy pragmatist in Nadezhda Iakovlevna and their relationship consequently evolved into an interesting variation on certain traditional marriage roles. Mandel'shtam intended from the very outset both to supervise and to support his wife. He acted as the protector of a vulnerable, helpless girl: "In his eyes I was always the younger one who had to be soothed, protected and, if need be, taken in hand to stop me from doing silly things" (*Hope Abandoned,* 127).[22] He wished her to cultivate a "dignified wifely charm," while he retained his primary position as nurturing, providing husband. Yet, as their living conditions worsened, his health flagged, and his persecution became more apparent, Mandel'shtam was compelled to rely on the domestic and *professional* ministrations of his wife. He had always presumed his wife's function as his literary secretary, but he did not anticipate *her* role as provider. Having abandoned her career as an artist for a more absorbing life with Mandel'shtam, Nadezhda Iakovlevna suddenly found herself forced to improvise a livelihood. Under such extenuating circumstances, she became, by her own admission, "the breadwinner" in their household (125), taking on the translating and editing jobs Mandel'shtam could or would not perform.[23] Thus their relationship partially, involuntarily reenacted the plot of weak male artist and provident female helpmate—a plot we find featured in such contemporary fictional works as Mikhail Bulgakov's *Master and Margarita* and Boris Pasternak's *Doctor Zhivago*—and at the same time evinced an interdependency in which the roles of caretaker and charge were shared over the years.

It is remarkable, too, that Nadezhda Iakovlevna comes to identify her caretaking ability as a female strength. She has intimated it as a family trait in her sketches of childhood; in *Hope Against Hope* she conveys it more specifically as maternal legacy. After Mandel'shtam's first arrest, when she and Akhmatova were struggling to cope, it was her mother, just arrived from Kiev, who immediately sized up their situation and put the household in order (21). When the couple was sent into exile, she gave them all her money and tried to keep their Moscow apartment until their return. Although her presence is intermittent in her daughter's narrative, we know from letters and other testimony that Vera Iakovlevna regularly substituted as Mandel'shtam's caretaker when her daughter had to be away.[24] Paying brief tribute to her mother's resourcefulness, lauding the similar industry and solicitude of other women (the women who visit them after Mandel'shtam's first arrest, the noble figures of Anna Akhmatova and Vasilisa Shklovskaia), Nadezhda Iakovlevna eventually draws this bold conclusion in *Hope Abandoned:*

> When the hard times came it became clear that women, who had affected the part of lady or little bird, were the main organizers of daily life and, indeed, were the builders and mainstay of the family. . . the women were always stronger than the men, as everybody sees well enough today. (105)

Yet as powerful as she became in providing for her husband, Nadezhda Iakovlevna was never fully developed or objectified as a typical "Soviet wife"—that is, an amalgam of housekeeper, breadwinner, and ambitious materialist.[25] Though Mandel'shtam eventually lived in dependence on Nadezhda Iakovlevna, he neither desired nor encouraged her to become "the high-powered, protective" spouse his friends urged him to marry (141). By running off with Mandel'shtam, Nadezhda Iakovlevna had renounced, in effect, all goals of worldly accomplishment, all hope of domestic stability. Just as she forsook her own career, so she rejected the vicarious career of ambitious wife. She demanded none of the rewards distributed by the new Soviet cultural establishment—the nice apartment, good salary, special goods and privileges. She still longed for the domestic well-being of her childhood years, but, in contrast to the materialism of the "wives," her longing is linked with a general enjoyment of life rather than a desire for status: "We were not at all ascetics by nature and neither of us had a tendency toward self-denial. It simply turned out that we had to renounce everything because they demanded too high a price for an increase in one's rations" (236). She and her creator-husband appeared to live according to the same world view—one that combined a free aesthetic sensitivity with ethical concern and earthly pleasure.[26] And as their relationship matured and Mandel'shtam had to yield more responsibility to his "foolish" younger wife, the two of them achieved a kind of balance of nonstatus, an equal level of childlike helplessness and "lightheadedness." In her last letter to her husband Nadezhda Iakovlevna offers a most apt description of their state:

> Osia, what joy it was living together like children—all our squabbles and arguments, the games we played, and our love. . . . Like two blind puppies we were nuzzling each other and feeling good together. (620)

For all its difficulty, then, life with Mandel'shtam did not transform the playful child—the "little foolish creature"—into an official writer's materialistic wife. Although Nadezhda Iakovlevna evinced a greater capacity for pragmatic action, she acted out of necessity, not ambition; her mild materialism, in turn, was shared with and endorsed by her husband. By maintaining her childhood values and temperament, she thus voluntarily resisted the role of wife in a Stalinist-bourgeois marriage. Her mentality and self-image were not so much made by Mandel'shtam as intersecting at crucial junctures with his authoritative model. Furthermore, she indicates that she was able to progress from being the "kitten" or "puppy" kept in tow by her husband to a partnership in which husband and wife alternated in the roles of parent and child and, in their happiest moments, managed to live as children and "puppies" together. She reconstructs Mandel'shtam as a kind of husband/brother—a "man who would understand"—who has been conditioned by outside circumstances and the give-and-take of their close relationship. As such, Mandel'shtam is shown to exist in part as a product of *her* hands and "an alternative to patriarchal power and dominance," the more so since their partnership is never unbalanced by children.[27]

Nadezhda Iakovlevna avoided yet another occupational hazard: in contrast to the lovers and wives of other male poets, she was never scripted and silenced as an icon of female beauty. With characteristic acumen, she pinpoints this essential difference between Mandel'shtam and the archsymbolist Russian poet, Aleksandr Blok:

> In his personal life M. was the complete opposite of Blok. I would even say that he was by nature anti-Blok. The highest aspect of love was not, for him, service to the "Beautiful Lady," but something quite different which he summed up in the words "my you." His anti-Blok nature was also reflected in his choice of a wife—not a "beautiful lady," not in fact even a "lady" at all, but a mere slip of a girl, someone belonging to a lower order of womanhood with whom everything was funny, simple, and frivolous, but with whom he gradually attained to relations of such supreme closeness that he could say: "I feel free with you." (245)

As we have seen, Mandel'shtam did fix his wife with various images and plots, but he conceived of her mainly as an extension of himself, not a female Other or an embodiment of the Eternal Feminine.[28] Nadezhda Iakovlevna was not beautiful and not idolized; although she was sexually attractive, she refused to mystify her appeal in the fashion of the symbolists and she rejected the rituals and mannerisms of the "great lady" as exemplified by Anna Akhmatova. In fact, despite her deep affection for Akhmatova, Nadezhda Iakovlevna criticizes her constant posing as a leftover habit from the early twentieth-century cult of "beauties" —women who took pains with their grooming and were worshiped as the belles of Petersburg high society. To Nadezhda Iakovlevna these "beauties" are another defining antipode for her own image and conduct. In place of artful games, high melodrama, and worship of the Beautiful Lady, Nadezhda Iakovlevna expresses her preference for sexual frankness, casual liaisons, and the easy company she can offer and employ as the "girl friend."[29] In this regard, she is for once proud of the "destruction" wrought by her contemporaries:

> My generation, which destroyed the institution of marriage (something I still regard as an achievement), did not recognize vows of fidelity. We were ready at any moment to break off a marriage (regarded anyway only as a protracted love affair) and get a divorce—or rather separate, because in fact there was no real marriage to begin with. It is amazing that such markedly casual relationships often resulted in lasting unions which were very much more stable than the marriages, founded on lies and pretense, of earlier generations. (136)

As a "girl friend," she argues, she was far more beneficial to Mandel'shtam than a conventional wife could be: she was a lighthearted companion who renounced all rights and demanded no care (139). And it is highly significant that Nadezhda Iakovlevna ventures to claim this attitude—with its emphasis on honesty and disregard for convention—as possibly her one creative contribution to their relationship: "Although [Mandel'shtam] influenced me greatly and molded me in his own image, I also affected him in certain ways with my impatience and readiness to pack up and leave at any moment" (137).[30]

Thus, by playing out the role of girl friend, Nadezhda Iakovlevna escaped the venality of the materialistic wife and the objectification of the beauty. At the same time, her "happy-go-lucky" role, sanctioned by Mandel′shtam's co-option of her as his "you," harbored a more aggressive power, a license for self-assertion. Since she alone had undergone his intensive, intimate training—had allowed him in part to remold her into an extension of himself—she was given both the duty and the right to speak in his name. She was the one who could and should tend to his archive; more, she was the one authorized spokesperson for his views. And her self-styled role as girl friend and the attitude it implies unmistakably shaped and extended her fulfillment of these tasks. As the unlovely, irreverent, impatient girl friend, Nadezhda Iakovlevna evinced a constant impulse to unmask and reassess people and events in plain and even provocative terms.[31] The companion and confidante of great poets such as Mandel′shtam and Akhmatova, she dared to write and elucidate what they said in private or uttered enigmatically; she functioned, in a sense, as their prosaic, uncensored alter ego, the truthtelling fool in their discreet royal court. With Mandel′shtam in particular, this role accrued from beloved precedent. Here she seemed to resume the stance she first learned with her father: Mandel′shtam's idiosyncratic authority not only exempted her from the more inhibiting patriarchal conventions of her society but finally inspired her to take the part of unabashed defender, to be provoked into speaking the "whole truth."

In this way, through childhood experience and marriage, Nadezhda Iakovlevna acquired the foundation for a complex self-conception and authorship. Her character took definite shape in childhood, when she developed the basic life patterns and values later canonized by her relationship with Mandel′shtam. Within the refuge of her family she enjoyed a tolerant atmosphere and an unconventional autonomy; she learned to appreciate a wide array of arts and pleasures. In her relations with her father she seemed to discover the makings of two productive roles—those of the wild girl brought to reason and the wild girl unleashed as righteous warrior. Reviewing the formative period of her childhood, I presume to amend her extreme conclusion: although Nadezhda Iakovlevna confesses that she is "the work of [her husband's] own hands," she was constantly negotiating her life text in relation to beloved, authoritative male figures—vacillating between obedience and wildness, altruism and a complex self-indulgence.

Her "submission" to Mandel'shtam, then, comprised an intriguing combination of self-renunciation and self-assertion. Giving up her independence, she acquired through him an articulation of her own world view and a most compelling and ennobled mission. Nadezhda Iakovlevna's iconoclasm and joie de vivre came already embodied and approved in the poet. Her selfless mission to preserve him and his work granted her a powerful public image and, most surprisingly, a speaking part she would never have otherwise assumed. Moreover, in the course of serving and then preserving Mandel'shtam, Nadezhda Iakovlevna gradually recognized her own distinctive strengths and position. She discovered her greater ability to cope and endure, an ability she even identifies as female. She proved her own empowering singularity as a woman; resisting material entrapment and objectification (as well as the docility her husband demanded), she maintained an unusual freedom of action and expression. And by pursuing her own creative variant of the role of girl friend and confidante, she developed into a powerful, distinctive writer who displayed great storytelling and rhetorical skills, a liberating irreverence toward convention, and an almost self-indulgent passion for telling the whole truth.

Yet however fulfilling her relationship with Mandel'shtam proved to be, it is important to note that Nadezhda Iakovlevna could become an author only after she was widowed.[32] Their relationship created the impetus and essential source for her writing, but she could not presume to write until her husband's authoritative voice and person—for her, the greatest values of their marriage—were absent. In a sense, her bereavement provided her with a crucial detachment, the necessary space in which to write in her own way. And once Nadezhda Iakovlevna began to write, the process of self-realization gained incredible momentum: in *Hope against Hope* and *Hope Abandoned* she progressed to grander thematic vistas and bolder, more idiosyncratic assertions of her authority. We have come full circle to the most familiar (and most neatly contained) segment of her biography, the time when the poet's widow has at last surfaced as writer and public figure and wins the accolades of various cultural authorities after years of suffering and political repression. Yet, as I have tried to show, this "unique phenomenon" arose through no simple sequence of martyrdom and reward or through the male-centered "widow's" plot of submission and service. Nadezhda Iakovlevna came to produce her works of art through a complex series of sanctions, compromises, and collaborations. Like so many Soviet women, she was caught up in that determining opposition of patriarchal structures—between official Stalinism and the norms and premises of unofficial Russian society—and both disrupt and divert the story of her creation. Therefore, unique as her achievement is claimed to be, I contend that her creative biography reveals important patterns and strategies that recur in the development of other Russian women writers: their allegiance to mediating male authorities, especially within more repressive official contexts; their self-liberating critique of certain traditionally feminine traits and behaviors; their intermittently managed detachment and self-assertion; their productive, sometimes paradoxical combination of assigned and self-styled roles and images. If we are not to fall into the old (and still effective) traps set to contain and dismiss women's writing, we need to reread the life and work of Nadezhda Iakovlevna Mandel'shtam as a telling model rather than as an unpredictable anomaly.[33]

Notes

1. Conquest, esp. 291; Tucker, esp. 479.

2. Tvardovskii deftly summarizes the book's merits: "I read [the book] in 'one gulp' for there's no other way to read it. It is written as if it was being related one night to a good friend before whom there is nothing to hide or

prove. . . . But at the same time it is written with exceptional strength and talent and, judging it from a literary point of view, with a special sense of the necessary in its exposition, for despite its length nothing seems superfluous. Even the peculiar repetitions, flashbacks, flashforwards, digressions or distractions—it all appears to be natural and justified" (10).

3. All of the quotations from these memoirs are Max Hayward's translations (1970, 1974) with my revisions based on the Russian originals (1982, 1987).

4. These notions of women's autobiography have been explored extensively by American and Western European critics. For a few useful sources, see Friedman; Smith; Jelinek.

5. In contrast, see how childhood and adolescence are explored in the well-known autobiographical narratives of other Russian women: the soldier Nadezhda Durova (1783–1866), the mathematician Sofia Kovalevskaia (1850–1890), and the poet Marina Tsvetaeva (1892–1941). All are available in English translation. Although female political activists tend to write most about their political involvement as adults, their earlier phases often are clearly marked in their autobiographies. For a sampling of these texts in English, see Engel and Rosenthal.

6. See, e.g., *Hope Abandoned*, 236, for a recapitulation of this story. On Nadezhda Iakovlevna as Europa, see 116.

7. Nadezhda Mandel'shtam offers an interesting version of the syndrome Carolyn Heilbrun identifies in *Writing a Woman's Life*. Heilbrun points out that in the absence of stories recapitulating women's distinctive lives and vantage points, women have had to make do with the often highly circumscribed narratives and roles men have assigned to them (37–40).

8. During the fall of 1989 I was privileged to conduct interviews with several members of Nadezhda Iakovlevna's circle in Moscow—the psychiatrist and Mandel'shtam scholar Iurii Freidin; Varvara Shklovskaia (daughter of Viktor and Vasilisa Shklovskii, close friends of the Mandel'shtams) and her husband, the poet Nikolai Panchenko; the poet Nina Belosinskaia; Liudmila Sergeeva, an editor for the publishing house Sovetskii pisatel'; and Mikhail Polivanov, a physicist and Mandel'shtam scholar. I am also indebted to Carl Proffer's account of his relationship with Nadezhda Iakovlevna.

9. From his reading of the *Third Book* (*Kniga tret'ia*), in which these sketches appear (79–91), Donald Fanger gleans the same valuable information I do: for all her claims to have been "made" by Mandel'shtam, she "was not quite a tabula rasa" when she met him (219–20). The translations from the *Third Book* are mine.

10. Despite her indignation about certain slanderous remarks in *Hope Abandoned*, the critic Emma Gershtein has many positive things to say about Nadezhda Iakovlevna's character. She remarks, for example, on Nadezhda Iakovlevna's strong family feeling and fond memories of her childhood (26).

11. Liudmila Sergeeva, one of her close friends in later years, remembered that Nadezhda Iakovlevna often contrasted the current food situation with the wonderful meals she relished in childhood.

12. Iakov Arkad'evich Khazin died in the early 1930s; her mother, Vera

Iakovlevna, who survived until World War II, appears in both volumes of the memoirs as a resilient partner, aiding her daughter through the trials of arrest and exile. Mother and daughter form an implicitly seamless network of support, and Vera Iakovlevna—a "mite" (*kroshka* [*Third Book*, 79])—never attains the separate stature of her husband. Although Nancy Chodorow's research on mothering is confined to Western families, her account of the more fluid relationship obtaining between mother and daughter (166–67) certainly coincides with Nadezhda Iakovlevna's family experience. No precisely correspondent research on the Russian family has been published, but Lynne Attwood provides an account of how sex roles and sex differences in personality have been addressed in the Soviet Union.

13. Nadezhda Iakovlevna refers to this impressive fact obliquely in *Hope against Hope:* "My mother, who as a doctor was mobilized after the Revolution to help with famine relief in the Volga region, told me that the peasants just lay quite still in their houses, even in parts where there was already something to eat and people were not totally exhausted by hunger" (185). Nadezhda Iakovlevna's legal heir, Iurii Freidin, confirmed this information when I interviewed him in Moscow in 1989.

14. Although Nadezhda Iakovlevna does not allude to it, one other important family character needs to be mentioned in this connection. Emma Gershtein recalls that both Nadezhda and her brother Evgenii cultivated a keen storytelling ability: "both she and Evgenii Iakovlevich had a particular relish for events and people. 'That's good,' they'd say to each other, repeating some well-turned phrase" (26).

15. For a brief introduction to Ekster's life and work, see Bowlt; Marcade.

16. Gershtein remembers the stories Nadezhda Iakovlevna told of her years as a "lively, mischievous girl" in Kiev (26).

17. Isenberg notes these roles without identifying their secondary status (1990, 196–97). Gail Lapidus notes that Stalinist policy tended to reinforce a traditional gender division of labor; although women were encouraged to enter the labor force, they still bore primary responsibility for family and home (103, 108, 110). On the Stalinist devaluation of domestic labor and reinstitution of a more patriarchal social model, see Heitlinger 25, 84.

18. Nadezhda Iakovlevna notes that after her husband's death she "was sustained by the memory of his words 'Why do you think you ought to be happy?' and by the passage in the *Life* of the Archpriest Avvakum when his exhausted wife asks him: 'How much further must we go?' and he replies: 'Until the very grave, woman.' Whereupon she gets to her feet and walks on" (*Hope against Hope*, 57).

19. Isenberg generally observes that Nadezhda Iakovlevna is empowered by the tradition of women's memoirs ("*the* central genre of female writing in Russia"), but it is important to specify her connection with this variant, particularly since she will venture beyond its "selfless" boundaries (1990, 197).

20. When I interviewed Varvara Shklovskaia, Nikolai Panchenko, and Nina Belosinskaia, they mentioned that Nadezhda Iakovlevna liked to read about "women's essence" (*zhenskaia sushchnost'*) and, in this connection, had read the memoirs of Princess Dolgorukaia.

21. For general accounts of how Russian women eschewed the "selfish" course of feminism for devotion to a "greater" political cause, see Stites; Engel, esp. 196–98.

22. She also maintains that Mandel'shtam preferred a younger, dependent partner and "was angered by the least display of [her] independence" (*Hope Abandoned*, 142).

23. Gershtein recognizes the terrible burden of Mandel'shtam's neediness and the tension of their daily lives (25, 89). Iurii Freidin remarked that Nadezhda Iakovlevna frequently helped her husband with his purely "money-making" translations.

24. In April 1937, for example, Vera Iakovlevna wrote to her daughter from Voronezh, where she was staying with Mandel'shtam while Nadezhda Iakovlevna was in Moscow on business. She complained in a joking way about Mandel'shtam's improvidence: "In domestic matters we do not agree. But Osia is convinced that he is as good a household manager as he is a poet" (Osip Mandel'shtam). Natasha Shtempel' remembers the Voronezh visits of Vera Iakovlevna—a "small, thin little old lady, very lively and sharp-witted," who treated the poet like a sick child (219).

25. For an interesting discussion of this new "type" as well as the rise of bourgeois values in Soviet culture, see Dunham.

26. For one of her discussions of Mandel'shtam's joie de vivre, see *Hope Abandoned*, 239: here she remembers how his "love of life grew stronger" even during the most terrible period.

27. The "man who would understand" is a character type elaborated by Marianne Hirsch, who in turn borrows the term from Adrienne Rich. Hirsch identifies this recurring figure in nineteenth-century realist writing by women: "The male object in this transformation of the marriage plot takes the form of a 'brother' who can be nurturing even as he provides access to the issues of legitimacy and authority central to plotting. Most importantly, perhaps, his fraternal/incestuous status can protect the heroine from becoming a mother and can thereby help her, in spite of the closure of marriage, to remain a subject, and can help her not to disappear from the plot as the object of her child's fantasy" (58).

28. "Even in the smallest things he was always to expect the same from me as from himself, and he could make no distinction between my life and his own: if I am given a permit to live in Moscow, then so will you be; what happens to me will happen to you; you will read this book, if I read it. . . " (233).

29. Carl Proffer comments on Nadezhda Iakovlevna's salty language and sexual candor (17, 23).

30. As my second epigraph makes clear, for Gershtein her charm could be traced also to her "bold language," "self-assuredness," and "daredevil tricks" (27).

31. Isenberg identifies her intention to unmask people but he does not go so far as to connect it with her development of a distinctive and (for many readers) problematic persona. He interprets her "unmasking" as largely effective social commentary, the strategy of "an acute field anthropologist" (1990, 205).

32. Isenberg remarks on this important sequence: ". . . the death of the poet

Mandel'shtam is represented as the originary act that brings the writer Nadezhda Mandel'shtam into being" (1990, 201).

33. For the liveliest discussion of these traps devised for dismissing and denigrating women's writing, see Russ.

References

Attwood, Lynne. *The New Soviet Man and Woman: Sex-Role Socialization in the USSR*. Bloomington, IN: Indiana University Press, 1990.

Belosinskaia, Nina. Interview, 3 October 1989, Peredelkino.

Bowlt, John. "Biography, Bibliography." In *Kunstlerinnen der russischen Avantgarde, 1910–1930*, 112. Cologne: Galerie Gmurzynska, 1979.

Brodsky, Joseph. "Beyond Consolation." *New York Review of Books,* 7 February 1974, 13–16.

Brown, Edward J. *Russian Literature since the Revolution*. Rev. and enl. ed. Cambridge, MA: Harvard University Press, 1982.

Chodorow, Nancy. *The Reproduction of Mothering: Psychoanalysis and the Sociology of Gender*. Berkeley, CA: University of California Press, 1978.

Chukovskaia, Lidiia. *Zapiski ob Anne Akhmatovoi*. Vol. 2, *1952–1962*. Paris: YMCA, 1980.

Conquest, Robert. *The Great Terror: A Reassessment*. New York: Oxford University Press, 1990.

Dunham, Vera. *In Stalin's Time: Middle-Class Values in Soviet Fiction*. New York: Cambridge University Press, 1976.

Durova, Nadezhda. *The Cavalry Maiden: Journals of a Russian Officer in the Napoleonic Wars*. Trans. Mary Fleming Zirin. Bloomington, IN: Indiana University Press, 1989.

Engel, Barbara Alpern. *Mothers and Daughters: Women of the Intelligentsia in Nineteenth-Century Russia*. Cambridge: Cambridge University Press, 1983.

Engel, Barbara Alpern, and Clifford N. Rosenthal, eds. and trans. *Five Sisters against the Tsar*. New York: Knopf, 1975.

Fanger, Donald. Review of Nadezhda Mandel'shtam's *Kniga tret'ia. Russian Review*, 48, no. 2 (April 1989): 219–20.

Freidin, Iurii. *Interview, 15 October 1989, Moscow.*

Friedman, Susan Stanford. "Women's Autobiographical Selves: Theory and Practice." In *The Private Self: Theory and Practice of Women's Autobiographical Writings*, ed. Shari Benstock, 34–62. Chapel Hill, NC: University of North Carolina Press, 1988.

Gershtein, Emma. *Novoe o Mandel'shtame*. Paris: Atheneum, 1986.

Heilbrun, Carolyn. *Writing a Woman's Life*. New York: Ballantine, 1988.

Heitlinger, Alena. *Women and State Socialism: Sex Inequality in the Soviet Union and Czechoslovakia*. Montreal: McGill-Queen's University Press, 1979.

Heldt, Barbara. *Terrible Perfection: Women and Russian Literature*. Bloomington, IN: Indiana University Press, 1987.

Hirsch, Marianne. *The Mother/Daughter Plot: Narrative, Psychoanalysis, Feminism*. Bloomington, IN: Indiana University Press, 1989.

Isenberg, Charles. "The Rhetoric of Nadezhda Mandel'shtam's Hope against Hope." In *New Studies in Russian Language and Literature,* ed. Anna Lisa Crone and Catherine V. Chvany, 168–82. Columbus, OH: Slavica Publishers, 1987.

—. "The Rhetoric of *Hope against Hope.*" In *Autobiographical Statements in Twentieth-Century Russian Literature,* ed. Jane Gary Harris; 193–206. Princeton, NJ: Princeton University Press, 1990.

Jelinek, Estelle. *The Tradition of Women's Autobiography: From Antiquity to the Present.* Boston, MA: Twayne, 1986.

Kovalevskaya, Sofia. *A Russian Childhood.* Trans. Beatrice Stillman. New York: Springer-Verlag, 1978.

Lapidus, Gail. *Women in Soviet Society: Equality, Development, and Social Change.* Berkeley, CA: University of California Press, 1978.

Mandel'shtam, Nadezhda. *Vospominaniia.* 4th ed. Paris: YMCA, 1982. Published in English as *Hope against as Hope,* trans. Max Hayward. New York: Atheneum, 1970.

—. *Kniga vtoraia.* 4th ed. Paris: YMCA, 1987. Moscow: Moskovskii rabochii, 1990. Published in English as *Hope Abandoned,* trans. Max Hayward. New York: Atheneum, 1974.

—. *Kniga tret'ia.* Paris: YMCA, 1987.

Mandel'shtam, Osip. Correspondence and materials in fond 2833, n. 7, ed. khran. 544, in TsGALI, Moscow.

Marcade, Jean-Claude. "Alexandra Exter, or The Search for the Rhythms of Light-Colour." In *Kunstlerinnen der russischen Avantgarde, 1910–1930,* 124–28. Cologne: Galerie Gmurzynska, 1979.

Polivanov, Mikhail. Interview, 21 October 1989, Moscow.

Proffer, Carl. *The Widows of Russia and Other Writings.* Ann Arbor, MI: Ardis, 1987.

Russ, Joanna. *How to Suppress Women's Writing.* Austin, TX: University of Texas Press, 1983.

Sergeeva, Liudmila. Interview, 14 October 1989, Moscow.

Shklovskaia, Varvara, and Nikolai Parchenko. Interview, 3 October 1989, Peredelkino.

Shtempel', N.E. "Mandel'shtam v Voronezhe." *Novyi mir,* 1987, no. 10, 207–34.

Smith, Sidonie. *A Poetics of Women's Autobiography.* Bloomington, IN: Indiana University Press, 1987.

Stites, Richard. *The Women's Liberation Movement in Russia: Feminism, Nihilism, and Bolshevism, 1860–1930.* Princeton, NJ: Princeton University Press, 1978.

Tsvetaeva, Marina. *A Captive Spirit: Selected Prose.* Ed. and trans. J. Marin King. Ann Arbor, MI: Ardis, 1980.

Tucker, Robert C. *Stalin in Power: The Revolution from Above, 1928–1941.* New York: Norton, 1990.

Tvardovskii, Aleksandr. Letter to Nadezhda Mandel'shtam. Box III, m. 91–92, Osip Emilyevich Mandelshtam Papers, Firestone Library, Princeton University. Published with the permission of Princeton University Library.

6

THE CANON AND THE BACKWARD GLANCE
Akhmatova, Lisnianskaia, Petrovykh, Nikolaeva

Stephanie Sandler

> A glance is accustomed to no glance back.
> —Joseph Brodsky, *A Part of Speech*

Can one talk about creating a canon of Russian women poets? The mere question might produce unease, for most twentieth-century Russian women poets have said that they do not belong to a separate, gendered category when they write. What would it mean to create a canon of people who don't want to be there? Being wary of canon creation itself—the very activity of including, excluding, picking and choosing according to criteria that themselves deserve interrogation—I shall describe the activity of canon creation in a way that expresses my anxiety: canon creation involves a look to the past, a backward glance that reveals things at once important and disturbing. This glance seeks works that merit preservation, interpretation, even rigorous rethinking; and in stating preferences, loyalties, and values, it also defines the dispositions of the present.[1] I will look at three poetic texts that variously narrate and enact the turn to the past; their versions are fraught with prohibition, conflict, and danger. I will defend their ambivalences toward the work of retrospection, in part because of my own ambivalence toward the creation of a canon, feminist or otherwise.[2] These poems ask how the sanctioned backward glance at Russia's cultural tradition has regarded con-

113

tributions by women. The poems are by two contemporary women poets, Inna Lisnianskaia and Olesia Nikolaeva, about whom virtually nothing has been written, so they have not been brought into any sort of canon, and by Anna Akhmatova, who ranks among "even" the great male poets of this century. A fourth poet, Maria Petrovykh, appears as the addressee of one poem, and as an important measure for the process by which poets are considered for canonical status in the first place.

I begin with Anna Akhmatova (1889–1966). Her presence in contemporary letters was intensified in 1989, the hundredth anniversary of her birth and the year when her great poem *Requiem* (1935–40) finally saw publication in Russia (some people viewed it as the most important publication of the year [Shaitanov 22]). *Requiem,* a memorial to the victims of Stalin's purges, may now be canonized as Akhmatova's most enduring achievement, but I want to consider a poem that predates it by more than a decade, one that takes up a similarly paradoxical position of iconoclasm and loyalty and is also very well known: "Lot's Wife" ("Lotova zhena," 1924), from a cycle of three biblical poems that Akhmatova wrote and revised at various times in her life.

Lotova zhena

Zhena zhe Lotova oglianulas' pozadi ego i
stala solianym stolbom.

—*Kniga Bytiia*

I pravednik shel za poslannikom Boga,
Ogromnyi i svetlyi, po chernoi gore,
No gromko zhene govorila trevoga:
Ne pozdno, ty mozhesh' eshche posmotret'

Na krasnye bashni rodnogo Sodoma,
Na ploshchad', gde pela, na dvor, gde priala,
Na okna pustye vysokogo doma,
Gde milomu muzhu detei rodila.

Vzglianula, i, skovany smertnoiu bol'iu,
Glaza ee bol'she smotret' ne mogli;

I sdelalos' telo prozrachnoiu sol'iu,
I bystrye nogi k zemle prerosli.

Kto zhenshchinu etu oplakivat' budet,
Ne men'shei l' mnitsia ona iz utrat?
Lish' serdtse moe nikogda ne zabudet
Otdavshuiu zhizn' za edinstvennyi vzgliad.

24 fevralia 1924
(Akhmatova 1977, 160)

"Lot's Wife"

Lot's wife looked back from behind him
and became a pillar of salt.

—Book of Genesis

And the righteous man followed the envoy of God,
Huge and bright, over the black mountain.
But anguish spoke loudly to his wife:
It is not too late, you can still gaze

At the red towers of your native Sodom,
At the square where you sang, at the courtyard
      where you spun,
At the empty windows of the tall house
Where you bore children to your beloved husband.

She glanced, and, paralyzed by deadly pain,
Her eyes no longer saw anything;
And her body became transparent salt
And her quick feet were rooted to the spot.

Who will weep for this woman?
Isn't her death the least significant?
But my heart will never forget the one
Who gave her life for a single glance.

February 24, 1924
(Akhmatova 1990, 567–68)

Akhmatova here looks back at what is perhaps the most canonical text in Russia and the West, the Bible, but her poem

about the destruction of Sodom differs importantly from her source. She cites the Bible's only sentence about Lot's wife as an epigraph, as if without it we would miss her change in emphasis.[3] Whereas the Bible shows both the wrongdoing of Sodom's inhabitants and the sight of cities destroyed, Akhmatova shows us a world of family intimacy and domestic habit—thus the second strophe's condensed images of home, nurture, and childbirth. This is *rodnoi Sodom,* both a native city and a place that is dear to Lot's wife.

Rather than lamenting the loss of the city, then, and rather than chronicling the errant ways of its inhabitants, Akhmatova mourns the loss of Lot's wife. Lot's wife refuses to turn her back on her dear and native city, for all its evil, as Akhmatova will refuse to abandon Russia.[4] Her backward glance becomes an emblem of the poet's calling, in part because it is replicated by Akhmatova's own defiant gesture of weeping for this woman.

One cannot help recalling another forbidden glance, Orpheus's gaze back at Euridyce as he is rescuing her from Hades, a gaze that costs him his love.[5] Singer of songs (his song made Underworld spirits listen to his plea for Euridyce), Orpheus has often been taken as a figure for the poet (by Marina Tsvetaeva, for example, and by Rainer Maria Rilke, whose work Tsvetaeva so prized).[6] Yet Akhmatova's less conventional choice of Lot's wife has a compelling alternative logic. It is typical of her use of women as poetic doubles (such as Cleopatra and Dido),[7] and thus offers us some opportunity to consider how being a woman matters in the particular representation of the poet found in "Lot's Wife." That is not a question much asked in studies of Akhmatova, nor is it one that Akhmatova makes easy to answer, given her many and contradictory comments about women, poets, and "poetesses."[8]

"Lot's Wife" seems to demand a reading that accounts for its asymmetries of gender. A woman walks in the shadow of the righteous man and of the angel of the Lord. These masculine figures of authority pull her to turn her back on what is described as an all too feminine world. Her resistance is based on emotion, another "feminine" trait, but it is one that Akhmatova affirms, by her loyalty to Lot's wife in the last lines. This loss, Akhmatova reminds us, has been seen as trivial, but she swears she will never cease to mourn it.

Akhmatova thus changes the ethical problem central to the destruction of Sodom: she criticizes a tradition that overlooks the death of Lot's wife, and she seeks in her own poem to undo the omission. What her backward glance reveals, then, is the exclusion and trivialization of this woman, and potentially of woman in general. Recall that this poem is from 1924, a period of transition for Akhmatova as a poet: she was no longer the author of love lyrics that earned her the adulation of women readers, but she was not yet the poet who would write of her nation's fate under Stalin's terror in *Requiem*. Akhmatova is in the process of becoming that poet here: she identifies with the woman who refuses to turn her back on her country, no matter how evil it has become. That loyalty marks Akhmatova's verse, yet here she catches herself wondering if anyone will remember, much less honor, such fidelity when it is couched as a larger act of disobedience.

The fear of being forgotten also marks a poem by Inna Lisnianskaia (b. 1928). She writes to her friend Maria Petrovykh (1908–79), who was also a poet and noted translator. Note the way Lisnianskaia disclaims her connection to the past.

> Umeite domolchat'sia do stikhov . . .
> > Mariia Petrovykh

Mariia Sergeevna! Ia domolchalas',
I ia do togo domolchat'sia sumela,
Chto vremia byloe vo mne skonchalos',
Kak mozhet skonchat'sia bol'noe telo.
Proshedshee ia skhoronila besslezno,
Bezrechno, bespamiatno i bessvechno,
Vpolne veroiatno, ono bylo grozno,
No ne iskliuchaiu, chto bylo bespechno.
I Vas by ne vspomnila, esli b ne knizhka

Inna Lisnianskaia

> V chernoi oblozhke s belym portretom,
> Pokhozhim na oblako. Dazhe s izlishkom
> Vospol'zovalas' ia poleznym sovetom.
> I vot do chego ia teper' domolchalas':
> Menia zanimaet lish' den' tekushchii,
> Perekhodiashchii v nebesnuiu zhalost'
> Ne vedat', chto bylo v den' predydushchii.

Mariia Sergeevna! Vot i pis´mo Vam,
Ne znaia, gde rai i o chem tam poete,
Pishu ia v svoem sostoianii novom,
V kotorom net mesta tragicheskoi note.

("Neotprovlennye pis´ma," 5)

Know how to keep silent till there is poetry . . .

Maria Petrovykh

Maria Sergeevna! I have kept silent,
And knew how to keep silent until
Past time had died in me,
As a sick body can die.
The past I have buried tearlessly,
Speechlessly, without memory and without candles,
In all probability, it was terrible,
But I don't rule out that it may have been careless.
And I would not have remembered you were it not
    for the little book
In the black cover with a white portrait
That looks like a cloud. I even excessively
Made use of the helpful advice.
And here's the point up to which I have now
    kept silent:
My attention goes only to the present day,
Flowing, turning into a heavenly pity
Of not knowing what happened the day before.
Maria Sergeevna! Here is a letter to you, too;
Without knowing where paradise is, or what
    you sing about there,
I write in my new state,
Where there is no place for the tragic tone.

The "silence" broken in this poem is presumably Lisnian-skaia's absence from official publications: she resigned from the Soviet Writers' Union after the 1979 *Metropol* scandal, and only in 1987, the year of this poem, did her works reappear in journals.[9] The epigraph from Petrovykh also suggests a more general time of blockage or aridity, and it comes from a 1971 poem advising poets not to make excuses for periods of silence, and not to fear to confront the causes of poetic silence.[10] Certainly it is not a silence toward Petrovykh herself, since this is the third poem Lisnianskaia addressed to her since 1976.[11] But there is a certain self-consciousness in the act of address, despite its familiarity, seen in the ending's anxiety as to where Petrovykh is now, what language she now speaks (or sings), whether she will understand Lisnianskaia's song, deprived as it is of her customary tragic tone. That same obstacle marks the 1983 poem to Petrovykh, an even more difficult attempt at communication beyond the grave.[12]

We might pause for a moment over the difficulty here, the focus of the particular backward glance in Lisnianskaia's poems to Petrovykh—a glance back at a friendship in the past, but also at an exemplary poet who has now died. Lisnianskaia seems determinedly uninterested in the past: she says that it has died in her "as a sick body can die," that she has buried the past without tears. This stance is in sharp contrast to Akhmatova's insistent mourning for the lost past, but perhaps we should not take Lisnianskaia too much at her word. When she claims that she would not have remembered Petrovykh at all were it not for the book before her, can we believe that assertion from a poet whose published comments affirm the deepest loyalty and gratitude to Petrovykh—and one who is writing her third poem to Petrovykh?[13] Surely we are not to accept Lisnianskaia's claim that she can no longer write in tragic tones, given the searing new poetry she published during and after 1987.[14]

I shall suggest some reasons for these duplicities in a moment, but for now I want to return to what I take to be the heartfelt uncertainty that closes the poem—heartfelt in that this poem articulates a sense of danger hidden in its glance at the past: what is revealed is like the revelation that Lot's wife has seemed a trivial loss, and it is as psychologically disturbing.

Why? Well, Maria Petrovykh was little published in her lifetime, at least as a poet. She worked as a translator and editor, positions that provide an apt spatial metaphor for the way Petrovykh is thought to have lived: she always took a secondary position to other, more important writers and poets, she lived her life in the background. One friend compared her to "a plant that prefers the shade" (Petrovykh 377). Others have noted how little she spoke about herself, that she was a wonderful listener, that she was extremely attentive to others (Petrovykh 336, 351, 373). Here, alas, is the ideal woman poet for a patriarchal culture: quiet, modest, never seeming to have sought glory, fame, or even much pleasure, ever willing to work for others.

That diminished self may be one reason that Petrovykh so steadfastly refused to see her poems to publication, but it also tells us why Lisnianskaia might find it troubling to consider Petrovykh's example too closely. The spectacle of such reduced subjectivity would have been trouble enough, but the spectacle of a poet who was nearly not published is still worse. Petrovykh's advice about keeping silent reduces to more pain than irony. When we consider the first poem that Lisnianskaia wrote to Petrovykh, the scary act of identification becomes even more palpable. That short poem, which begins with questions as to what Lisnianskaia and Petrovykh will remember as time passes, ends by asking whether, as time passes, anyone will remember them. It seems to Lisnianskaia that what Akhmatova feared for Lot's wife has nearly come true for herself and for Petrovykh. Lisnianskaia, typically, ends with none of Akhmatova's sense of affirmation.

The desire to pay attention "only to the present day" was one resolution that allowed this poem to get written in the first place. In Lisnianskaia's case that resolution is undermined; it characterizes less equivocally Olesia Nikolaeva's 1987 poem "Seven Beginnings" ("Sem′ nachal"). Nikolaeva (b. 1955) here fuses and transforms the two kinds of backward glance found in Lisnianskaia and Akhmatova: she uses the story of Lot's wife obliquely, and she also enacts a turn to a previous poet.

Sem´ nachal

I

Vykhodia iz goroda,
gde khoziainichaiut novostroiki, novosely i nuvorishi,
zhelanie vybit´sia v liudi, byt´ schastlivym,
   ubedit´ sebia, chto ne strashen ad,
o derznovenneishaia iz zhenshchin—dusha moia,
   ne podnimai gordelivuiu golovu eshche vyshe,
ne ogliadyvaisia nazad!

II

Vykhodia iz goroda,
gde kto-to, liubil kogo-to,
gde kto-to igral komu-to luchshuiu iz Motsartovykh sonat,
i roial´ byl sovsem rasstroen, i u Erota oblupilsia nos,
   i s Orfeia osypalas´ pozolota,
o, ne ogliavyvaisia nazad!

III

Vykhodia iz goroda,
gde prazdnovali dni rozhdenii, dorozhili mneniem mody,
gde, na panikhide vstretivshis´, govorili:
   "Ba, davnen´ko ne videlis´!"—pili vino
   i otshchipyvali vinograd,
gde boleli khandroi i rakom,
   ubivali detei vo chreve i prinimali rody,
o, ne ogliadyvaisia nazad!

IV

Vykhodia iz goroda,
gde tshheslavilis´ obil´nym stolom, nariadom i bashmakami,
zadavali sebe voprosy "zachem eto vse mne nado?"
   i "chto eto mne daet?",

dokazyvali, chto dobro obiazano byt´ s kulakami,
o, ne ogliadyvaisia, dusha moia, no smotri vpered!

V

Vykhodia iz goroda,
na kotoryi i zhena pravednika oglianulas´
ibo ne vsiakaia liubov´ ostyla,
    i vospominaniia razryvaiut grud´,
i ne vsiakaia strela propala,
    i ne vsiakaia struna prognulas´,
no ty, o dusha moia, o dusha moia,
    ob etom zabud´!

VI

Vykhodia iz goroda,
v kotorom khot´ odin kupol eshche zolotitsia
i khot´ odin kolokol na vysokoi bashne uveriaet v tom,
chto ne kazhdoe slovo pogiblo
    i ne kazhdaia sleza v prakh vozvratitsia,
no ty, dusha moia, ne ogliadyvaisia—
    zamresh´ solianym stolbom!

VII

Vykhodia iz goroda,
uzhe poverzhennogo, uzhe lezhashchego v peple,
gde dazhe oplakat´ nekomu svoego mertvetsa,
o, ne ogliadyvaisia, dusha moia,
    zabud´, oglokhni, oslepni,
kogda tvorets vyvodit tebia iz goroda tvoego otsa!
                ("Vykhodia iz goroda," 62–63)[15]

Seven Beginnings

I

Leaving the city,
where new buildings, new neighborhoods, and the
    newly rich keep house,

the desire to make one's way, to be happy,
   to be convinced that Hell is not scary,
O most insolent among women—my soul,
   do not raise your proud head any higher,
do not glance back!

II

Leaving the city,
where one loved another,
where one played Mozart's best sonata for another,
and the piano was completely out of tune and
      Eros's nose chipped off,
   and the gilding crumbled on Orpheus,
oh, do not glance back!

III

Leaving the city,
where birthdays were celebrated and views of
      fashion prized,
where those who saw each other at a funeral said
   "Ohhh, it's been ages!"—and drank wine,
      plucked grapes,
where diseases of boredom and cancer struck,
   children were killed in the womb, and babies
      were delivered,
oh, do not glance back!

IV

Leaving the city,
where the riches of table, of dress, and of boots
      drew vanity,
   one asked oneself the questions "Why do I need
      to bother with all this?"
   and "What will this give me?"
It proved that good must always come with force,
oh, do not glance around, my soul, look ahead!

V

Leaving the city,
at which the righteous man's wife had also glanced
    back,
because not all love had cooled away,
    and memories rip through the breast,
and not all the arrows had missed,
    and not all the strings were sagging,
but you, oh my soul, oh my soul,
    forget this!

VI

Leaving the city,
in which at least one cupola still sparkles gold
and at least one bell in the lofty tower reassures
that not every word perished
    and not every tear is returning to dust,
but you, my soul, do not glance back—
    you will die a pillar of salt!

VII

Leaving the city
already prostrate, already lying in the ashes,
where there was not anyone even to cry for the
    dead,
oh, do not glance back, my soul,
    forget, go deaf, go blind,
when the creator leads you out of the city of your
    father!

With its repetitions, its seven beginnings, this poem more than most glances back upon itself, and in this respect it formally resembles Nikolaeva's poem, appropriately titled "The Ring" ("Kol'tso") (untitled, 1989, 112–13), about another woman in the Bible (Rachel, Jacob's wife). It can hardly be accidental that Nikolaeva writes about two of the three women who are also Akhmatova's subjects in her biblical poems, despite the fact that

Nikolaeva has said publicly that of all Akhmatova's verses, this cycle is the only text she dislikes.[16] This is a backward glance that is critical but also revisionary, in Harold Bloom's terms. Nikolaeva seeks to correct Akhmatova in ways not unlike Akhmatova's correction of the Bible.[17] Nikolaeva's work is partly an act of restoration—she prefers the original biblical ethos, and indeed, when an interviewer asked her about influences on her work, Nikolaeva listed the Old and New Testaments first.[18]

To cite a concrete example of how the correction works, one might note that Nikolaeva repeats Akhmatova's domestication of the city in her use of "to keep house" (*khozianichat'*) as early as the second line, and again in images of music-making, laden table, fine clothes. But she renders these scenes empty; she records with dry irony a concern for fashion and the consumption of food and wine at funerals that are used as social occasions. These details are continuous with the violence of "children killed in the womb" and with the crumbling away of culture in untuned pianos and statues in decay (note that one of them is a statue of Orpheus).

The voices, indeed all the sentences of this poem, are peculiarly disembodied (a point to which I'll return in a moment), but it's not as if we can't make out who is doing what in this poem. The sins of the city are the sins of women.[19] Petty concerns for house and dress, the dangers of abortion and childbirth, of cancer and boredom—these interests are gender-specific in a way that rehearses, I believe, a kind of parody of the social construction of women, and does so with remarkably little sympathy for the women involved.

Women are not just the objects of this poem, they are also its subject, if in a spectacularly ambivalent way. The speaker identifies herself, her soul, as "the most insolent of women," at once calling up a stereotype of the uppity and proud woman. Pride is a sin in this poem, not a strong response to external threat (as it would be in Akhmatova or in Lisnianskaia). Such a reading of the poem is supported by Nikolaeva's advocacy of the Orthodox tradition of humility and submissiveness.[20] Religious belief translates into sentence structure in "Seven Beginnings," so that the poem markedly avoids first-person grammatical constructions and any other syntax of specific subjectivity.[21]

One of the things Nikolaeva has in common with Lisnianskaia is this complex rendering of beliefs about subjectivity, though Lisnianskaia struggles more appealingly (at least to my sensibilities) toward a strong statement of self.[22] Nikolaeva hardly laments any reduced sense of self; indeed, one could argue that hers is an extraordinarily strong voice: she has so deeply internalized God's will that the repeated command not to turn back is her own.[23] The backward glance barely tempts Nikolaeva; indeed, her gaze is more generally fixed on the present (and a recent volume of poems is titled *Here* [*Zdes'*]). A line in another poem, "the soul, when it looks back, turns to stone" (dusha, ogliadyvaias', kameneet),[24] could be read as reversing any assertion that the retrospective glance offers any spiritual benefits. The commitment to keeping memories at the forefront of one's imagination, by contrast, inspires much of Akhmatova's poetry after 1921; that is, after the death of her first husband, Nikolai Gumilev. Perhaps in this rejection of a poetics of memory, Nikolaeva rejects once again the possibility that she resembles Akhmatova; that is, that she resembles the woman who wrote about Lot's wife before she did. I take that, among other things, as Nikolaeva's direct refutation of the idea that this poem takes its place in a continuous tradition of women's verse.

That, as I said at the outset, is not a position that much troubles me, or even much troubles my feminism, but Nikolaeva's Orthodox self-definition might challenge us to reconsider a slightly different aspect of feminist approaches to Russian culture. I have in mind the history of division and attack that marks Russian feminist thinking about women and religion—it is chronicled in the important work of Tat'iana Mamonova.[25] Mamonova's position, with which I respectfully disagree, is that Orthodox women betray the politics of feminism with their ethos of submissiveness. I suggest, on the contrary, that feminist thinking about Russian culture is incomplete if it declares a poet such as

Nikolaeva beyond the bounds of its canon. If we are to have a full sense of, for example, female subjectivity in the Russian lyric, a question tangential to my investigation here but one that I consider quite important, we can hardly afford to ignore the writing of women who think of themselves as committed religious beings. Among these women are such important contemporary poets as Natal'ia Gorbanevskaia and Irina Ratushinskaia. These poets also contribute to the urgent debate about spiritual renewal in Russian culture, and they do so in ways that challenge the dangerous nationalist tendencies of some participants in this debate. It is possible, then, that religious women poets may also offer important political insights.

Let me conclude on a less generous note. An ambivalence about turning back emerges in all three poems discussed here. In itself ambivalence constitutes a fine lesson for feminists who would create a canon. The business of deciding who's in and who's out only mimics the goings-on at the authoritarian institutions of masculine scholarship—institutions more worthy of criticism than of imitation. If I were inclined to prophesy, I would warn that creating a canon of women writers is not just a waste of time, it's dangerous: it will turn us to pillars of salt, root us in the moment of turning back, freeze our gaze on the errancy that destroys righteousness, blind us to the sight that Akhmatova sees, that the canon has never served the interests of women. We risk missing the recognition so startling in Lisnianskaia's poem, that the women who were there before us sometimes practiced survival strategies of reticence that look like, and felt like, strategies of self-destruction. And we may be less able to see how to do, as Nikolaeva so urgently entreats us to, the spiritual work of the present—and of the future.

Notes

1. This formulation animates an essay by Frank Kermode that I found useful in thinking about canons and their control of reading, particularly as he described the literary community's hierarchy: "its continuance depends on the right of the old to instruct the young" (Kermode 73).

2. The work on the "female canon" that I have found most consonant with my own views is that of Jan Montefiore, which persuasively refutes the position taken by Sandra Gilbert and Susan M. Gubar, for example, in positing an essentializing category of "woman" (*The Madwoman in the Attic* [New Haven, CT: Yale University Press, 1979]). See Montefiore 57–64.

3. The change has been formulated well by Nikolai Skatov in an essay commemorating the hundredth anniversary of Akhmatova's birth. Note his attribution of a "feminine" quality to her revision (the quotation marks, thankfully, are his): "And what an unexpected 'feminine' and sharply polemical turn has the story of Lot's wife acquired [. . .]. For centuries it was understood only as a fable about women's relentless curiosity and disobedience. Akhmatova's Lot's wife cannot but turn back. . . . The biblical story becomes in Akhmatova's hands a story of self-sacrifice that emerges from the very essence of women's character—not curious, but loving" (3).

4. This is the point Akhmatova makes in a 1922 poem, "Ne s temi ia, kto brosil zemliu" ("I am not among those who abandoned this land"), and in the epigraph to *Requiem*. Amanda Haight makes the point that "Lot's Wife" is intended to correct the harsh judgment that readers who emigrated from Russia after the Revolution found in the 1922 poem (87–88).

5. As recounted, for example, in bk. 10 of Ovid's *Metamorphoses*.

6. See, e.g., Tsvetaeva's 1923 poem "Evridika—Orfeiu" (Tsvetaeva 3:56). Given what I say below about Akhmatova's choice of a woman as a poetic double, it bears mention that Tsvetaeva speaks through Euridyce in this poem, though she chose historical and mythic men as subjects quite often in both her lyric and narrative verse.

7. For a good example of this approach to Akhmatova, with an extended discussion of her identifications with Dido, see Amert 133–43. In a dense but very suggestive essay, Tat'iana Tsiv'ian has surveyed Akhmatova's use of female doubles from antiquity.

8. Akhmatova particularly reacts to the way a certain vision of the woman poet was projected onto her as a result of her early love lyrics. Among the many relevant texts are comments scattered throughout her conversations with Lidiia Chukovskaia, in which Akhmatova distinguishes herself from other women writers (Chukovskaia 1:70, 159; 2:42, 409–10) and notes that she has always hated the wives of great men (2:283–84). These moments of distancing herself from the category "woman" are balanced by others, as when Akhmatova calls men a "lesser race," in part because few men stand in the prison lines (1:23, where Chukovskaia takes the occasion to refer to Akhmatova, with some surprise, as a *zhenofilka*—literally a lover of women); many years later, Akhmatova traces her dislike of Islam to its humiliating treatment of women (2:362). Akhmatova's attacks on Tolstoy for his treatment of Anna Karenina are also to the point.

9. A selection of journal publications of Lisnianskaia's verse since 1979 is included in my list of references, as is her 1991 volume of verse. For a review of some of these works, see Stepanian; for the interview with Lisnianskaia, see

Lisnianskaia and Stepanian. I have not treated here her publications abroad or her many publications in Russia before 1979.

10. The eight-line poem begins "Odno mne khochetsia skazat' poetam" (I want to say one thing to poets); see Petrovykh 124.

11. The first two poems to Petrovykh are "Vot kniga tvoia predo mnoiu lezhit" (1983) in Lisnianskaia, *Stikhotvoreniia*, 32, and "A vspomnim li my" (1976) in *Dozhdi i zerkala*, 99.

12. The poems have other traits in common, including the juxtaposition of a face with a book in the 1983 and 1987 poems. These two poems' formal resemblance also marks them as more closely connected than either is to the 1976 poem. Both the 1983 and 1987 poems are twenty lines long (not an uncommon length for Lisnianskaia's poems, which usually run twenty to thirty lines); both use an amphibrache verse line; the 1987 poem has all feminine rhymes, the 1983 poem has all masculine rhymes—both schemes are unusual for Lisnianskaia.

13. Lisnianskaia has said, "Probably many of my poems would not have been written were it not for her. No poet except for her so believed in my vocation and so supported me in my times of deepest doubt" (Lisnianskaia and Stepanian 33–34).

14. For memorable examples see "Neotpravlennye pis'ma," 6, for a poem dated 1988 that begins "Zakruzhilas' zemlia, zakruzhilos' i nebo, i akh,—" (The earth started to spin, and the heavens started to spin, and ahh—); and a poem dated 1989 about Jewish and Orthodox identity, "Razvalilos' vse, chto dolgo dlilos' " ("Everything that has lasted a long time has fallen apart"), in "Chetyre stikhotvoreniia," 7. Most of the poems Lisnianskaia has published since 1987 were written before then, but I have counted fifteen poems dated 1987–90 as of this writing.

15. The reference list includes some of Nikolaeva's other poetry and prose publications. She remains a prolific, visible poet. For reviews of her work, see Marchenko; Rodnianskaia.

16. See "Anketa 'Vestnika,' " 109. It is interesting to note that Nikolaeva offered this thought in response to a request that she indicate her favorite Akhmatova poem or poems—something she said she found it impossible to do. She also ranked Akhmatova after Blok, Mandel'shtam, Pasternak, and Khodasevich among twentieth-century poets, but above Annenskii and Tsvetaeva.

17. This is also a case in which Nikolaeva makes the subtextual references clear. "Seven Beginnings" uses lexical repetitions to remind us of Akhmatova's poem—*pravednik* (the righteous man), for example, and *oplakat'* (to cry for or to mourn). The latter term, given its pivotal role in Akhmatova's revision of the Bible, is crucial.

18. See Nikolaeva, "Poniat' zamysel zhizni," 44. In asking the question, Mikhail Pozdniaev was suggesting that Nikolaeva's poetry has fewer cultural and literary allusions, citations, and paraphrases than the works of her contemporaries.

19. In fact, the relevance of gender has always been disputed in reviews of

Nikolaeva's verse. See Marchenko, who places Nikolaeva's work in the context of women's poetry and also suggests how she moves beyond that context (234–36); and Rodnianskaia, who polemicizes with Marchenko to stress Nikolaeva's affinities with medieval spiritual traditions (250–52). Rodnianskaia's approach to Nikolaeva is also interesting for her comments about form: she appropriately notes Nikolaeva's use of a long verse line, and suggests links to free verse as it is practiced in contemporary American poetry, as well as to a larger tendency within Russian verse toward what she calls "*stikhoproza*" ("verseprose").

20. See Nikolaeva's contribution to the forum "Natsiia. Iazyk. Literatura" ("Natsionalizm," 232–35). Her advocacy of spiritual humility has an important political context—a strong rejection of Russian national chauvinism.

21. I am reminded of Marjorie Perloff's description of the poetry of the American Susan Howe, whose work, unlike "much contemporary feminist poetry," does not take "as emblematic its author's experience of power relations, her personal struggle with patriarchy, her sense of marginalization, her view of social justice," but instead substitutes an " 'impersonal' narrative—a narrative made of collage fragments realigned and recharged—for the more usual lyric 'I' " (310). Perloff takes this point to indicate that "the personal is always already political." I would argue instead that for Nikolaeva (as for Lisnianskaia), the effect of the politics of gender is to render the personal virtually inaccessible.

22. It may be fruitful to compare Lisnianskaia's and Nikolaeva's poems involving mirrors. Nikolaeva's "Pered zerkalom" ("In front of the mirror"), reproduced in Rodnianskaia's 1988 essay, is a memorable poem that describes a woman dressing and making up her face as she gazes at her reflection. Typically for Nikolaeva, there is no first-person commentary. Compare Lisnianskaia's 1980 poem that begins "Ia v zerkalo glianu, byvalo" (I will glance into a mirror) (*Dozhdi i zerkala,* 204), in which the poet stares into a mirror and sees not her own face but a dreamed tale of exile and execution.

23. Compare Johnson's comments on the passive pose adopted by the American poet Phyllis Wheatley as a form of resistance.

24. This line is in a poem that begins "I vdrug stanovitsia toshno ot mnenii svoikh i pesen" (And suddenly one grows sick from one's opinions and songs). See "Zhizn'iu auknetsia," 53–54.

25. *Zhenshchina i Rossiia,* the Russian original of *Women and Russia,* was expanded and changed in Mamonova's version with the same title (and both claim to be first). She opposed the Mariia group: "[. . .] a nationalistic tendency is peculiar to the right wing, which encompasses Russian Orthodox women whom we consider elitist and affected. Orthodox women are now attempting to Christianize the feminist group Marya, which advances the ideals of the Virgin Mary. We consider these ideals inappropriate for contemporary women" (xxi). Mamonova has reiterated these views in a 1985 essay, "Regeneration or Degeneration," in her *Russian Women's Studies,* 151–60. See esp. 155 for an unfortunate attack on Tat'iana Goricheva, whose work merits serious attention.

References

Akhmatova, Anna. *The Complete Poems of Anna Akhmatova.* Ed. Roberta Reeder. Trans. Judith Hemschemeyer. 2 vols. Somerville, MA: Zephyr, 1990.

————. *Stikhotvoreniia i poemy.* Leningrad: Sovetskii pisatel', 1977.

Amert, Susan. *In a Shattered Mirror: The Later Poetry of Anna Akhmatova.* Stanford, CA: Stanford University Press, 1992.

"Anketa 'Vestnika.' " *Vestnik russkogo khristianskogo dvizheniia,* 1989, no. 156, 109.

Bloom, Harold. *The Anxiety of Influence.* New York: Oxford University Press, 1973.

Chukovskaia, Lidiia. *Zapiski ob Anne Akhmatovoi.* 2 vols. Paris: YMCA, 1976, 1980.

Goricheva, Tat'iana. "O religioznom i postmodernizme." *Kontinent,* 1987, no. 53, 277–89.

Haight, Amanda. *Anna Akhmatova: A Poetic Pilgrimage.* New York: Oxford University Press, 1976.

Johnson, Barbara E. "Euphemism, Understatement, and the Passive Voice: A Genealogy of Afro-American Poetry." In *Reading Black, Reading Feminist: A Critical Anthology,* ed. Henry Louis Gates, Jr., 204–11. New York: Meridian/Penguin, 1990.

Kermode, Frank. "Institutional Control of Interpretation." *Salmagundi* 1979, no. 43: 72–86.

Lisnianskaia, Inna. "Chetyre stikhotvoreniia." *Kontinent,* 1990, no. 64, 7–9.

————. *Dozhdi i zerkala.* Paris: YMCA, 1983.

————. "Iz liriki." *Znamia,* 1987, no. 9, 127–30.

————. "Neotpravlennye pis'ma." *Znamia,* 1990, no. 12, 3–8.

————. "Novye stikhi." *Oktiabr',* 1988, no. 11, 130–32.

————. "Novye stikhi." *Oktiabr',* 1990, no. 9, 66–69.

————. "Postskriptumy: Poslanie B. Ia. B." *Druzhba narodov,* 1990, no. 1: 41–49.

————. *Stikhotvoreniia.* Moscow: Sovetskii pisatel', 1991.

————. *Stikhotvoreniia: Na opushke sna.* Ann Arbor, MI: Ardis, 1984.

————. [Untitled selection of poems.] *Iunost',* 1990, no. 11, 26.

————. "V gospitale litsevogo raneniia," *Druzhba narodov,* 1988, no. 1, 242–47.

————. *Vozdushnyi plast.* Moscow: Pravda, 1990.

Lisnianskaia, Inna, and Elena Stepanian. "O zhizni i o knige." *Literaturnoe obozrenie,* 1990, no. 4, 30–34.

Mamonova, Tatyana. *Russian Women's Studies: Essays on Sexism in Soviet Culture.* Oxford: Pergamon, 1989.

————, ed. *Women and Russia: The First Soviet Anthology of Feminist Writing.* Trans. Rebecca Park and Catherine A. Fitzpatrick. Boston, MA: Beacon, 1984.

Marchenko, Alla. "U zhizni zhenskoe litso," *Novyi mir,* 1987, no. 12, 234–36.

Montefiore, Jan. *Feminism and Poetry: Language, Experience, and Identity in Women's Writing.* New York: Pandora, 1987.

Nikolaeva, Olesia. "Invalid detstva." *Iunost'*, 1990, no. 2, 34–61.

————. "Iz novoi knigi." *Literaturnoe obozrenie*, 1990, no. 3, 45.

————. *Na korable zimy*. Moscow: Sovetskii pisatel', 1986.

————. "Natsionalizm i russkaia dukhovnaia traditsiia." *Druzhba narodov*, 1989, no. 6, 232–35.

————. "Poniat' zamysel zhizni." *Literaturnoe obozrenie*, 1990, no. 3, 43–45.

————. "Popytka tolkovan'ia." *Novyi mir*, 1988, no. 8, 2–4.

————. "Proshchanie s imperiei." *Znamia*, 1992, no. 7, 3–6.

————. *Sad chudes*. Moscow: Sovetskii pisatel', 1980.

————. [Untitled selection of poems.] *Vestnik russkogo khristianskogo dvizheniia*, 1989, no. 155, 110–16.

————. "Vykhodia iz goroda." *Novyi mir*, 1987, no. 3, 61–63.

————. "Zhizn'iu auknetsia—krov'iu otkliknetsia slovo!" *Druzhba narodov*, 1988, no. 3, 53–57.

Perloff, Marjorie. *Poetic License: Essays on Modernist and Postmodernist Lyric*. Evanston, IL: Northwestern University Press, 1990.

Petrovykh, Mariia. *Cherta gorizonta*. Erevan: Sovetakan grokh, 1986.

Rodnianskaia, Irina. "Nazad—k Orfeiu!" *Novyi mir*, 1988, no. 3, 234–54.

Shaitanov, Igor'. ". . . No trudnee, kogda mozhno: Poeziia–89." *Literaturnoe obozrenie*, 1990, no. 1, 21–29.

Skatov, Nikolai. "Ia—golos vash. . . ." *Literaturnaia gazeta*, 21 June 1989, 3.

Stepanian, Elena. "Dar samootrechen'ia." *Literaturnoe obozrenie*, 1988, no. 10, 46–48.

Tsiv'ian, T.V. "Antichnye geroini—zerkala Akhmatovoi." *Russian Literature*, 1974, nos. 7/8, 103–19.

Tsvetaeva, Marina. *Sobranie sochinenii*. 5 vols. to date. New York: Russica, 1980–.

Women and Russia: First Feminist Samizdat. London: Sheba, 1980. Published in Russian as *Zhenshchina i Rossiia*. Paris: Editions des Femmes, 1980.

7

SPEAKING BODIES
Erotic Zones Rhetoricized

Helena Goscilo

Feminists routinely charge male authors with mediated appropriation of women's bodies through literary inscriptions that deny women authentic physical being by reducing the female body to trope.[1] Masculine representations of woman and her body, according to this view, instance the mirror effect, whereby "the question of the woman reflects only the man's own ontological doubts" (Doane 75).[2] Ontology yields a troped topography, when, for example, the female body becomes figured as land— Freud's "dark continent," mysterious and untamed, awaiting male discovery, mastery, and possession—what feminists are wont to call "colonialization."[3] Problems of inscription are compounded by entrenched yet contradictory and ambiguous precedent. Long-standing philosophical traditions link women with metaphor and rhetoric (language), on the one hand, and simultaneously with the body and the physical, as opposed to the intellect, on the other.[4] And while some feminists (such as Simone de Beauvoir, Kate Millett, Nina Auerbach, and Elaine Showalter) deplore the equation of woman with her physicality as regressive biologism, contemporary French feminists (including Luce Iragaray, Sarah Kofman, Michèle Montrelay, and Hélène Cixous) exalt the overwhelming "presence-to-itself" of the female body. Cixous, for instance, asserts, "More so than men[,] who are coaxed toward social success, toward sublimation, women are body" (343). In either feminist variant, the plaint that troping

"feminine" physicality—which precludes female subjectivity—
characterizes specifically male-authored texts implies that
women writers who have not internalized their culture's ruling
assumptions and authorial practices inscribe the female body differently. Indeed, such artists as Georgia O'Keefe and such writers as Rita Mae Brown, Erica Jong, and Monique Wittig
programmatically endeavor to rescue women's self-as-body from
male politico-aesthetic straitjacketing by pointedly subjectivized
recastings of the female form.[5] Yet, as Ann Rosalind Jones has
demurred, although psychoanalytic models of sexuality admittedly bypass individual differences by universalizing "woman,"
they nonetheless acknowledge sexuality as culturally constructed. In ignoring the role of social arrangements and symbolic systems in its formation, Cixous, Irigaray, and other
utopian proponents of "feminine writing" who proceed from
these psychoanalytic models and thus generalize womanhood[6]
inevitably essentialize female sexuality. They thereby yoke
women's creativity to procreativity (Cixous's "she writes in
white ink"—that is, mother's milk), even when their own writings rely heavily on *cerebral* play and consciously respond to
socioliterary realities.[7] Commentators on *l'écriture féminine* such
as Arleen Dallery argue that American privileging of actual experience (which presupposes a simple referentiality) ignores the
body's mediation by language, which is crucial to the French
feminists' concept of radical alterity. That concept posits the
feminine as sign, so that Cixous and Kristeva, for example, can
credit such avant-garde writers as James Joyce and Jean Genêt with
producing feminine writing that undermines phallocratic discourse
(Dallery 54–62). Yet that sign cannot be completely divorced from
lived experience, hence is not arbitrary, so to examine it exclusively
in terms of discourse means to isolate discourse from the concrete
conditions that partly generate and shape it. To complicate the issue,
some commentators deem feminist efforts to reclaim the female
body through any means necessitating its display or representation
extremely hazardous, on the grounds that associations attached to
that body in contemporary culture overwhelmingly encourage

masculinist reappropriation (Wolff 121–22)—an opinion that seems partly confirmed by responses to Judy Chicago's vaginal "mistresspiece" in the *Dinner Party* Project.

In light of this continuing and often prickly debate, it is instructive to examine how Liudmila Petrushevskaia, Tat´iana Tolstaia, and Valeriia Narbikova—arguably the three most original female practitioners of Russian fiction today[8]—write bodies into their texts. Although feminism remains alien (and largely incomprehensible) to the former Soviet Union, these writers' colorful independence from conventional categories and paradigms breeds cautious Western expectations of at least revisionist (detroped) textual bodies. What militates against those expectations in fascinating and paradoxical ways, however, is the trio's endlessly complex implication in haloed traditions and the realia of their culture.

Reviews in the former Soviet Union of recent women's fiction have lamented the authors' sudden adoption of presumably unmotivated frankness in matters of physiology, which has long been considered gender-specific: bold for men but unimaginable for women.[9] Indeed, the prose of writers as otherwise dissimilar as Larisa Vaneeva, Marina Palei, Elena Tarasova, Nina Sadur, Svetlana Vasilenko, and Nina Gorlanova teems with unblushingly direct references to, or descriptions of, women's physicality, anathemized throughout the Soviet period.[10] Interpreting their unprecedented explicitness as a failed and wrongheaded strategy of self-legitimation through mimicry of empowered masculinist writing, critics have urged women to retain their own "feminine" mode of artistic expression. This outcry against female authors' lack of inhibitions in inscribing the body presumes a literalness of representation ("the body is the body"), denying it literariness. That reduction of a writer's creativity to naive empirical transfer, which conflates text with life and treats them as one and the same, reflects the long-standing encroachment of journalism on Russian literary criticism. Such an approach to Petrushevskaia, Tolstaia, and Narbikova is particularly unhelpful, for in their case a literalist stance must ignore precisely what constitutes the inimitable prose signature of each: a highly indi-

Svetlana Vasilenko

vidualized deployment of language's rhetorical powers that invites a more meticulous and complex analysis than has been offered so far by Russian commentators.

Perhaps no contemporary Russian prosaist has explored the textual possibilities of the narrated body more profoundly and productively than Petrushevskaia; and so puritanical readers deem her prose offensive or indecent. Although she makes sparing use of dysphemistic terminology, Petrushevskaia's fiction shrinks from few physiological realia and breaks most sexual taboos. In short, its focus falls on the grotesque, not the classical

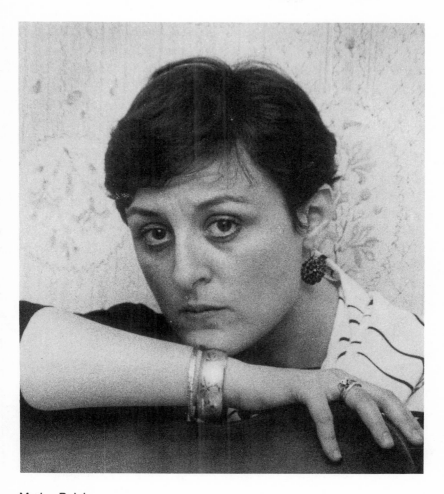

Marina Palei

body, as characterized by Bakhtin. Petrushevskaia overtly acknowledges an entire range of physical phenomena that other
writers hesitate to register and she accepts the body as in some
significant way central both to human experience and to literary
representation.[11] Prostitutes, alcoholics, nymphomaniacs, sui-
cides, and murderers (who, in a sense, all violate their own and
others' bodies) figure prominently in her stories, which matter-

of-factly record how people urinate—in bed (the neglected boy
Alesha in "Our Crowd" ["Svoi krug," wr. 1979, pd. 1988], the
young alcoholic in "Ali-Baba" [1988], who cannot control his
body functions); excrete—outside the toilet (in "Svoi krug," in
the sea; and in "Hygiene" ["Gigiena," 1990] we read: "The little
girl . . . relieved herself sloppily, not on the paper, she didn't
manage to keep track of her needs" [Devochka . . . isprazhnialas'
neriashlivo, ne na bumagu, ne uspevala sama sledit' za svoimi
zhelaniiami (28)]); vomit (during a drunken orgy in "Svoi krug"
Marisha empties her stomach through the kitchen window, and
Petrushevskaia adverts casually to the remains adhering to the
wall outside); arouse each other and subsist on a regular diet of
sexual surrogates ("Svoi krug," "Such a Girl" ["Takaia devochka," 1990]). "Svoi krug" alone condenses a host of references to
false eyes rolling out of sockets, knocked-out teeth, a ripped-up
body with a hole in the stomach, a bleeding nose, a ruptured
hymen, dildos, D-cup breasts, impotence, nymphomania, one-
night stands, incestuous relations between parents and children,
group sex, sexual play between children, near-rape, bedwetting,
childbeating, and on and on.[12]

Here, as elsewhere, Petrushevskaia conceives of the body as a
site of violence, of hyperbolized ingestion and regurgitation—ins
and outs of every sort through all available orifices. This un-
checked traffic of people and things in and out of bodily aper-
tures spills the self out of its vessel of containment. It breaks
down boundaries (of every sort), so that activities become dif-
fused and indiscriminate: spouses copulate not only with each
other but with others' spouses (the wife of the habitual adulterer
in "Takaia devochka" avidly participates in her husband's post-
mortems on his sexual escapades as they drink champagne; she
encourages her married next-door neighbor Raisa, a former prostitute who earlier serviced a penal colony of men, to have intercourse with her husband so as to deter him from straying farther
afield);[13] children (Marisha's and Tania's offspring in "Svoi
krug," for instance) not only sleep together but "sleep together"—
that is, share some form of sexual experience.[14] The multiple

couplings in Petrushevskaia's fiction ironically underscore the iterability and replaceability of bodies in a culture that has invested heavily in the valorization of the group over the (expendable) individual.[15]

If, as Claude Lévi-Strauss has posited, exogamy (with its corollary, the incest taboo, which "enables man to locate himself— and his goods—in relation to others" [Cowie 60]) is the prerequisite for the formation of culture and hence of the social group (Cowie 57), then in Petrushevskaia the prohibitions demarcated by that exchange, which are fundamental to the social order of a natural kinship system, have evaporated. Petrushevskaia erases the body barriers enabling kinship, to confront incest between mothers and sons, fathers and daughters (Serzh and his daughter, Tania and her son in "Svoi krug"). Bodies intermingle more or less at random in an environment no longer regulated by taboos. To apply to body economics Carole Pateman's terminology in her study of contract theory, Petrushevskaia may be said to treat the body as private property into which owners permit overly democratic trespass without discretion or precautions against damage.[16] That undifferentiatedness leads to devaluation and attests to the disintegration of social norms.

Assessing the pertinence of Bakhtinian categories to contemporary Russian women's fiction in chapter 2 of this volume, Natal'ia Ivanova contends that Bakhtin's concept of carnivalization, with its hyperbolized, grotesque body and effacement of distinctions, finds fictional exemplification in Petrushevskaia's and Tolstaia's prose. Yet Petrushevskaia's narratives (and Tolstaia's a fortiori) emphasize the absence of two elements essential to Bakhtinian carnival: an authentically celebratory dimension (replaced in Petrushevskaia by desperate febrility) plus a sense of community, of group relations cemented by shared values, if only for the duration of carnival. The communal body of carnival yields in Petrushevskaia to the body that invariably remains isolated and instrumentalized. Its materialization does not bear an individual stamp, for the Petrushevskaian body is generalized rather than collective. Readers remember not the person involved but the action performed. And what makes the action memorable is its shocking, repugnant nature.

Two-directionality (which mimics the in/out of the sexual act and of the biological sequence of eating/excreting, drinking/urinating or vomiting) is one of Petrushevskaia's major stratagems: it enables her to structure the tonality of narrative and dialogue that conceal in the midst of disclosure and vice versa, to interfuse horror with comedy, and to punctuate periphrastic abstraction with a single concrete detail, so that reinforcement through contrast struggles with semi-erasure. As a consequence, presence may dissolve into insignificance, while absence and silence acquire tremendous force. Hence the curious synthesis of illicitness and apparent candidness in Petrushevskaia's works, which stems from the inverse proportion between the length and particularization of an individual's diatribe or confession and the degree of its revelation. As Dostoevskii, following Rousseau, demonstrated with unassailable conviction, ostensible confessions may constitute yet another, new act of transgression.[17]

Unlike writers who tend to foreshadow instances of physiological dysphemism and sexual explicitness through framing and an assortment of other textual signals, Petrushevskaia elicits her strongest reader responses by purveying formerly bypassed body details abruptly and explicitly, but neutrally. What another author might bracket in the premonitory emotional aura of horror or shock she records in a flat, uninflected tone indistinguishable from descriptions of, say, a teacup or the weather. The technique has a leveling effect; it strips the body of illusion, demystifies it, to expose its parts and its activities as commodities, as merely items in an endless series—thus enabling the paronomasia of such titles as *A Raw Leg* (*Syraia noga,* wr. 1973–78) for a play in which people's flesh does indeed get treated as raw meat.[18]

This process of dehumanization externalizes the spiritual violation and suffering that are Petrushevskaia's ruling concern. If nineteenth-century Russian literature discoursed freely on the soul and eschewed corporeality, the erstwhile taboo body is, paradoxically, Petrushevskaia's euphemism for the devastation of the psyche.[19] She inverts conventions by censoring displays of the inner self and unconstrainedly recording externals, disclosing repellent physical minutiae (signifiers) so as to camouflage what is truly obscene—psychological and spiritual pain and desolation (signified). These internal states her narratives communicate through displacement onto the body and a perpetual deferment of the correspondence between the named and the unarticulated or unrepresentable. On the rhetorical level, then, Petrushevskaia duplicates the in/out movement of her personae. Thus her narrators and characters speak breezily of abortions (in *Smirnova's Birthday* [*Den' rozhdeniia Smirnovoi,* wr. 1977] during the fifth month of pregnancy!); miscarriages ("Father and Mother" ["Otets i mat' "], "Bohemians" ["Bogema"]); sickness and death (hospitalized mothers are a major topos in both her drama and her prose); rotting limbs and dismemberment (*Love* [*Liubov'*], "The New District" ["Novyi raion"], "The Hand" ["Ruka"]); beatings (*Music Lessons* [*Uroki muzyki,* wr. 1973], *Syraia noga*), and the like, with the disengaged equanimity of the journalist on the spot, while either omitting or distancing through irony all mention of shame, humiliation, pain, loss, love. Tabooing the expression of feelings and a genuine analysis of psychological motives, Petrushevskaia transforms the body into the materialization of psychic trauma, of unspeakable, inhuman desires, thoughts, and acts. Whereas a nineteenth-century writer would avoid specifying the visible physical data of the body as an improper object of literary representation, Petrushevskaia treats the invisible, emotional aspect of human experience as the unmentionable. Body language is her medium of permissible communication. In a sense Petrushevskaia's revenge on an avowedly materialist culture is to render any material phenomenon narratable but all intangibles taboo. What you see is what you get. But her inordinate degree of selectiveness in specifying anatomical zones singles out those parts less as synecdoches representing the entire body but as representing—standing in for—something else. In short, it metaphorizes them.

Such an approach complicates the status of figuration in her work, urging the reader to a tropological reading of physical elements in general. In "Svoi krug," for instance, the narrator's blindness, which accompanies her inherited illness, points simultaneously (through cultural analogue) to her Teiresias-like insights and to her limited, skewed point of view on events, her failure at adequate self-scrutiny, owing to the various censoring mechanisms in her psychology. In the same story, Serzh's incestuous closeness to his daughter exteriorizes his inability to love anyone but himself. Abortions metaphorize the elimination of one's "humanity within"; prostitution represents a similarly degrading commodification of self, and so forth. Petrushevskaia, in fact, addresses the vexed issue of tropology when she encloses "Takaia devochka" in parallel formulations that spotlight the ambiguity of statements susceptible to both metaphorical and literal readings: "Now for me it's as if she [Raisa] died, and maybe she actually did die, though this last month we've not buried anyone in our apartment building" (Teper' ona [Raisa] kak by dlia menia umerla, a mozhet byt', ona i na samom dele umerla, khotia za etot mesiats v nashem dome nikogo ne khoronili [144]);[20] "And for me she stopped existing, as if she'd died" (I ona perestala dlia menia sushchestvovat', kak budto ona umerla [158]). Given Raisa's vulnerability (emphasized throughout—she resembles a newborn animal, trembles, cries, and so on), the vicarious, pragmatic exploitation of her body by the narrator (her sole friend, according to the latter) may well have broken her psychologically and precipitated her literal death. Yet the likelihood that the narrator decided to expunge Raisa from her life and the narrative not only to avoid self-confrontation but also because she foresees little benefit to be gained from prolonging the relationship is sufficiently strong to make a figurative reading of the passage equally persuasive. Indeed, "Takaia devochka" instances and highlights the ambiguities generated by the metaphoricity of an ostensibly "naturalistic" text.

An individual biography in Petrushevskaia's fictional world essentially records the body's misadventures, which, through Petrushevskaia's device of hyperbolic accumulation, often approach mythic proportions. In the four-page story paronomastically titled "Ali-Baba," for instance, when the eponymous protagonist steals alcohol from her drinking lover, he tosses her over the balcony, deforming her hands in the process. To purchase alcohol, she pilfers books from her mother (sick, of course, in the hospital—the quintessential domain of Petrushevskaian mothers), picks up a male alcoholic while waiting in line at the beer hall, and accompanies him home. His urinating in bed wakes her from a drunken sleep, whereupon she takes an overdose of sleeping pills, has her stomach pumped, and ends up in a psychiatric ward, where she regales her fellow patients with stories about her previous suicide attempts.[21] Figuring the body as a halfway house for substances that invade and vacate it in rapid succession (alcohol, urine, sleeping pills, stomach contents, a cascade of words) encourages a view of Petrushevskaia as the high priestess of dysphemism. Although her style reaps the rhetorical profits of indirection, allusion, and the verbosity of calculated obfuscation disguised as candidness, she usually reserves forthrightness for physical matters.

Petrushevskaia's seemingly programmatic commitment to dysphemism draws attention all the more dramatically to those moments when she has recourse to euphemism, particularly because she intensifies the effect through repetition. Her reticence may take the form of a familiar trope, as in "Mania," where she develops in her typically tautological manner the traditional synecdoche of hair as a clue to female sexuality or desirability.[22] Alternatively, she may substitute a purposely nebulous phrase (rendered meaningful only by maximal contextualization) for a more precise and explicit expression. The narrator of "Takaia devochka," for example, has no scruples about recounting her husband's multiple infidelities, her own pleasurable curiosity about the details of his conquests, and the readiness with which their neighbor, the former prostitute Raisa, has sex with any stranger who knocks on her door. Yet Petrushevskaia not only uses euphemisms when she refers to sexual intercourse; of the many at her disposal, she chooses the most semantically vague and blatantly circumambient: "that business" (*eto delo*), which, outside of the story's context, could refer to virtually anything. From a sociolinguistic standpoint, Petrushevskaia's use of *eto delo* is, quite simply, accurate, for, as Iurii Poliakov points out, owing to the paucity of Russian terminology for sexual activity, "even among people who are close we're used to speaking in hints, nods, half-smiles, and in extreme cases resorting to the all-powerful word 'that' " (u nas dazhe mezhdu blizkimi liud'mi priniato iz"iasniat'sia namekami, kivkami, poluulybkami, v krainikh sluchaiakh pribegaia k vsemoguchemu slovu "eto" [238]). Euphemisms, paradoxically, acquire almost obscene overtones in a text that unblinkingly calls things by their names. The code words transform the activity into something unnameable enshrouded in coyness, partly because behavior of a possibly more questionable order is spoken of freely and directly. Instead of palliating our perception of the activity, it perversely singles it out and rehearses the euphemistic distancing of the most reprehensible act in the story: the narrator's instrumentalization of Raisa's body for her own purposes, followed by her hypocritical projection onto Raisa of the very betrayal of which she herself is guilty. Thus in Petrushevskaia's fiction the sophisticated interplay between euphemism and dysphemism, condensation and tautology, periphrasis and direct statement, presence and absence coheres into a strategy of rhetoric centered in the body.[23] Among the elements issuing from that corporeal space is the oral language that, Petrushevskaia contends, "never lies."

Dualism of a different order marks Tolstaia's body inscriptions. Whereas for Petrushevskaia the body is the site of displacement (from within), the Tolstaian body serves as insurmountable barrier, a hyperbolized sign of disjunction. In this regard Tolstaia appears as a radical Platonist for whom the invisible internal self is the Ideal, its perceptible physical encasement at such a remove as to be wholly at odds with the quality and workings of its spiritual counterpart. What tragedy informs Tolstaia's world stems from the discrepancy between the inner and outer—or between the significantly profound but imperceptible and the adventitiously superficial but palpable in a universe where the latter inhibits recognition of the former. To invoke an overworked metaphor, Tolstaian bodies are houses whose ramshackle exteriors contradict their luxurious contents. It is no accident that Evgeniia Ivanovna (Zhenechka) in "The Most Beloved" ("Samaia liubimaia" [1986]) is implicitly analogized with the narrator's dacha throughout: both of them provide nurture and sustenance, yet in appearance grow increasingly dilapidated and cumbersome with time's passage. Tolstaia's gargoyle-like old women, in fact, exemplify this fracture between essence and appearance, especially in "Samaia liubimaia," "Sweet Shura" ("Milaia Shura" [1985]), "Okkervil River" ("Reka Okkervil' " [1985]), and "Sonia" (1984).

In each instance Tolstaia employs a variety of devices to render the persona in question grotesque enough to estrange her simultaneously from the putatively normal people around her and from the reader, who in the act of reading mimics their totalizing interpretive habits. In rhetorical terms, the dichotomy between the invisible and the corporeal sets the stage for what Paul de Man has called the allegory of reading.[24] Tolstaia's texts instance our submission to the irresistible pleasure of a mythical unity by demonstrating how rapid surface reading on the basis of immediately accessible evidence (the fact of a physically "alienating" or "depersonalized" individual) suppresses contradictory elements that a closer perusal would take into account. Just as the butts of traditional satire are ridiculed and reduced by summarizing behavioral tics or phrases (such as Uriah Heep's hand-rubbing and "I'm 'umble" in *David Copperfield* and Wemmick's "portable property" in *Great Expectations*), so the crumbling or hulking edifices of old women's bodies in Tolstaia make a durable, ludicrous impact through an estranging decoration or appendage (Zhenechka's constantly malfunctioning hearing aid and orthopedic shoe ["Samaia liubimaia"], Aleksandra Ernestovna's oversized fruit salad of a hat ["Milaia Shura"], the mustache on Vera Vasil'evna's fat, black-browed face ["Reka Okkervil' "], Sonia's identification with a horse and a rag doll, as well as her fat legs, enormous feet, sunken chest, and outlandish clothes).[25]

Tat'iana Tolstaia

Tolstaia's narrators are our representatives in the texts. Especially in her retrospective stories, they negotiate their uncertain way between simplistic misreadings of body texts and subsequent correctives, producing a bifocal perspective that highlights the seeming inevitability of misperception.

Whereas oversized bizarre bodies house poetic dreams and generous, loving spirits (what Tolstaia calls a "crystal-pure soul"), beautiful exteriors, conversely, camouflage barren and shriveled psyches. In other words, the disjunction may operate in reverse. Physical beauty tends to be suspect in Tolstaia's world, an alluring but fake passport to undeserved benefits or a source of delusions abetted by manipulation of others. A passage in the story "The Circle" ("Krug" [1987]) laments the inhuman price paid for women's efforts to enhance their appearance, which includes the suffering of animals and, by implication, loss of the women's own selfless compassion ("inner beauty"): "High up a Siberian tree your hat blinks its eyes in fear; a cow gives birth screaming so you can have boots; a lamb is sheared screaming so you can warm yourself with its fleece; a sperm whale is in its death throes; a crocodile weeps; a doomed leopard pants, fleeing. Your pink cheeks come from boxes of flying dust, your smooth skin from tubes of grease, your gaze from round transparent jars."[26] The majority of Tolstaia's externally attractive women—Zoia in "Hunting the Woolly Mammoth" ("Okhota na mamonta" [1985]), Nina in "The Poet and the Muse" ("Poet i muza" [1986]), Ada Adol'fovna in "Sonia," and Vera Mikhailovna in "The Heavenly Flame" ("Plamen' nebesnyi" [1987])—instance the rupture that an aesthetic ideology, according to de Man, strives to disguise through legerdemain.[27]

And in "Fakir" (1986) and "Reka Okkervil'" Tolstaia deconstructs the apparently inescapable human desire for an aesthetic ideology that in the interests of unity generalizes corresponding spiritual traits from the limited tangible data of physical beauty or vice versa.[28] Thus on the basis of Vera Vasil'evna's lush voice Simeonov spins romantic fantasies about her seductive visual beauty that struggle against his disillusioning encounter with the aged whalelike chanteuse. Similarly, Galia (in "Fakir"), having invested her frustrated romantic yearnings in the ambiguous Filin, resists surrendering her illusions about his imposing looks and magical powers, for such a differentiated reading would necessitate a wholesale disavowal of her entire view of life. In each instance Tolstaia showcases the illusory nature of organic, unruptured being and seeing. Discontinuity is a condition of Tolstaian life that militates against metonymical (or metaphorical) readings from body to unembodied, just as Tolstaia's texts instance the disjuncture between a rich poetic language and the bleak, gray life it unfurls into a narrative.

Unlike Petrushevskaia, Tolstaia euphemizes, domesticates, or subordinates all bodily appetites. The locus of naked hunger and pregnancy in her fiction is the imagination, which consumes and breeds undeterred by the observable facts of life. Explicit sexual couplings occupy a minor place in her writings at best (an exception is "Rendezvous with a Bird" ["Svidanie s ptitsei"]), and references to the body (when their function is not to defamiliarize) lie for the most part within the bounds of nineteenth-century propriety (no buttocks, breasts, or genitalia; no vomiting, excreting, abortions, beatings). The body in Petrushevskaia ceaselessly acts (functions in the dynamic narrative mode), while the Tolstaian body looks a certain way (exists in the passive descriptive mode). Whereas Petrushevskaia's bodies offer access to the inner self via displacement, Tolstaia's block the route to that intangible realm by emitting false clues—false in the context of a culture that reflexively ascribes to beauty a complex of corollary attributes. For both writers the body carries a tremendous tropological weight, insofar as it provides a means of illustrating the alluring but destructive potential of aesthetic mythologies (in Tolstaia's case) and (in Petrushevskaia's) of documenting the bottomless well of horrors that constitutes the human self.

Somewhat fancifully dubbed the first female practitioner of erotica, Valeriia Narbikova rhetoricizes the body for purposes different from Petrushevskaia's and Tolstaia's, although, like Petrushevskaia, she exploits the ambiguous effects of euphemism in the midst of explicitness (see Nadya Peterson's commentary in this volume). The furor over the much-quoted opening sentence of her novel *The Equilibrium of Light of Diurnal and Nocturnal Stars* (*Ravnovesie sveta dnevnykykh i nochnykh zvezd*) lent it a notoriety that would be utterly bewildering to Western readers of, say, Philip Roth or Erica Jong.[29] As context-dependent as Petrushevskaia's *èto delo,* the "emptiness in waiting" of Narbikova's introductory euphemistic statement becomes filled only retroactively, by the events that ensue. Thus from the outset bodily activity is implied through absence and the subjunctive mood of desire, its fleshly possibilities abstracted through a paronomasia given to symmetry: "She wanted you know what with you know who. But 'you know who' didn't call, but you don't know who did" (Ei khotelos´ izvestno chto, izvestno s kem. No "izvestno kto" ne zvonil, zato zvonil neizvestno kto [5]). Its implication in language is precisely what shields the Narbikovian body from the reader; enshrouded in intertexts and layers of rhetorical devices even when naked, that body emerges not as physical entity but as palimpsestic text. Accordingly, the protagonist Sana conceives a child over the telephone—that is, she is impregnated through an exchange of words, not fluid—and the Sleeping Beauty of fairy tales proves, indeed, to belong to the ever-elusive oral/fantastic realm, for no physical kiss can awaken her. Although Narbikova wants to rehabilitate the body as a means of expressive communication,[30] the materialization of that body constantly trips over language, from which Narbikova cannot escape, even as she mourns the slippage inherent in verbal "representation" ("Words express thoughts very approximately, and express feelings even more approximately" [Slova ochen´ priblizitel´no vyrazhaiut mysli, eshche priblizitel´nee oni vyrazhaiut chuvstva (70)]).

Not unlike Aleksandr Ivanchenko's equally cerebral "Safety Procedures I" ("Tekhnika bezopasnosti I" [1988]), Narbikova's work deals with entrapment through cultural baggage, whether in the form of comprehensive clichés, ironclad hierarchies, paradigmatic situations, or words vitiated through overuse. Both writers' concern with incarceration yields a highly individualized chronotope, where time loses specificity (despite Narbikova's protracted meditation on its resistance to logical organization and capture by human categories [104–6]) but space receives extravagant elaboration.[31] In Narbikova's case, extensive spatial movement reflects the genre of a utopian voyage, a search for authenticity, for "lived life," à la Gide's *Immoraliste*. She essentially seeks to restore the world to a prelapsarian state, in which the heuristic capacities of body and language are still intact and attuned to the Primary, pre-Saussurean Wor(l)dmaker ("in what language, one asks, should one pray so as to reach His heart? Where is there such a language and who knows it?" [na kakom, sprashivaetsia, iazyke molit′sia chtoby doshlo do Ego serdtsa? Gde takoi iazyk i kto ego znaet? (60)]).[32] Debased by inertness, passivity, and mechanical repetition, both body and language now toil under the burden of stale, meaningless formulations that oppress without expressing. To break out of this prison of language and lymphocytes, Narbikova attempts to jettison the physical and verbal trappings that entrap (hence the shedding of clothes and standard grammatical markers),[33] to dismantle overly familiar authoritative constructs made authoritarian by entropy.

Narbikova negotiates her way out of the impasse by reconfiguring existent components in combinations that introduce the illicit into the conventionalized. Thus formerly taboo words such as *blevat′* (to throw up) and *sisat′* (to pee) consort with a poetic lexicon, just as dirty underclothes witness the "sublime" conjoining of two lovers; a third party (Otmatfeian: redolent of the biblical Matthew ["high" text] and of sperm [*malofei*—"low" body stratum]) invades a marriage, and the ménage à trois of Sana-Avvakum-Otmatfeian becomes reconfigured by the substitution of the lover's linguistically illegitimate friend Chiashchiazhyshyn (illegitimate insofar as his name violates Russian spelling rules) for the husband (illicitness squared). In parallel fashion, a shift in punctuation and the omission of a word fundamentally revise a concept ("Perhaps or definitely?" [Mozhet byt′ ili tochno?] becomes "Perhaps, definitely" [Mozhet byt′, tochno (5)]); the three unities in the authoritative classical poetics of Boileau become transformed by their irreverent application to the pragmatic logistics of a love affair (three in *dis*unity).

The illusion of eroticism in Narbikova's narrative derives from the conflation of sexual with textual, whereby bodies and literary citations copulate, in a drive for originality ("a nude Adam" or "a new word"). In fact, Narbikova makes quite explicit the interchangeability of sex and text:

> Language is, as it were, the materialization of a shift in sex. Human relations displayed sex, a shift in sex, and this manifested itself in language. But when language itself pointed to the sex of the elements, of forces, of heavenly bodies, their relations resulted from language. The wind chased a group of clouds [Pushkin]. A star spoke with a star [Lermontov]. The hermaphroditic Russian sun settled for a long time behind the androgynous Russian sea.
>
> Iazyk [both language and tongue?] iavliaetsia kak by materializatsiei perekhoda pola. Chelovecheskie otnosheniia vyiavliali pol, perekhod pola, i eto proiavlialos' v iazyke. No kogda sam iazyk ukazyval na pol skikhii, sil, svetil, ikh otnosheniia vytekali iz iazyka. Veter gonial stai tuch [Pushkin]. Zvezda gorovila so zvezdoi [Lermontov]. Russkoe germafroditicheskoe solntse nadolgo zaselo za russkim androginnym morem. (39)

The symbiosis between sex and text (phenomenon and word) leads Narbikova *as author* to a blind alley: anything physically new relies on verbal means for representation, but in a world of fallen language, naming "from the beginning" is impossible:

> At first there was the word "sea," and it materialized into a sea, and the word "mountain," and it—into a mountain. . . . The object didn't give birth to the word, but the word gave birth to the object. And the object proved larger than the word. The sea was larger than "sea," the tree larger than "tree." You could screw/strike [*trakhnut'*] with the word, it was the spirit, you could conceive from it [*zachat'*], but who now can conceive over the phone?
>
> Snachala bylo slovo "more," i ono materializovalos' v more, i slovo "gora," i ono—v goru. . . . Ne predmet porozhdal slovo, a

slovo porozhdalo predmet. I predmet okazalsia bol'she slova. More bol'she "moria," derevo bol'she "dereva." Slovom mozhno bylo trakhnut', ono bylo dukhom, ot nego mozhno bylo zachat', a seichas kto mozhet zachat' po telefonu? (42)

One of numerous sequences spotlighting the sex/text correspondence,[34] the passage climaxes in a rhetorical question that is answered approximately thirty pages later, when Sana conceives over the telephone. That ideologically willed impregnation places in proper perspective the role of the body in Narbikova's novel. She makes repeated disclaimers about logos, positing the priority of natural phenomena over language: "Nonetheless, at first there was rain, then later a verse about the rain . . . and never the opposite" (Vse-taki snachala byl dozhd', a potom stishok pro dozhd'. . . i nikogda naoborot [60]); "What are we arguing about? About naming a feeling that exists and a word that doesn't. 'Love,' after all, is a word, but the word's transparent, it's the most authentic apparition, which roams about at night and frightens the imagination, a phantom and nothing more" (O chem my sporim? O nazvanii chuvstva, kotoroe est', o slove, kotorogo net. Ved' "liubliu"—eto slovo, a slovo prizrachno, ono samyi nastoiashchii priznak, kotoryi shataetsia po nocham i pugaet voobrazhenie, fantom, i bol'she nichego [189]). Yet logos emerges as Narbikova's hero ("the object recedes, and only the name of the object remains, that is, the word, that is, the spirit . . . in the end there'll be the word, as there was the word in the beginning, and the word was everything" [otkhodit sam predmet, i ostaetsia tol'ko nazvanie predmeta, to est' slovo, to est' dukh . . . v kontse budet slovo, kak i v nachale bylo slovo, i slovo bylo vse (44); "the word is larger than the event" [slovo bol'she sobytiia (88)]) or the antihero, tainted, insufficient, but irresistible and, more important, ineluctable. And when constraints of decorum lead Narbikova to censor *zhopa* (ass) into *zh* . . . and *bliad'* (whore) into *b* . . . , despite the relentless iteration of *blevat'*, continuous eating, drinking, and urinating (*sisat'* and *pisat'* [pissing]), we find the body screened and semi-erased by linguistic propriety. Tellingly, *tufta* (nonsense) becomes a euphemism for *bliad'*,

by association, presumably, with promiscuity, random surfeit.
The epitome of prolonged, meticulous disembodiment occurs
early in the novel in Narbikova's description of Sana and
Otmatfeian's copulation: the thick web of associations, poetic
allusions (Pushkin and Lermontov), and abridged polemics about
the superiority of the organic (divine nature) over the inorganic
(of human creation) raise insuperable barriers between the reader
and the sexual act, itself euphemistically metaphorized as riding—Narbikova's own fall into time-worn literary patterns of
displacement. True to the novel's master trope, postcoital reflections turn not to but *into* textual matters, suggestively focusing on
subtexts—what lies beneath the "exposed" surface of a poem (8).
Thus *la petite mort* yields to the literal death of a poet (Lermontov) whose palm tree/birch leaf becomes the hypothetical cover
for Sana's naked body—the immediate subtext withheld from the
reader.

In his essay on the Marquis de Sade, Roland Barthes contends
that language, "being analytical," can "come to grips with the
body only if it cuts it up; the total body is outside language, only
pieces of the body succeed in writing; in order to *make* a body
seen, it must either be displaced, refracted through the metonymy
of clothing, or reduced to one of its parts" (127).[35] Language is
not *exclusively* analytical, however, and while the total body may
elude its compass, a writer intent on a rehabilitative amplitude of
representation may signal omissions through the careful creation
of space. This is Monique Wittig's solution in her prize-winning
Lesbian Body (1975), a rare attempt at just the kind of exhaustive
body-writing Barthes judges impossible. The integrity of the female body, the interdependence of its parts, and "the necessity
for these parts to create a space for themselves in language" are
installed visually in Wittig's text. Various female body parts in
capital letters, strategically spaced to accommodate the insertion
of what has been omitted and to register body cavities and gaps,
punctuate the narrative. Wittig travels around and inside the entire body, tracing its contours, organs, and fluids in a progression
that collapses distinctions between inner and outer areas, thereby

exploding the Barthesian reduction of the body "to one of its parts," which all too often slides into fetishism (Michie 144).

Such detailed mapping of the female body, however, presumes the author's desire to materialize its physicality for the reader to the fullest possible extent. That desire is lacking in Petrushevskaia, Tolstaia, and Narbikova, for whom body language represents a treasure-trove of rhetoric invigorated by suppression. Indeed, both Tolstaia and Narbikova show ironic awareness of the cultural uses to which the female body has been hostage, and their works capitalize inventively on the associative enrichment that with time has accrued to the body "trope." Instead of "literalizing" the body, however, they exploit its tropological potential according to the needs of their own aesthetics, which, mutatis mutandis, operates within the framework of a recognizable tradition and thus may be said to propagate "masculinist" conventions.

Any reader seeking a Russian woman's text that, while not reclaiming women's physical form, firmly distances itself from the mythology surrounding it through an irony intent on exposure instead of play might do well to read Marina Palei's miniature story "Rendezvous" ("Svidanie"). In a few trenchant pages Palei deconstructs the relationship between male "creativity" and the female body/beloved/muse as one-way traffic between a solipsistic subjectivity and an object denied not only all humanity but any identity apart from instrumentality (172–75). The narrative reads like a fictional gloss on John Berger's *Ways of Seeing*, a pioneering analysis of gender politics in visual male presentations and perceptions of the female form.[36] Palei caps her satirical survey of Western male artists' hypostatization of the ideal female body parts (Botticelli, Leonardo, Velásquez, Ingres, Picasso) with a striking realization of metaphor, whereby the "living" female body becomes a mechanism to be dismantled once its Purpose—as speculum for male *Angst*—has been fulfilled (or, more accurately, exhausted). She then proceeds to objectify the male, a move that, predictably, reveals his "mechanical" nature, functioning no differently from the female's and "constructed" according to the same principles.

"Svidanie" and some of the stories by the younger generation of women writers included in Larisa Vameeva's collection *Ne pomniashchaia zla* (*The Woman Who Doesn't Remember Evil*) show resistance to standard troping of woman's body in their emphasis on the very process of rhetoric formation and their determination to document the body's experience in painstaking detail.[37] Petrushevskaia, Tolstaia, and Narbikova, by contrast, work within the much-debated tradition—vilified by many feminists—of drawing upon the female body as a repository of rhetorical devices. They are therefore, doubtless, vulnerable to accusations of colluding with oppressive patriarchal habits. Yet their originality and techniques of defamiliarization transmute what might otherwise seem hackneyed and sexist into revisionist, fresh, and subversive formulations. Perhaps their prose best corresponds to Julia Kristeva's sense of "woman" as an attitude that resists conventional culture and language while operating within them in a revolutionary capacity (Jones 358–59). As Leonard Barkan and others have remarked, the body in general, whether male or female, lends itself to rhetorical extrapolation.[38] And through the textual bodies of Petrushevskaia, Tolstaia, and Narbikova sound three unique authorial voices whose distinct qualities set them apart from the hum of homogenized thought and "manspeak." In their case, trope gives cause for hope.

Notes

Parts of this chapter were first presented as a talk at the second annual meeting of the Working Group on Contemporary Soviet Culture (Berkeley, June 1991), sponsored by the Joint Committee on Soviet Studies with funds provided by the American Council of Learned Societies and the Social Science Research Council. I thank these agencies and the members of the group. The essay as first delivered in Berkeley ("Body Talk in Current Fiction: Speaking Parts and [W]holes") will appear in an issue of *Stanford Slavic Studies*, forthcoming, 1993.

1. Kate Millett first voiced this sense of gendered appropriation, in her watershed study *Sexual Politics* (1969). Probably the most sustained and impassioned argument in this vein is offered by Gubar and Gilbert.

2. In her story "Rendezvous" ("Svidanie"), Marina Palei makes explicit and ironizes this masculine habit: "And here she is, his one and only, and that's why she's wonderfully neither this nor that, neither beautiful nor ugly.

He perceives her as he does himself in a mirror, she's his creation, the crowning achievement of his many efforts and experiences" (174).

3. The pioneer of this concept and taxonomy probably is Hélène Cixous, who in "The Laugh of the Medusa" (1975) speaks of "a fantasized obligatory virility meant to invade, to colonize" (Warhol and Herndl 349). For elaborations of the notion, see, e.g., the signally titled article by Judith Williamson. For a thorough examination of the topic, see Kolodny.

4. Spelman's survey traces somatophobia to Plato's influential writings, which foreground the mind/body distinction along gendered lines. That binary cast of mind generates multiple oppositions, the most relevant here, perhaps, being culture/nature. On the female body perceived as nature, free of conventions, see Scholes. On gendered binarism, see Cixous.

5. See Michie 124–50. For women's reclaiming of their bodies through explicitly sexual artworks, see the essay by Maryse Holder, "Another Cuntree: At Last, a Mainstream Female Art Movement," in Raven et al. 1–20.

6. Cixous asserts, in fact, "When I say 'woman,' I'm speaking of [. . .] a universal woman subject" (334).

7. Jones, esp. 260. For an examination of writing that ties creativity to procreativity, see Friedman.

8. All three would categorically dissociate themselves from a taxonomy that genders literary categories, for reasons discussed in Goscilo, "Domostroika or Perestroika?"

9. One critic complains, for example: "Women writers now present such instances of 'frank writing' where recently even 'male' prose used ellipses that it seems as though the only thing female left in it [their writing] is the authors' names" (Zhenshchiny-pisatel'nitsy nyne demonstriruiut takie primery "otkrytogo teksta" tam, gde nedavno i v "muzhskoi" proze stavili mnogotochie, chto, pokhozhe, zhenskogo v nei tol'ko i ostalos', chto familii avtorov [Shcheglova 23]). For a similar opinion, see Pavel Basinskii's review of Vameeva, in Goscilo, *Skirted Issues*.

10. See Goscilo, "Inscribing the Female Body."

11. Key devices in Petrushevskaia's fiction rest on the division between the body and soul traced by Francis Barker, who analyzes the increasing privatization of the body and denial of its "base" appetites throughout history. Stallybrass and White perform a similar examination, with the aid of Bakhtinian concepts.

12. Petrushevskaia's long-rejected works illustrate the discrepancy between journal versions of texts (usually bowdlerized) and their later publication in books (with the author's original phrasing restored). Passages previously omitted from *Liubov'*, "Svoi krug," and "Takaia devochka" (references to rotting limbs in a cemetery, to a dildo, and to incestuous antics; the words *der'mo, bzdet'*, and *prostitutka*) are reinstated in the most recent collections of Petrushevskaia's drama and prose. On this phenomenon of expurgation and restoration in Petrushevskaia, see Goscilo, "Alternative Prose," 123.

13. The sinuous Byzantine manner in which the narrator reports her own manipulation recalls Dostoevskii's treatment of Ivan Karamazov's highly

coded ratification of Smerdiakov's murder of the old Karamazov. This is but one of innumerable echoes of Dostoevskii, Petrushevskaia's favorite writer, in her works.

14. For an incisive analysis of the changing connotations and euphemistic aspect of the expression "sleeping together," see Robinson 409–11.

15. On the iterability and replaceability of the female body, see Michie.

16. Pateman's organizing thesis is that contract invariably generates political right in the form of domination and subordination, so that it is impossible to put contractarian theory to progressive use. She challenges conventional notions about the contracts implicit in both prostitution (chap. 7) and marriage (chap. 6), among other practices.

17. On the unrepentant brand of confession, see Belknap; also Goscilo, "Gilded Guilt."

18. The body as a source of nourishment receives macabre treatment in two of her latest and grimmest stories, evocatively titled "Novyi Gulliver" and "Medeia," just as the cycle "Pesni vostochnykh slavian" exploits a grisly dismemberment of the sort that the censor excised from the play *Liubov'* when it was first published.

19. Whether in private conversation, in her drama, or in her prose, Petrushevskaia's preoccupation with psychology and especially with the "lacerated soul" à la Dostoevskii, but now overlaid with a veneer of toughness, emerges quite clearly. Petrushevskaia is constitutionally incapable, I believe, of projecting an unproblematic, adjusted, or reasonably happy individual.

20. Petrushevskaia's narrators in both her stories *(istorii)* and her monologues *(monologii)* typically combine vagueness and claims to uncertainty with wordiness and what at first glance strikes the reader as a plethora of extraneous detail. These devices work to conceal while urging discovery, stress the insignificant while sidestepping the primary. The synchronization of these two conflicting impulses gives Petrushevskaia's narratives a tension that recalls the bifurcations in Dostoevskii's emotionally charged confrontations.

21. Petrushevskaia presents the act of narrating as a seizure of anxious power whereby the mode of telling (through subterfuge, omission, deferment, misplaced emphases, etc.) can reshape reality according to the narrator's psychological needs. The verbal articulation of an experience gives the speaker command of that experience and alters its significance in the telling. That phenomenon is most clearly visible in "Svoi krug," "Takaia devochka," and "Vremia noch'."

22. On the sexualization of hair in body discourse, see Brownmiller 55–76; on hair as synecdoche, see Michie 99–102: "Hair is a particularly involuted figure because, like metaphor itself, it both covers and reveals, dresses and undresses the body. . . . [Hair] figures the body it hides" (100). St. Paul contributed to the troping of women's hair: "But if a woman have long hair, it is a glory to her: for her hair is given her for a covering" (1 Cor. 11:15).

23. By and large Petrushevskaia's stories operate by gigantic omissions and deflections that are camouflaged by the garrulity of the narrating persona, whose forays into crudity and explicitness give a false sense of frankness.

Although Petrushevskaia's narrators feel compelled to confess through narration, they withhold unpalatable truths from themselves and from their audience, while supplying enough clues to enable the percipient reader to grasp the unspoken. Their postponement and obfuscation are also Petrushevskaia's, as is evident in the tortured delay in "Medeia," where the title immediately prepares one for the mother's murder of her husband's beloved daughter but the man's extended cryptic comments to his passenger keep deferring the revelation until virtually the narrative's end.

24. De Man's efforts to undo totalizing readings have produced some major revisions in critical responses, above all to what he calls the aesthetic ideology of the Romantics.

25. The male protagonist of "Peters" and Natasha in "Vyshel mesiats iz tumana" represent younger variants of the type.

26. Tolstaya, *On the Golden Porch,* 65 (amended for accuracy). The original reads: "Vysoko na vershine na sibirskom dereve ispuganno blestit glazami tvoia shapka; korova v mukakh rozhaet ditia—tebe na sapogi; s krikom ogoliaetsia ovtsa, chtoby ty mogla sogret'sia ee volosami; v predsmertnoi toske b'etsia kashalot, rydaet krokodil, zadykhaetsia v bege obrechennyi leopard. Tvoi rozovye shcheki—v korobkakh s letuchei pyl'tsoi, ulybki—v zolotykh futliarakh s malinovoi nachinkoi, gladkaia kozha—v tiubikakh s zhirom, vzgliad v kruglykh prozrachnykh bankakh" (62).

27. On Zoia and Nina, see Goscilo, "Monsters"; on Ada Adol'fovna and in general Tolstaia's penchant for binary oppositions (e.g., of the material and the intangible), see Goscilo, "Tolstajan Love as Surface Text."

28. That tendency, of course, originates in the unitive impulse of religious iconography (the One God) and had its heyday during Romanticism. Victor Hugo's *Notre Dame de Paris* relied on the paradigm so as to invert and subvert it through the antitheses personified by Quasimodo and Phoebus.

29. As Nadezhda Azhgikhina has remarked: "Critics exalted and reviled the author, accused her of a lack of talent and called her the first modernist of the Five-Year Plan, and—since she'd decided to write 'about that'—collectively placed her at the head of the tradition of erotic literature that is being revived in our country" ([K]ritiki pisatel'nitsu voznosili i nizvergali, obviniali v otsustvii talanta i narekali pervoi modernistskoi piatileki, i—koli reshila pisat' "pro eto"—druzhno postavili vo glavu vozrozhdaiushcheisia v otechestve traditsii eroticheskoi literatury [224]). Before the novel was published in *Ravnovesie*, excerpts from it appeared in *Iunost'*, 1988, no. 8, 15–29.

30. In an interview Narbikova singled out the erotic as the sole respite from everyday banality and tension. Yet only someone unfamiliar with eroticism would ascribe that quality to her (insistently cerebral) prose. Readers' subliminal recognition of Narbikova's attachment to the Edenic myth may explain their misprision of her as an erotic writer. Motifs from the myth intercalated in the novel include the garden, hunger for the forbidden, eating, the trio of dramatis personae (Adam/Eve/snake) enmeshed in knowledge of sex, nakedness and covering, and the inability to return to a former state or space. See Veselaia 14.

31. Various spatial categories figure prominently in the novel. In addition to the journey from their apartment to the beach, where they roam ceaselessly back and forth, Narbikova's protagonists experience difficulty locating each other, leaving and entering their temporary dwelling, finding "their places," etc. We witness seemingly pointless movement in and out of contained space, especially apartments and bodies. Verbs for eating, drinking, urinating, and regurgitating, particularly *blevat'* (throw up), recur frequently, sometimes modifying unusual direct objects: "'We have no money, we have nothing to throw up'" (Deneg u nas net, blevat' nam nechem [68]); "to throw up nature" (*vyblevat' prirodu*), etc.

32. See also the passages treating prisons and Adam (127–30).

33. In her story "Ad kak Da/aD kak dA," conventional punctuation, name differentiation, and the like are cast off. See Vaneeva 315–62.

34. See the related passage: "Male writers always mean the active principle, whereas heroines always the passive; there are no live women. All men wanted to have to do only with Natasha, Sonechka, and Tania Larina, starting with kindergarten—with the golden fish, the ideal woman, whereas all women wanted to do only with Pushkin himself, with Tolstoi and Dostoevskii" ([P]isateli—vsegda aktiv, a geroini—vsegda passiv, zhivykh zhenshchin net. Vse muzhchiny khoteli by imet' delo tol'ko s Natashei, Sonechkoi, Tanei Larinoi, nachinaia s detskogo sada—s zolotoi rybkoi, ideal'noi zhenshchinoi, i vse zhenshchiny zato s samim Pushkinym, Tolstym i Dostoevskim [163]).

35. Barthes, then, conceives of the body as a linguistic problem requiring enabling dismemberment.

36. Berger's classic study presents in simple, graceful prose many of the ideas that have become fundamental to feminist thought; e.g., the conventionalized differences in male and female presence, the concept of female internalization, the voyeurism of male artistic depiction/spectatorship, the distinction between nakedness and nudity. See esp. chap. 3 (45–64).

37. See, e.g., Svetlana Vasilenko's "Shamara" and the title story by Elena Tarasova, which, however, ultimately relies on trope.

38. See esp. chap. 1. See also the classic work by Mary Douglas, demonstrating how the body has served historically as a symbol of society across cultures.

References

Azhgikhina, Nadezhda. "Razrushiteli v poiskakh very." *Znamia*, 1990, no. 9.
Barkan, Leonard. *Nature's Work of Art: The Human Body as Image of the World*. New Haven, CT: Yale University Press, 1975.
Barker, Francis. *The Tremulous Private Body: Essays on Subjection*. London: Methuen, 1984.
Barthes, Roland. *Sade/Fourier/Loyola*. New York: Hill & Wang, 1976.
Basinskii, Pavel. "Pozabyvshie dobro?" *Literaturnaia gazeta*, 1991, no. 7 (20 February), 10.

Belknap, Robert L. "The Unrepentant Confession." In *Russianness: In Memory of Rufus W. Mathewson*, ed. Robert L. Belknap, 113–23. Ann Arbor, MI: Ardis, 1990.

Berger, John. *Ways of Seeing*. London/New York: BBC and Penguin, 1972/1977.

Brownmiller, Susan. *Femininity*. New York: Fawcett Columbine, 1984.

Cixous, Hélène. "Sorties: Out and Out." In *The Newly Born Woman*. Trans. Betsy Wing, 63–132. Minneapolis, MN: University of Minnesota Press, 1986/1988.

Cowie, Elizabeth. "Woman as Sign." *m/f*, 1978.

Dallery, Arlene B. "The Politics of Writing (the) Body: Ecriture féminine." In *Gender/Body/Knowledge*, ed. Alison M. Jaggar and Susan R. Bordo, 52–67. New Brunswick, NJ: Rutgers University Press, 1989.

de Man, Paul. *Allegories of Reading*. New Haven, CT: Yale University Press, 1979.

Doane, Mary Ann. "Film and the Masquerade: Theorizing the Female Spectator." *Screen* 23, nos. 3–4 (1982).

Douglas, Mary. *Purity and Danger: An Analysis of the Concepts of Pollution and Taboo*. (1966.) London and Boston: Routledge & Kegan Paul, 1984.

Friedman, Susan Stanford. "Creativity and the Childbirth Metaphor: Gender Difference in Literary Discourse." In *Feminisms*, ed. Robyn R. Warhol and Diane Price Hendl, 371–96. New Brunswick, NJ: Rutgers University Press, 1991.

Goscilo, Helena. "Gilded Guilt: Confession in Russian Romantic Prose." *Russian Literature* 14, no. 2 (August 1983): 149–81. (Special Issue: Russian Romanticism I.)

———. "Tolstajan Love as Surface Text." *SEEJ* 34, no. 1 (1990): 40–52.

———. "Alternative Prose and Glasnost Literature." In *Five Years That Shook the World*, ed. Harley D. Balzer. Boulder, CO: Westview, 1991.

———. "Inscribing the Female Body in Women's Fiction: Cross-Gendered Passion à la Holbein." *Gender Restructuring in Russian Studies*, ed. Marianne Liljeström, Eila Mäntysaari, and Arja Rosenholm, 73–86. Tampere: Slavica Tamperensia II, 1993.

———. "Domostroika or Perestroika? The Construction of Womanhood under Glasnost." In *Late Soviet Culture: From Perestroika to Novostroika*, ed. Thomas Lahusen. Raleigh, NC: Duke University Press, 1993.

———. "Monsters Monomaniacal, Marital, and Medical: Tat'iana Tolstaia's Regenerative Use of Gender Stereotypes." In *Sexuality and the Body in Russian Culture*, ed. Jane Costlow, Stephanie Sandler, and Judith Vowles. Stanford, CA: Stanford University Press, 1993.

———, ed. *Skirted Issues: The Discreteness and Indiscretions of Russian Women's Prose*. Armonk, NY: M.E. Sharpe, 1992. Spring issue of *Russian Studies in Literature*.

Gubar, Susan, and Sandra M. Gilbert. *The Madwoman in the Attic*. New Haven, CT: Yale University Press, 1979.

Jaggar, Alison M., and Susan R. Bordo, eds. *Gender/Body/Knowledge*. Femi-

nist Reconstructions of Being and Knowing. New Brunswick, NJ: Rutgers University Press, 1989.

Jones, Ann Rosalind. "Writing the Body: Toward an Understanding of *l'écriture féminine.*" In *Feminisms,* ed. Robyn R. Warhol and Diane Price Herndl, 57–70. New Brunswick, NJ: Rutgers University Press, 1991.

Kolodny, Annette. *The Lay of the Land: Metaphor as Experience and History in American Life and Letters.* Chapel Hill, NC: University of North Carolina Press, 1975.

Michie, Helena. *The Flesh Made Word.* New York: Oxford University Press, 1987.

Narbikova, Valeriia. *Ravnovesie sveta dnevnykh i nochnykh zvezd.* Moscow: Vsesoiuznyi molodezhnyi knizhnyi tsentr, 1990.

Palei, Marina. *Otdelenie propashchikh.* Moscow, 1991.

Pateman, Carole. *The Sexual Contract.* Stanford, CA: Stanford University Press, 1988.

Petrushevskaia, Liudmila. "Takaia devochka." *Ogonek,* 1988, no. 40 (October), 9–11.

―――. "Gigiena." *Ogonek,* 1990, no. 28, 27–29.

Poliakov, Iurii. "Ob eroticheskom lizbeke i ne tol'ko o nem." *Inostrannaia literatura,* 1989, no. 5 (May).

Raven, Arlene, Cassandra Lager, and Joanna Frueh, eds. *Feminist Art Criticism,* New York: HarperCollins/Icon, 1991.

Robinson, Douglas. "Henry James and Euphemism." *College English* 53, no. 4 (April 1991).

Scholes, Robert. "Uncoding Mama: The Female Body as Text." In *Semiotics and Interpretation,* 127–41. New Haven, CT: Yale University Press, 1982.

Shcheglova, Evgeniia. "V svoem krugu." *Literaturnoe obozrenie,* 1990, no. 3.

Spelman, Elizabeth V. "Woman as Body: Ancient and Contemporary Views." *Feminist Studies* 8, no. 1 (Spring 1982): 109–31.

Stallybrass, Peter, and Allon White. *The Politics and Poetics of Transgression.* London: Methuen, 1986.

Tolstaia, Tat'iana. *"Na zolotom kryl'tse sideli. . . "* Moscow, 1987. Published in English as *On the Golden Porch,* trans. Antonina W. Bouis. New York: Knopf, 1989.

Vaneeva, L.L., ed. *Ne pomniashchaia zla.* Moscow: Moskovskii rabochii, 1990.

Veselaia, Elena. "Dunovenie erosa: Beseda s Valeriei Narbikovoi." *Moskovskie novosti,* 1 April 1990.

Warhol, Robyn R., and Diane Price Herndl, eds. *Feminisms.* New Brunswick, NJ: Rutgers University Press, 1991.

Williamson, Judith. "Woman as an Island: Femininity and Colonialization." In *Studies in Entertainment,* ed. Tania Modleski, 99–118. Bloomington, IN: Indiana University Press, 1986.

Wolff, Janet. *Feminine Sentences: Essays on Women and Culture.* Berkeley, CA: University of California Press, 1990.

8

GAMES WOMEN PLAY
The "Erotic" Prose of Valeriia Narbikova

Nadya L. Peterson

> In a system in which the marginal, the avant-garde, the
> subversive, all that disturbs and "undoes the whole" is
> endowed with positive value, a woman artist who can identify
> these concepts with her own practice and metaphorically with
> her own femininity can find in them a source of strength and
> self-legitimation.
>
> —Susan Rubin Suleiman, *Subversive Intent*

Valeriia Narbikova, a young Russian author of "erotic prose,"
was ushered into the literary limelight by the Russian writer Andrei Bitov in 1988 (*Ravnovesie,* 15). "Discovered" and praised by
one important man of letters, she was denigrated and verbally
abused by another, the prominent Soviet critic Dmitrii Urnov. As
in Narbikova's own stories, the woman appeared at the center of
a controversy, at the apex of a triangle, between two men.

To Andrei Bitov, Narbikova's world appeared "astonishingly,
enchantingly transparent and tender" (15). To Dmitrii Urnov, Narbikova's density and unusual technique were proofs of her inability
to deal with erotic themes. In Urnov's opinion, to compensate for a
lack of philosophical depth, Narbikova takes "a trivial situation"
and "complicates it by purely verbal gymnastics" (4).

Other critics joined in the fight over the significance and value
of Narbikova's contribution to Russian literature, generally echo-
ing the arguments of the two principals. Critics tended to agree
on the main features of Narbikova's work—its complexity, its

deliberately shocking, insatiable interest in sex and physiology, and the triviality of some of its situations and language.[1] They disagreed vehemently on the general worth of such literature—a clash of opinions that is indicative of the traditional value-oriented ways of Soviet criticism but that has very little to do with Narbikova as a serious writer or innovator.

I am not concerned here with the unresolvable issue of merit. According to Narbikova herself, her work is in demand (in 1991 a copy of her first published novel brought 100 rubles or so on the black market).[2] She is being read, perhaps even widely, and this is sufficient for my purposes.

What is immediately apparent to anyone who attempts to make sense of Narbikova's work, however, is that she does everything possible to hinder such an endeavor. The critic who sets out to decipher Narbikova's convoluted, ostensibly erotic language is engaged in a labor of love. And I mean not to imply that her prose is intended to excite one's libidinal impulses (it generally does not—an issue to be addressed in due course) but rather to emphasize the arduousness of the critical task at hand.

Narbikova's work is a permanent exercise in transgression, which, by virtue of its predictability, subverts its own transgressive intent. The first reaction to Narbikova's prose is an intense involvement with the shocking distortions in her compacted language; her narrative configurations are an inducement to guess, to crack the code, to find the rules of the game she is playing with the reader. Then, inevitably, the novelty wears off, her devices become predictable and automatized; the cross-fertilization of other texts within her text, Narbikova's "intertextuality," is no longer a refreshing revelation, and the deliberately meager story line can no longer sustain interest.

The principal player defeats herself at her own game: the work becomes too dull to read. This is the predicament in which a modernist writer finds herself when her text becomes "all too readable—not in the sense of readability imposed on [it] by the traditional reader, but in the sense in which [it has] codified [its] own transgressive procedures, and codified as well the commentary on those procedures" (Suleiman 43). If, however, one views Narbikova's work in the context of the contemporary Soviet avant-garde, as a modernist work aimed at upsetting artistic standards and challenging the dominant ideology, then the automatization of her transgressive procedures is the price she has to pay for being subversive. Then the questions I pose below may yield a broader view of Narbikova's work—not as an isolated incident but as a trend, the result of intense cross-pollination of ideas and techniques between East and West, between visual and narrative arts.

What is the significance of Narbikova's innovative focus on the commonplace? How important are the clichés of Soviet speech in Narbikova's writing? Why does she constantly engage in what Urnov called "verbal gymnastics"? Equally intriguing is the issue of her work as an example of "erotic" prose written by a woman. What norm does Narbikova use as a platform for transgression in the language she employs and the situations she describes? Is her prose erotic, pornographic, or realistic in some new sense? Does her work have a message? What kind of message?

In Narbikova's view, socially oriented literature (what she calls "the literature of great ideas") turns ideas into stale slogans (Veselaia 14). Alternative literature, in contrast (Soviet critics apply the term to a broad spectrum of unorthodox contemporary Soviet works), tends to mask its social agenda.

In Narbikova's debut work, *Ravnovesie sveta dnevnykh i nochnykh zvezd* (*The Equilibrium of Light of Diurnal and Nocturnal Stars*), which can serve as a paradigm for her writing in general (particularly because her narratives emphasize their "uninterruptedness" and elasticity), she does not spell out her ideas directly.[3] Following her own prescriptions for writing alternative prose, she conceals her message by weaving it into the dense fabric of the narrative. At the core of *Ravnovesie* we find a familiar love triangle, a standard arrangement for Narbikova's stories. The main character, Sana, is married to Avvakum but is seeing Otmatfeian (an allegorical name with allusions to the gospel of Matthew—"Ot Matfeia"). The names of Sana's men are deliberately

Valeriia Narbikova

recognizable allusions, but their significance is limited to their recognizability. Neither Archpriest Avvakum's famous *Life* nor Matthew's account of the life of Jesus contributes in any way to an understanding of the characters or of the author's philosophical position. Rather, the allusions are intended to disturb readers, to jolt them out of the complacency that comes with passive consumption of "easy" texts. Such "empty" allusions, "snares," abound in Narbikova's writing; consider her use of the name of the False Dmitrii for one of the characters in "Probeg—pro beg" ("Rally about Running"), or of Dodostoevskii (which can be loosely rendered as Foredostoevskii) and Toest'lstoi in "Plan pervogo litsa. I vtorogo" ("First Person. And Second").

After a bitter argument with Sana, her lover escapes to a seaside resort under the pretext of a business trip. She and her husband follow and find themselves in the same house with Sana's lover and his friend. The group discovers a Sleeping Beauty and, after unsuccessful attempts to rouse her, decide to take her along. Sana abandons her husband, gives birth to a child conceived over the telephone, and lives with her lover in an old museum. In the end, Sleeping Beauty is released back into the sea, Sana's lover returns to his wife, and Sana reunites with her husband.

This summary is only the bare bones of the novel as it was excerpted in the journal *Iunost'*. In the full version, the veiled messages are elaborated on, and certain themes are more directly expressed as the plot dissolves into a series of very loosely related episodes (in fact, chapter 4 of the full version was published separately in the émigré publication *Strelets*).[4]

Narbikova's style is very dense, aware of its own literariness, and seemingly aimed at puzzling the reader. Her narrative principle has a lot in common with one strand of the Soviet avant-garde, conceptual art (*kontseptualizm*), associated primarily with such artists as Il'ia Kabakov and Erik Bulatov and such poets as Dmitrii Prigov and Lev Rubinshtein. (Narbikova is a close friend of Kabakov and repeatedly refers to his work in her writing.)

In Soviet conceptual art, as Mikhail Epshtein has pointed out, "everything that exists is transcribed in the mode of banality, all utterances appear as quotations" (229). In this process the author/artist does not simply use ready-made verbal clichés but imitates, consciously and skillfully, entire world views, situations, characters, elements of plot, and ideas (*suzhdeniia*) about life. Epshtein sees this "humiliation of speech" as a means of debunking the myths of Soviet society, as a "solemnly cheerful interment of those ideas that for so long have tortured people's souls with vain dreams [*tsheta*] of unbounded power, happiness, unity, and victory" (235).

It should be noted that Russian conceptualism is a blend of

indigenous and extrinsic trends: American pop art and conceptualism on the one hand and Soviet *sots art* on the other. *Sots art* as
a movement began with the work of Vitaly Komar and Alexander Melamid and a group of underground artists of the *aptart*
(apartment exhibitions) of the early 1970s. Epshtein's definition
of conceptualism ("everything that exists is transcribed in the
mode of banality, all utterances appear as quotations") is perhaps
too narrow for conceptualism itself; it defines *sots art,* however,
with utmost precision. Here, as Elisabeth Sussman explains, banality appears as a "signifier of the social," and the artifacts of Soviet
politicized mass culture are used for avant-garde purposes (64).

Sots art and pop art both employ the proliferating signs of
their respective mass cultures to subvert the process of "naturalization"—the process by which, as Roland Barthes showed in his
work on modern mythologies, artificial constructs of dominant
cultures strive to appear as "Nature." Whereas pop art responded
aesthetically to the symbols of Western culture's mass consumption, however, *sots art* acted in opposition to the advertising of
the "building of socialism" and to the redundancy and overabundance of ideological propagandistic graphic production.

The mutual influences exerted by Eastern and Western art
have created what Sussman calls a "state of hybridity" (64). She
points out parallel descriptions of a shift from expressive to conceptual attitudes in the writings of Soviet conceptual artists and
some American critics. The Soviet conceptualist Sergei Anufriev
refers to the replacement of "artistic pathos" by "investigative
pathos," and the American Hal Foster, writing in 1983, points to
"anti-aesthetic" gestures in Western art, so that "a poem or picture is not necessarily privileged, and the artifact is likely to be
treated less as a work in modernist terms—unique, symbolic,
visionary—than as a text in a postmodernist sense—'already
written,' allegorical, contingent" (Foster x–xi). According to
these observers, the shared tendencies in Western and Soviet art
in the last twenty years point to an art layered with meanings,
organized by strategies of irony and parody, an art that is self-referential, resisting a single meaning or interpretation (Sussman 64).

This assessment can very easily be applied both to the conceptualist art of Il'ia Kabakov and to Valeriia Narbikova's narratives.

Il'ia Kabakov's early work might be seen as an example of *sots art,* but in the 1970s it acquired the more depoliticized elastic dimensions of Russian conceptualism. Kabakov's mature art, then, can no longer be easily contained within the ironic boundaries of quotational *sots art.* Writing becomes an important element of his artistic design, linking Kabakov to the Western conceptualists of the late 1960s (Joseph Kosuth, Douglas Huebler, and Lawrence Weiner). Here concept, information, language, and system are foregrounded through the use of narrative texts, photographs, and objects (Sussman 65).

Through installations and narratives Kabakov creates a fictional cosmos—a communal Soviet apartment shared by ten fictional characters—in the process constructing, in his own words, a "metaphysics of the commonplace."[5] Kabakov's purpose here is to expand the limits of *sots art,* to move from a straightforward ironic undercutting of the myths of socialist realism to an almost existentialist world view in which the emptiness, purposelessness, and wastefulness of life occupy center stage. If garbage in Kabakov's art has been interpreted to signify the waste of ideology, of words, of the environment—the failure of the human "experiment"—than the always white last page of a Kabakov album is there to undercut any attempt at a one-dimensional interpretation of anything.

Narbikova's work is similarly constructed to resist a single interpretation. Epshtein notes that in the works of the avant-garde (that is, the Soviet experimental art of the last three decades) the absurd dominates over the meaningful, the individual is alienated from the self, and we observe "a crisis of reality impossible to contain in forms available to humans, reality that melts, disappears, becomes less perceptible and knowable" (226). In Narbikova this barely perceptible and knowable reality emerges through the defamiliarization of the quotidian, through the deliberate debunking of the myths of the Soviet and Russian state.

In Narbikova the waste of ideology and environment is presented, exemplified, and amplified as the waste of words. Trivial language is mimicked, forcibly stripped of its logic, and torn out of the normalized system of speech:

> You know, she wanted you know what with you know who. But "you know who" didn't call, and you don't know who did. No one knew what was happening outside either. Yesterday they promised something and it happened the way they promised. (*Ravnovesie*, 15)

Or:

> They had an unhappy marriage: while she was his mistress, she wanted him to love her as a wife; when she became his wife, she wanted most of all for him to love her as a mistress; he couldn't do this, he loved her as he could; when she was his mistress, he loved her as a mistress, when she became his wife, he loved her as his wife. (Ad kak Da, 319)

Narbikova rearranges clichés in striking combinations and shifts the emphasis in set expressions to reveal the texture of the language of which they are composed, and so to defamiliarize notions about reality embedded in truisms of everyday life. As one prominent Soviet critic has noted, this technique betrays the direct influence of Sasha Sokolov (Chudakova 34). And like Sokolov, Narbikova likes to invert the standard hierarchy of styles by trivializing aspects of high culture and placing the cultural vernacular on a pedestal. Boileau and Aristotle are brought in, for example, to support the notion that for an act of physical love one needs unity of time, place, and action. Since the protagonist is married, it is rather difficult for her to satisfy two of the requirements—a time and a place—to arrange a rendezvous with her lover. Similar and striking shifts of emphasis occur when a discussion of myths and religious beliefs appears next to a description of dirty underwear, and when the story of the Holy Family's flight into Egypt is retold in the gossipy tone of a discussion in a communal apartment:

> He left his son in the care of people. What can one say, then, about the young girl, the mother of his son, whom he left in the care of her husband, her son's stepfather; he didn't even take her to Egypt

himself, but just told Iosif Iakovich to take her to Egypt, didn't even say it himself, just left a message with the holy ghost. If he could do that to the people close to him, what then about the people completely unknown to him. Although people he didn't know he sometimes treated better than those close to him, and people themselves sometimes treat those they don't know better than the ones close to them. (*Ravnovesie*, 105)

Rearrangement, reaccentuation of clichés (what Helena Goscilo refers to as "reversed syllogisms"), "empty" allusions (historical tags used to disorient rather than orient in meaning), and deliberate trivializing of situations and actions work together in Narbikova's writing to create a sense of plasticity and transparency that has nothing to do with mimesis. The appropriate word here is "interchangeability"—characters, sexes, situations, spaces, interpretations, even historical periods are interchangeable. Two passages in "Ad kak Da/aD kak dA" (as well as the title itself, "Hell as Yes heLL as yeS," with an allusion to dadaism imbedded in it) illustrate this point nicely:

> Parts of her face were arranged in an order that created an illusion of complete interchangeability: where she had her nose, her mouth could have been easily located; where she had her eyes, she could have had her ears; the chin could have been where the forehead was; no matter how the parts of her face were moved around, the face itself retained its natural harmony. (326)

And:

> It was Popoff himself; and only Popoff could attract by this rare combination of the plebeian and the refined; and women (men) were won over by the refinement he inherited from his father (mother), and the men (women) were won over by his plebeian qualities given to him by his mother (father): for women (men) he was an absolute whore, for women—a gentleman, for gentle women—a man [dlia zhenshchin—dzhentl'menom, a dlia dzhenshchin—zhentl'menom]. (358–59)

Nothing changes, there is no tangible plot in which to anchor your reader's expectations, yet everything might and does change. Banality, Kabakov's trivial constant garbage of life, becomes an object of contemplation, an aesthetic object; the component parts of this refuse of life, however, can and do undergo an infinite number of transformations.

Narbikova's spaces shrink and expand, her characters merge and emerge, they surface in the times of Napoleon, or go back to the period of Henry IX in France, and suddenly appear in a new guise in modern Leningrad. The guidelines are elusive, the movement is perceived not at the level of a plot but at the level of words—in the incessant game with meaning that leads one to conclude that there can be no meaning because the author can always rephrase, emphasize, and laugh at the reader's willingness to narrativize, to make sense:

> What are they talking about? It's hard to catch the meaning. This meaning has another meaning hiding behind it, which reaches a zero and then changes its sign to the opposite one: she attempts to convince him about something he has been trying to propose just a while ago, she denies what she asserted just a minute ago, he denies what he has just asserted, they are talking simultaneously, and when she is the voice he is the background, and when he is the voice she is the background, and then it is one voice over another and one background against another background. . . . (*Ravnovesie*, 140)

The author is in complete control over these permutations of meaning. Prohibitions are broken, norms transgressed—through the violation of the word, defamiliarization of the commonplace, the infinite game of emphasis. That is why Narbikova's love triangles are narratively unanchored; situations described in traditional narratives indeed occur, but can and do occur somewhere else, at other times. That is why what is stated needs always to be restated in a different way.

The few fixed areas of representation are lovesickness, wives/husbands/lovers, adulterous situations, sex, eating, nature, water, body fluids and waste, certain mythical landmarks (such as the beautiful Helen of Troy), certain historical figures (such as Peter the Great), writers (such as Pushkin—he stands for God in literature), and God. The present tense environment is recognizable; it is probably in Soviet Russia, probably in Leningrad/Petersburg, probably within the last ten years.

The only departure from the overall movement of Narbikova's prose into unintelligibility and dissolution of meaning as a philosophical stance is her directly expressed indignation at what can be called the fruits of civilization. Narbikova emphasizes the notion that people are part of nature by recasting human bodies and the attributes of everyday life in terms of nature. Instead of personifying nature—a familiar device of traditional narratives—she "naturalizes" persons and their environment. This strategy imparts a surrealistic quality to Narbikova's descriptions. In *Ravnovesie* the central character adorns her legs with brooks and covers herself with clouds. Similarly, human clothes are compared to mountains and forests protecting the earth.

The device of naturalization of persons serves to underscore several philosophical points in *Ravnovesie*. If one were to disregard the novel's innovative technique for a moment, the closeness of Narbikova's position to that of the "ecologically aware" village prose of Valentin Rasputin or Sergei Zalygin, or to the prose of Andrei Bitov, for example, becomes startlingly apparent. In addition, the emphasis on the absurdity of humanity's attempts to mold nature to suit its own purposes is consistent with the views espoused by the Soviet conceptualist Il'ia Kabakov, and can also be found in the recent paintings of Vitaly Komar and Alexander Melamid (the New Jersey cycle).

Ravnovesie's narrator points out that although people have been part of nature from the very beginning, in assuming divine powers they have lost their sense of belonging to it. People have become poor imitators of God; they have been able to create, but on a much smaller scale. Having imbued nature with their own petty desires, they have defiled it. Peter the Great, the great imitator of nature, built his city on a swamp, but nature has not been conquered—it is always there. In Narbikova's view, human attempts to tame nature are absurd. This absurdity is demonstrated through the striking image of people living, like animals, on little hills and under bushes, but provided with electricity and telephones.

A note of warning is sounded in the final pages of the journal version of *Ravnovesie,* evocative of the apocalyptic pronouncements of Soviet "publicistic literature." The atmosphere will soon leave the earth as the soul leaves a dying body; we are living the first of those millions of minutes before the end of the world.

The ecological anxiety that pervades the journal version of the novel is even stronger in the book version. Here we find one of those rare instances when Narbikova's narrator insists on her "reliability," and the points expressed are not completely embedded in the maze of inverted clichés. Rather the tone here is bitter and ironic:

> We live in a society where everything is fine: it's raining radioactive waste, and everything is fine; birds will fly over us and die over Finland, and everything is fine; tomatoes are picked, brought somewhere and thrown away, and bread too is thrown away; potatoes and sausage they won't throw away because those won't be delivered in the first place. Everything that grows well on its own we throw away, and what we have to do ourselves we do badly, but everything is fine with us. (80)

For Narbikova—and here her position begins to veer away from the concerns of village prose and of "publicistic literature"—only love can make the earth more noble and only lovers are able to perceive fully their links to and dependence on nature. Narbikova's ideal love is the spiritual and physical connection, almost an interchangeability, between a man and a woman. This idea, consistent with Narbikova's philosophical emphasis on the principle of substitution, is elaborated in the expanded version of *Ravnovesie,* where the two lovers become so thoroughly one that all gender differences between them disappear.

What appears unusual at first in Narbikova's representation of spiritual and physical love, ostensibly her central topic, is her characters' failure to express directly any pleasure (or any other feelings) in response to their emotional connection and sexual activities. Her approach is to show her characters' actions during a sexual act in a distanced, disembodied way. Within this defamiliarizing description the narrative is organized by means of what might be called associative jumps. In *Ravnovesie* the characters' lovemaking is presented, quite predictably, as an act of riding. Then the narrative shifts to a discussion of a dead palm tree, possibly a covert allusion to the state of her lover's sex organ after intercourse. The image of a dead palm tree resonates with allusions to Lermontov's "Three Palm Trees" (1839). Reference to the poem leads the narration toward a discussion of the phenomenon of subtext, which then turns into a dissection of the word "subtext." Narbikova sees subtext as a text laboring under the weight of all other existing texts; the idea acquires sexual overtones.

Feelings of uncertainty, of longing to possess the object of one's love, or of suffering are generally expressed in cliché-spiked dialogues or dealt with by silence—the two strategies that serve to neutralize emotions traditionally associated with infatuation. Pleasure is absent from descriptions of sexual acts; rather, Narbikova's basic organizing principle in representing sexual contacts is the woman's surrender to the male's aggressive force:

> Semiodin raised her arms, they froze in this position; he bent her head to the side, and the head froze like this. Lena was obedient, like a doll, and equally indifferent; when he moved her body forward a little, she didn't lose her balance [. . .] her face remained calm, like a mask, no matter what he did to her, no matter what position her body assumed. All his embraces rolled off of her, not one kiss stayed on her cheeks. He sprained his neck examining her from all sides. Looking at her, he hit her to break her into pieces, and she fell down to the floor; but there was no punch, she just rocked smoothly and slowly went down to the floor, like a wave. (Ad kak Da, 321)

I said earlier that Narbikova's prose is deliberately transgressive. The transgressive intent is immediately apparent in the distortions of her narrative—in the reemphasis of clichés, the empty allusions, the continuous deliberate reversals of the plot line, the reliance on interchangeability as the general philosophical and narrative principle. To understand Narbikova's violation of the norm in her descriptions of sexual practices, we have to consider the norm in traditional narratives.

Narbikova's prose touches on aspects of sexual behavior avoided by traditional Russian and particularly Soviet literary discourse. In her writing we find descriptions of various unorthodox sexual positions, of homosexual love, and incest. Narbikova's characters engage in oral sex, make love underwater and during the woman's menstrual period; they masturbate and urinate in each other's presence. There is also a considerable degree of violence in her prose, directed primarily at men: one male character is turned into a hedgehog, cooked, and eaten by his former mistress and her lover; another's head is torn from his body; yet another character's limbs are severed; a male character dies but comes to life again.

The intent here, however, does not seem to be to arouse libidinal or erotic/sadistic impulses in the reader, the aim of traditional pornographic and erotic literature. Admittedly, the reception of any narrative, even of the most prudish socialist realist novel, can be viewed as a process in which the initial narrative foreplay leads to the conflictual climax at the center, and finally to a narrative release in the denouement. The reading of fiction, as some perceptive soul has pointed out, is akin to masturbation. What differentiates erotic and pornographic literature from all other types of literature, however, is its primary focus on sexual practices, as well as the obvious intent of such literature to arouse the reader sexually. One can find neither aspect of erotic and pornographic literature in Narbikova's work.

In pornographic literature, moreover, as Vladimir Nabokov points out, the aim of arousal is achieved through description of an action that is "limited to the copulation of clichés." Nothing—style, structure, imagery—should ever distract the reader from "his tepid lust." The pornographic novel consists of an alternation of sexual scenes that "must follow a crescendo line, with new variations, new combinations, new sexes, and a steady increase in the number of participants" (315). The "copulation of clichés" is the general focus of Narbikova's narrative. If what Nabokov means here is actualizations (performances) of a certain erotic code, however, Narbikova takes the notion literally, and the "alternations, variations, and new combinations" in her work occur on the level of clichés embedded in everyday speech, related to commonplace occurrences, and not limited to sexual situations.

Another important vehicle for the transmission of pornographic intent is the obscene word (understood here as the word belonging to the vulgar linguistic register, employing anatomical vocabulary and clinical terminology avoided in polite conversation). As Lucienne Frappier-Mazur has observed, to achieve the pornographic effect most fully, the obscene word has to appear in a particular context. The pornographic impact is enhanced when crude and polite linguistic registers are "inappropriately" attributed; i.e., the effect of crude words is stronger in the mouths of aristocratic, especially female, characters; obscene words are more obscene in prose than in poetry, since so much depends on the narrative line here (Nabokov's "copulation of clichés"); a first-person story engages the reader more than other narrative forms because it promotes the reader's voyeurism; even dialogues in pornographic literature have to be padded with stories.[6]

Though erotic literature employs many of the same devices as pornography, it is less formulaic, more open to interpretation. The obscene word here becomes polysemic, and clinical terminology in its vulgar form is generally avoided. There is more emphasis on style, structure, and imagery, which (I agree with Nabokov) distract the reader from the blunt arousal techniques of pornographic literature.

Narbikova breaks taboos of traditional nonerotic literary practice by representing violations of established norms of sexual intercourse and, even more important, by distorting the rules of literary discourse related to sexuality, occasionally by innovative uses of obscene words. An obscene word in Russian literature is normally represented by the initial letter and an ellipsis. Narbikova plays with this norm: she confirms the norm by the traditional usage (she writes *bliad'* [whore], for example, as *b* . . .), then transgresses it by writing the same word in its full form. Or she establishes the transgressive intent by using the full form of the word, and then, unexpectedly, offering the same word in its customary abbreviation.

In Narbikova the obscene word as such appears extremely rarely; most often the anatomical parts involved in sexual activity are described metaphorically ("hedgehog" [*ezhik*] for a woman's genitals, for example, and "masculine finger" [*muzhskoi palets*] for a penis). Sexual acts are recounted in the third person, in metaphors that defamiliarize them. Thus scenes of sexual activity can be interpreted on various levels, and the pornographic impact is subverted. The crescendo arrangement of pornographic and erotic literature is absent, as is the acknowledgment of pleasure.

All of its uninhibited representation of sexual activities notwithstanding, Narbikova's prose cannot be considered pornographic or even erotic. The central tendency of her narrative to avoid straightforward interpretation, her focus on interchangeability, the deliberately polysemic nature of erotic words and sexual situations—all work together to mute and all but nullify the erotic impact.

Erotic situations in Narbikova serve to propagandize transgression of norms (I can do it with anybody at any time, in any way I choose, and if I love one, I love all). The text reigns. It is all in the language—I name, I distort, the only meaning here is that there is no meaning beyond my power to effect change and substitution (what Robbe-Grillet has termed the writer's "will to intervention"). I, as a writer, can go into free association; being in charge, I can embody in language my own wish to be violated, my own fantasy of voyeurism. And the pleasures I offer the reader have much more to do with intellectual than with sexual prowess.

The resulting effect of Narbikova's prose is not erotic but, curiously, didactic, indicative of a desire to instruct her readers about the nature of prohibition and control rather than to arouse them sexually. Overall, her work fits into the category of modernist, or perhaps "postmodernist," writing much better than into the narrow confines of "erotic prose" suggested by her Soviet critics and accepted by Narbikova herself. This is the case because, like the work of her conceptualist counterparts, Narbikova's writing privileges "heterogeneity, play, marginality, transgression, the unconscious, eroticism, excess" over "representation, the unitary subject, linear narrative, paternal authority, and Truth with a capital T" (Suleiman 13). Like conceptualist art, Narbikova's writing—self-referential, resisting a single meaning or interpretation—is layered with meanings, organized by strategies of irony and parody.

Sex is just one instrument Narbikova chooses with which to challenge the norms of her society, to break the taboo that "power" imposes to regulate it—the taboo that, as Michel Foucault has demonstrated, "plays on the alternative between two nonexistences," so that the existence of sex is maintained only "at the cost of its nullification" (84). Paradoxically, Narbikova's desire to engage in erotic play with language, thereby severing her ties to societal and representational norms, simultaneously plays into the hands of Foucault's "power" by virtually eliminating the erotic effect of her narrative. Nevertheless, the use of sex as a transgressive gesture is a powerful strategy, as powerful as the threatening "unreadability" of Narbikova's texts. Both aim to disturb, to disorient the reader, thereby exposing the fragility of the commonplace, of the norm, embodied in the language we all use, and possibly in the lives we all lead.

Narbikova's work strives to be what Roland Barthes has called "writerly prose—a process of production in which the reader becomes a producer, infinitely plural and open to the free play of signifiers and of difference, unconstrained by representative considerations, and transgressive of any desire for decidable, unified, totalized meaning" (Johnson 25). At the center of this writerly prose we find the unpredictability, fluidity, and oppressive emptiness of existence seen through the eyes of a woman narrator, shaped in an unorthodox narrative by a woman author—a doubly subversive gesture in a writing that privileges the marginal over the norm.

The game Narbikova plays with the reader is governed by the rules of transgression; the theme is prohibition; the result is a narrative that titillates at first but ultimately numbs. The reader dies a little death, satiated and fulfilled until that time when the author finds yet another way to challenge the reader's confirmed expectations. Her avant-gardist aim of disrupting the status quo, of arousing indignation and fear in some readers, curiosity and appreciation of her boldness in others, is nevertheless accomplished. The woman here does not want to be constrained by norms, reduced to a simplistic interpretation, or contained in the predictability of a traditional story line and language. She is at the center, a powerful manipulator and generator of meaning: referring to the patriarchs of Russian literature and history, but undercutting their importance by using them as empty signifiers; submitting to male desire but confirming her ultimate control through violence directed toward males; absorbing the clichés of Soviet life but playfully exposing their mythological underpinnings. The woman author plays freely, and the reader must join in the game.

Notes

1. See, e.g., Chuprinin; Shcheglova; Kondrat'ev; Vasilevskii.

2. This information was provided by Narbikova herself in an interview with me in March 1991 in New York.

3. In addition to the works I quote, Narbikova's bibliography includes "Probeg—pro beg," *Znamia*, 1990, no. 5, 61–87; "Plan pervogo litsa: I vtorogo," in *Vstrechnyi khod: Sbornik*, ed. by T.V. Del'sal' (Moscow, 1989), 119–56; and "Okolo ekolo. . . ," *Iunost'*, 1990, no. 3, 10–25. Her first written work, the novel "Skvoz'" ("Through"), was still unpublished at the time of my interview with her in March 1991. It is perhaps the most sexually transgressive of all Narbikova's narratives.

4. Published as "Vidimost' nas," *Strelets*, 1989, no. 3, 119–35. This information comes from Riitta H. Pittman, "Valeriia Narbikova's Erotic Prose," unpublished manuscript.

5. Il'ia Kabakov in an interview with Byron Lindsey in *Novostroika/New Structures: Culture in the Soviet Union Today*, ICA document 8 (London, 1989), quoted in Sussman 65.

6. Lucienne Frappier-Mazur, "Pornography and the Obscene in the Eigh-

teenth Century," paper delivered at the conference "The Invention of Pornography," University of Pennsylvania, 4 October 1991. My definition of the obscene word comes from Frappier-Mazur as well.

References

Chudakova, Marietta. "Put' k sebe. Literaturnaia situatsiia–89. Beseda korrespondenta LO Evgeniia Kanchukova s Mariettoi Chudakovoi." *Literaturnoe obozrenie*, 1990, no. 1.

Chuprinin, Sergei. "Drugaia proza." *Literaturnaia gazeta*, 8 February 1989, 4.

Epshten, Mikhail. "Iskusstvo avangarda i religioznoe soznanie." *Novyi mir*, 1989, no. 12.

Foster, Hal. "Postmodernism: A Preface." In *The Anti-aesthetic*, ed. Hal Foster. Port Townsend, WA: Bay Press, 1983.

Foucault, Michel. *The History of Sexuality*. Vol. 1. New York: Vintage, 1980.

Johnson, Barbara. "The Critical Difference: Barthes/Balzac." In *Contemporary Literary Criticism*, ed. Robert Con Davis. New York: Longmans, 1986.

Kondrat'ev, Viacheslav. "Sovetuem pochitat'." *Znamia*, 1990, no. 1.

Nabokov, Vladimir. *The Annotated Lolita*. New York: McGraw-Hill, 1970.

Narbikova, Valeriia. "Ad kak Da/aD kak dA." In *Nepomniashchaia zla*, ed. Larisa Vaneeva. Moscow: Moskovskii rabochii, 1990.

————. *Ravnovesie sveta dnevnykh i nochnykh zvezd*. Moscow: Vsesoiuznyi molodezhnyi knizhnyi tsentr, 1990. Excerpted in *Iunost'*, 1988, no. 8, 15–29, with Introduction by Andrei Bitov.

Shcheglova, Evgeniia. "'V svoem krugu: Polemicheskie zamechaniia o 'zhenskoi proze.' " *Literaturnoe obozrenie*, 1990, no. 3.

Suleiman, Susan Rubin. *Subversive Intent: Gender, Politics, and the Avant-Garde*. Cambridge, MA: Harvard University Press, 1990.

Sussman, Elisabeth. "The Third Zone: Soviet 'Postmodern.'" In *Between Spring and Summer: Soviet Conceptual Art in the Era of Late Communism*. Cambridge, MA: MIT Press, 1991.

Urnov, Dmitrii. "Plokhaia proza." *Literaturnaia gazeta*, 8 February 1989, 4.

Vasilevskii, A. "Bespredel'." *Literaturnaia gazeta*, 12 September 1990.

Veselaia, Elena. "Dunovenie erosa: Beseda s Valeriei Narbikovoi." *Moskovskie novosti*, 1 April 1990.

9

HAPPY NEVER AFTER
The Work of Viktoriia Tokareva and *Glasnost'*

Richard Chapple

Viktoriia Tokareva graduated from music school and taught singing before entering the Cinematography Institute with the hope of
becoming an actress. She majored in screen writing and was soon
so enthralled by that dimension of creativity that she abandoned
her desire to become a star.[1] Russian literature is the better for
that decision. Her first published collection of stories appeared in
1969, and she continues to comment on the human condition in a
creative and captivating way. In great measure her concerns and
perceptions are the same now as they were in the 1960s, thereby
suggesting that current literary concerns are not unlike those of
the second half of this century generally. For convenience of
discussion, however, her work may be divided into three periods:
the early Tokareva, dating from the 1960s and early 1970s; the
middle Tokareva, dating mostly from the 1970s; and the late or
glasnost' Tokareva, dating from the early 1980s. As phases in the
lives of writers and movements generally do, these three periods
in Tokareva's writing overlap, suggesting evolution rather than
distinct phases.

   The early Tokareva is evident in the collections *About That
Which Was Not* (*O tom, chego ne bylo* [1969]) and *When It
Warmed Up a Bit* (*Kogda stalo nemnozhko teplee* [1972]). Her
gallery of characters features men and women who are alone and
somehow mistreated by others. These characters feel depressed,
even outcast, and come to gain two broad insights—the stark

reality of their condition and the need to cast it off and succeed in life. They often have a dream, but that dream is not necessarily practical nor is it always consistent with any ultimate determination to overcome the debilitating reality of their lives. Thus her personae fall into the contrasting categories of those who determine to change their lot or realize their dream and those who lack the will or stamina to contemplate such an effort. The theme of love is significant in this first period and is frequently linked with characters' hopes and dreams. In fact, the generalization can be made that Tokareva writes stories of love. Anyone searching for happy endings, however, would be well advised to read someone else, despite the author's entertaining and wry humor.

The stories of love are colored by the characters' realization of how others perceive them and by the role they are seemingly destined to play in life. Spouses often treat each other poorly, the unmarried are ignored, used, or mistreated by the opposite sex, and family members judge one another harshly. Exemplary in this regard is the story "A Ruble Sixty Isn't Anything" ("Rubl' shest'desiat—ne den'gi"). The central male character is persuaded to buy a cap that will ostensibly make him invisible. The cost is trifling—1 ruble and 60 kopecks—but he soon learns why more people do not buy such caps. He comes to realize that others regard him as a nonentity, as if he were not really present. He learns that he is insignificant to his employer, fellow workers, and his wife, whether he is actually invisible or not. In "The Himalayan Bear" ("Gimalaiskii medved'") Nikitin crawls into the cage of the Himalayan bear at the zoo after his daughter challenges him to pet the beast. The thought occurs to him that this stunt may enable him to speak more honestly to his wife, from whom he maintains some distance so as not to learn anything about her that would require action on his part. When the bear blocks the door, Nikitin finds himself a prisoner. An appeal to the keeper proves useless. The keeper insists that nothing can be done, and he abandons Nikitin so as not to get involved in someone else's affairs. Ironically, this has been Nikitin's method of avoiding difficulties in life, and he now becomes a victim of his own avoidance tactic. The keeper's token response is to post a sign indicating the identity of the cage's new inhabitant. Nikitin muses:

> From one standpoint the bear really is unique, while the park is full of people like Nikitin. The bear has an obvious significance and strengthens ties between nations, while Nikitin has no significance at all. . . . As far as his wife is concerned, she will not even notice his absence. So the fact of the matter was that it was easy to replace Nikitin and very complicated to replace the bear.[2]

Nikitin ponders his seeming insignificance and eventually finds the courage to walk past the bear and leave the cage, at last having realized that he is actually more important than the bear.

In "The Law of Conservation" ("Zakon sokhraneniia") Tokareva further examines people's views of themselves and of what will make them happy. Giia, most recently a magician but now in charge of customer service for an enterprise, is beset by people who seek changes that will make them happy. A handsome man, for instance, wants to go abroad, become a model, and receive adulation for his appearance; a colleague wants Giia to persuade the object of her affection to marry her; Giia's boss wants to be thirty instead of fifty-eight, because he has fallen in love with a much younger woman. Giia's solution for his boss, drastic as it seems, is nonetheless accepted: the boss is obviously desperate. He agrees to swallow a tablet called the elixir of the instantaneous regeneration of the organism, and jump from a seventh-story window; this process will shatter and then regenerate him. All three petitioners are granted their wishes but none is the happier for it. A friend accuses Giia of being a trickster and cautions, "Happiness doesn't pass away, it is transformed from one form to another. This is the law of the conservation of energy."[3] The only happy petitioner is the secretary who asks Giia for a bag of onion peelings to fertilize her apple trees. It is noteworthy that she is the only one who does not seek something for herself or dream of some kind of love.

Deciding to succeed in life takes many forms in this initial period of Tokareva's creativity. In "There Will Be Another Summer" ("Budet drugoe leto") a young woman decides to leave a frustrating relationship with a married man and get on with her life. Nikitin decides that he is of greater value than a bear, and Tania in "The Swimming Teacher" ("Instruktor po plavaniiu") decides not only to dream but to participate actively in life. Giia and his boss, however, decide to disappear, to get away from the problems that may result from unrealizable hopes and dreams. Thus a firm decision is not always a positive one. Making positive decisions in post-October Soviet literature is quite routine, but Tokareva's characters do so without regard for social or political considerations. Indeed, her world in this first period is largely devoid of the trappings of Soviet life, and one would be hard pressed to fix her work firmly in the Soviet Union. Furthermore, her characters do more deciding than doing, because Tokareva not uncommonly ends her tale on or about the moment of the positive decision. In this way she maintains the emphasis on the individual and his or her personal world rather than upon any accomplishment—social, political, or otherwise.

Tokareva's favorite backdrop for positive resolve is the sky, with its aura of height and expanse or its sense of clearing. Not uncommonly it is the clear sky on a cool night. Nikitin realizes that he is of worth when he gazes into the night sky. Giia abandons his pessimistic view that happiness is only sought, never achieved, as he gazes into the expanse of the heavens. In "A Day without Lies" ("Den' bez vran'ia") the narrator awakes after a dream about a rainbow and determines to go through an entire day without being dishonest. He is distressed that people so seldom want to appear as they really are and vows to change that scenario at least for his own life for one day. The sky imagery is the impetus for decision here, as is the singing of a song about the lifting of the fog in "When the Fog Lifted" ("Uzh kak pal tuman"). The use of a natural symbol rather than human wiles is explained in the concluding paragraph of "The Law of Conservation" by reference to the effect of the bag of onion peelings on the secretary's apple trees: "But when people saw the apples, they stopped and gazed steadily and silently without any envy. They gazed and thought how wise nature must be if she cre-

Viktoriia Tokareva

ated such perfection, which is so lacking in people."

This lack of perfection and Tokareva's attitude toward it are central to her art. She draws people's attention to how poorly they live, exposes their interpersonal failings and their naive hopes for love, and shows how the natural works better than the human. These rather Tolstoian views are intensified in the middle period, which embraces the stories of the 1970s and the collection *The Flying Swing* (*Letaiushchie kacheli* [1978]).

In this period Tokareva shifts her focus from the outcast who has hopes to the theme of love. Her characters are perhaps no less depressed and ignored, but that dimension of their lives is no longer so vital. The theme of love fills that vacuum. Dreams and hopes are shown in both a positive and a negative light. In "Pirates on Distant Seas" ("Piraty v dalekikh moriakh") the male protagonist is mired in the humdrum of life despite his high aspirations, and his weak character compels him to do whatever others ask of him. Their self-centered lives contrast with his acts of service, yet for all his virtue, the reader never loses sight of the fact that his service stems from a weak character and a need for love and acceptance rather than a charitable orientation. As a final commentary, his death by suicide is overlooked by those he serves even at the moment of his poison-induced agony.

Tokareva responded to this problem later in the decade in the story "There Came a Greek" ("Ekhal greka"), in which the major character laments to his sister that no one seems to need him. Her reply—"But, really, you don't need anyone either"[4]—exposes one of the fundamental reasons for failed relationships. It is only at the end of the story that he and a manicurist, each lonely and somewhat hesitant, reach out to each other: "She suddenly became silent and serious. She looked at me with hesitation and at the same time with hope. I was new, the next person in her life, and new people mean new hopes" (247). He responds to her in like manner, and the author reinforces the idea that people appear as the most fundamental solution to problems. The reader is hopeful for the characters who seek to repair their lives through concrete individuals and the ideal of human understanding, and at the same time dismayed that characters insist upon seeking solutions through relationships rather than within themselves. This story professes to be more optimistic, and indeed it is, as the conclusion softens the naiveté of the search for love.

Love receives a thorough examination in this middle period and is found generally wanting. The emphasis in most of the stories is on the unhappiness found in marital, extramarital, and dating relationships. The quality of the relationship and the expectations it arouses are the same whether the couple is married or not; and the woman is just as likely as the man to seek love and fulfillment outside of marriage.

"The Flying Swing" is a symbolic representation of Tokareva's view of human perceptions. Two women converse about life and love while their young daughters wait in a long line to ride on an amusement park attraction. The narrator notes:

> The ride lasted four minutes. The wait was two hours.
>
> According to the most careful calculations waiting outstripped fun by a ratio of 30:1. That is like my entire life: the ratio of waiting and enjoyment is 30:1. People are erased, worn out by the commonplace. They stand in line so they can have four minutes of happiness. And what is happiness? The absence of the commonplace? But what if you love your commonplace?[5]

The women continue their conversation about love and the need to find the one relationship that will bring true happiness, while as a backdrop the children become bored and frustrated waiting in line. Their response is an ironic commentary on their mothers' frustration with love. When it is time to get into the large disk that holds the fun-seekers, the children complain because they do not get the seats they want, and one of them decides not to enjoy the ride. The ride parallels life: it begins and ends, goes up and down, and spins the riders. After the ride, the children react to the experience as adults do to love and life:

> Iul'ka, Lenka, and Natashka stood next to one another. Each reacted to the ride in her own way. Iul'ka was pale, almost green. The up-and-down movements bothered her and she now had a general aversion to life. Lenka stared at a single point in front of her, and a remnant of the thrilling experience remained on her face. Natashka had already forgotten about the Flying Swing. She wanted to go on the Ferris wheel. She folded her arms and began to negotiate hesitantly, not expecting success. (162)

Some people enjoy life and love, others are made sick and depressed by its disappointments and demands, and still others want to change the object of their love, albeit hesitantly. Simply growing up does not provide the keys to happiness.

This theme appears again in "Close Relatives" ("Glubokie rodstvenniki"), in which two male friends discuss love. The first complains that his wife, Irka, wears the pants in the family and continually makes him feel like a housewife. As he contemplates twenty to thirty more years of such a life, he gets depressed and no longer wants to live. Vera, by contrast, makes him feel special, as a man should feel, and so he has decided to leave his wife for her. The friend responds that that will not be necessary, because Irka has moved in with him that very morning. Her husband continually played the role of a housewife, she complained, and wanted her to wear the pants in the family. The thought of twenty to thirty more years of such a life depressed her, so she decided to move out. When the three of them gather to discuss the matter further, Irka decides to return to her husband, and they in turn propose that Vera go with the rejected friend. Vera hesitantly takes her suitcase and leaves with the stranger. They confess that even though they do not know each other and certainly do not love each other, with time they could become close, like the *glubokie rodstvenniki* of the title.

The tale is a parody of the tragicomic bartering for spouses and lovers that occurs in numerous comedies and operas. There is irony in the fact that the realigned couples do not differ appreciably from each other. If perfect strangers can ultimately become "close relatives," then spouses certainly can. The witness to the exchange is a Siamese cat who is dozing on the radiator in the stairwell. Animals, particularly cats, are not uncommon witnesses to and commentators upon human foibles in Tokareva's world. The final paragraph of the story—and one must acknowledge the brilliance of the author in her use of opening and closing paragraphs that set the tone and the theme of her work—contains the reflections of the cat:

> Having heard the people, he opened one eye, and the expression on his face seemed to say: "Perhaps from the point of view of fortu-

nate Siamese and Siberian cats I live in terrible circumstances. But from the point of view of common stairwell cats I am simply flourishing. This is a well-cared-for, well-ventilated stairwell, there are loyal boys and as many quality morsels as one would want."[6]

People would do well to be as content with their circumstances as is the cat. That contentment is rarely evident in Tokareva's fictional world, however.

"We Need Communication" ("Nam nuzhno obshchenie") further illustrates the themes of lack of communication, the failure of love, and coexistence rather than genuine marriage. The story begins:

> I left the house on 7 September 1976. This is how it happened. My wife and I were sitting and watching television. The program "In the World of Animals" began. Beautiful music began to play and ostriches began to dance. I understood that if I did not get up and leave that very second, I would do something drastic, for example, throw the television on the floor or jump out of the window. . . . Relations with my wife, as strange as it may sound, were strong, not in our acquisitions but in our losses. Because of me she lost her chance to be a mother and hated me for it. Because of her I lost the chance to be adventurous and remained the same as I am.[7]

The spouses tolerate each other and harbor hostilities that seldom find expression. The husband retreats to a dacha on the outskirts of the city, where he encounters one of Tokareva's cats, which miraculously verbalizes the need for communication in all dimensions of life. The owner of the dacha even sells his property so that the house will be full of the lives and chatter of new owners, because even buildings need communication. These insights prompt the husband to return home, where he learns that his wife intends to leave, because she cannot live without love. As he drives to this fateful meeting with his wife, frost accumulates on the car windows until he can barely see the road. He reflects that he is putting others in danger for no good reason and recalls the cat and its advocacy of communication. Ultimately even the cat prefers to stay at the dacha, where it can fulfill its role in catching mice, rather than come with him. If cats can fulfill roles, then husbands and wives should be able to do so as well, and there seems to be little excuse for going through life with poor visibility, thereby endangering oneself and others.

The decision to confront life's problems, change course, and succeed is present in this middle period, but it is not to be found in every work. The sky and heights again form the symbolic backdrop. In "You Don't Accomplish Anything Overnight" ("Srazu nichego ne dob'eshsia") the bureaucrat Fedkin decides that what he really wants to do with his life is to become a house painter. It is questionable, however, whether he will be decisive enough to leave his job. The fact that he is juxtaposed to several petitioners who are continually encumbered by red tape and who seldom get anything resolved may suggest, as the title of the story does, that nothing will be accomplished very quickly. When one adds the symbol of the heavens, however, the outcome is more optimistic. In "There Came a Greek" the ascent of a mountain represents the narrator's willingness to allow others into his life. In "Simply a Free Evening" ("Prosto svobodnyi vecher") the moon and the illuminated sky parallel Rita's resolve in life. In "Say Something in Your Language" ("Skazhi mne chto-nibud' na tvoem iazyke") Veronika leaves her egocentric date in the lurch and walks through the crisp night air, admiring the sky and making resolves for the future. In "The Japanese Umbrella" ("Iaponskii zontik") the narrator buys a Japanese umbrella that magically lifts him into the air above the crowd à la Mary Poppins. It is only there that he gains insight into life.

In "Between Heaven and Earth" ("Mezhdu nebom i zemlei") Lena observes that her life's dream is to make a parachute jump and be suspended between the sky and the ground. She suspects that she never will, though, because to do so she would have to join a sports club, and she is far too busy for that. She has taken refuge in being ostensibly busy but ultimately admits that she doesn't have much to do and is dissatisfied with her marriage. After an interview with an elderly professor, who at Lena's age had one adopted and three natural children, Lena is fired from her job. She leaves the building and looks up at the sky. "Not far away to the right was the television tower. It was taller than anything else, right between the sky and the earth. . . . Perhaps now I can sign up for a sports club and parachute."[8] In Tokareva's world one must also wonder what Lena will do with her husband, since personal resolve is seldom directed toward one's spouse.

Tokareva's work in the 1980s devotes even more attention to the theme of love as well as to several social and political observations that can be attributed to the influence of *glasnost'* and *perestroika*. Tokareva's characters are still on occasion the depressed outcasts of life, some still have dreams, and some resolve to succeed, but love and the concerns of the 1980s clearly predominate. This merging of personal, political, and social concerns may well characterize the literature of the 1990s, now that personal considerations are firmly entrenched in mainstream writing. This increased seriousness is not lost on the critic M. Prorokov, who in reviewing Tokareva's later work observed that "Tokareva's prose, which more than anything else wholeheartedly expresses a romantic and joyful response to the world, increasingly and decisively removes light-mindedness and a charming sense of the carefree from center stage."[9]

Now Tokareva more somberly examines love in its various forms. Dreams and hopes are still present as characters continue to view love or at least a romantic relationship as a desirable and plausible solution to life's problems. This dream is taken to the extreme in "A Star in the Mist" ("Zvezda v tumane"), in which Nina's goal is to isolate the hormone that produces happiness and make it available in tablet form. She ultimately determines that this cannot and should not be done. Such a pill would have been useful for Lil'ka in "Korrida," whose dream since fifth grade has been to marry someone talented and famous, acquire some nice things, have a son, and be noticed. She achieves all of these things but is overcome by isolation amidst her apparent happiness. Thus the attainment of what people think they want does not always bring happiness and contentment. The reason in this case is her husband, a filmmaker, who loves only the fantasy world that he himself creates and turns into a film. In this respect he epitomizes a large percentage of Tokareva's characters, for reliance on fantasy is an epidemic problem in her world.

In this period the necessity of love is verbalized. The taxi driver Prokushev in "Love and Travels" ("Liubov' i puteshe-stviia") observes that "living without love is a disease that you can't ignore under any circumstances; otherwise the soul will die."[10] His observation is partially inspired by his wife: ". . . after she gave birth [she] put on thirty kilograms, and a sleepy expression appeared on her face. . . . Lius'ka quietly sighed from the depth of her soul, lamenting her hopeless life. But the sigh didn't come out quietly; it sounded like the hollow sigh of a cow in a stall" (65–66). This may be enough to drive any taxi driver to greener pastures, but in the 1980s Tokareva sets some standards for relationships and measures her characters against them.

In "A Cat on the Road" ("Koshka na doroge") the male protagonist finds a cat in the woods and brings it to the sanatorium at which he is staying, but the institution's no-pets policy forces him to send it away. An eccentric old woman then observes: "If you begin to take part in another's fate, you must take part until the end. Or not take part at all."[11] The fact that the woman claims to have been a cat in a previous life does not minimize the validity of her observation and in fact unites the fate of people and cats. If people should take care of animals, they should also take care of one another, and it is noteworthy that a plethora of ignored dogs and especially cats around seldom-used dachas and elsewhere symbolically relate to ignored and lonely people.

This required constancy is also emphasized in the tale "The Old Dog" ("Staraia sobaka"), whose heroine, Inna, has come to a sanatorium to find a husband. She is thirty-two and has only two requirements for her future mate: he must be well placed in society and not over eighty-two. When she finds a candidate, she begins to think more seriously about the matter: "Happiness is now plus always. The immediate plus stability. She must be certain that it will be this way tomorrow and a year from now. To the grave and beyond."[12] Vadim, at the center of Inna's view of eternal love, is married, and he regrets having to leave his wife, who has been such a decent person during their twenty years together. Another impediment is an old dog. The dog is devoted to him, and Vadim insists on bringing it with him when he and Inna marry. Inna demands marriage, because her previous lover wanted to keep both Inna and his wife. She then receives an insight that removes the pleasant sensation of power and control that she is experiencing during the affair: "But this wasn't love. It was the desire for love masquerading as love" (113). The strange disappearance of the dog and Vadim's subsequent mourning result in the cancellation of any plans involving Inna. She in fact realizes that even if Vadim left his wife, he would return to her "because decency is conscience. And conscience is god. And Vadim is a believer" (126). Inna vows to continue living and hoping, having learned much about herself and love, and having been chastened by her insights.

Inna's realization of Vadim's loyalty to his wife, despite their affair, is significant. The idea of loyalty instead of diversion is strong in Tokareva's work of the 1980s. In "Friendship Transcends All" ("Druzhba prevyshe vsego") the betrayed wife insists on the preeminence of loyalty and the elevated friendship of marriage to counter her husband's passion for another woman. In "A Long Day" ("Dlinnyi den'") Veronika is married to a perfectly good man who would much rather sit and read than fulfill his domestic obligations. As Veronika struggles with the stress of her daughter's illness, she resents her husband's inaction and begins to have romantic fantasies about the eminent doctor who treats her child. When she returns home, she discovers that the elevator is not functioning, and she must climb several flights of stairs to their apartment. As she ascends to the symbolic height of insight, she is frightened by the sound of loud, stony footsteps in the stairwell, "as if the statue of the Commendatore [in Mozart's *Don Giovanni*] were descending."[13] The statue of the dead Commendatore came to life to seek vengeance against the man who betrayed his daughter. Veronika in fact has betrayed her husband emotionally, and in this scene gazes at potential retribution.

A more recent story, "A First Attempt" ("Pervaia popytka"), sums up Tokareva's assessment of love. The protagonist, Mara, goes through no fewer than five men, trying in each instance to make the man into what she wants. A relationship for her is the establishment of supremacy, and she recommends leaving one's husband as a good way to capture the exhilaration of life. The story is filled with betrayals, the illusion of greener pastures, and complex triangles, but love is most difficult to locate. Some standards and measures are expressed, however. Mara seduces Sasha, who comes to compare her with his wife, Sosha:

> Sosha is a good person. Mara is the embodiment of passion. He desired her. But he loved Sosha. As it turns out, they are not the same thing. A wise man once said that the flesh is like a horse. And the spirit is like a horseman. If one obeys only the horse, it will take him into the barn. One ought to obey the horseman.[14]

Tokareva thus establishes a dichotomy between love and passion. In the earlier stories some characters had felt themselves suspended between passion and loyalty or love but had not verbalized the predicament quite so clearly. Mara herself observes that "the family is the laboratory of durability and the home is its fortress. She thought up the laboratory herself, but the fortress came from the English" (140).

Mara ends her life riddled with cancer and attended by one of her former husbands, who has never lost his love for her. She is also surrounded by his cats and her dog, which get along famously and represent what a relationship can be. The animals are cared for and loved even as people ought to be, and despite their differences manage to live harmoniously, unlike their masters.

The 1980s and *glasnost'* introduced a new dimension to Tokareva's work. Her characters are still on occasion those rejected by life, some still have dreams, some resolve to change their lives and strive for a self-defined success, and the theme of love is perhaps even more crucial to her world. But in the Gorbachev years Tokareva inserts in the stories "The Happiest

Day" ("Samyi schastlivyi den'"), "Friendship Transcends All," "A Long Day," "Five Figures on a Pedestal" ("Piat' figur na postamente"), "Pasha and Pavlusha" ("Pasha i Pavlusha"), "Thou Shalt Not Create" ("Ne sotvori"), and "A First Attempt" topical themes and observations that were missing earlier. The reader encounters politicized school assignments, a sense of the virtue of physical labor, comments on the poor medical care available in the rural areas of the Soviet Union, husbands who do no domestic chores, the difficult role of women in society, alcohol and its relation to crime, the role of grandmothers in Russian homes, the bureaucracy and its interminable paper chase, the sacrifice of soldiers, the prison system, negative comments on life in the West, incompetent officials, the black market, a cynical view of heroine mothers with large families, *perestroika,* the need for more conscientious parents, the Stalin era, Brezhnev, Andropov, Chernenko, the housing situation, and the need for bribes to improve one's circumstances. Only religion and ecology are missing.

"Pasha and Pavlusha" demonstrates the impact of the 1980s upon her writing. Pasha is a virtuous man who works in a school for handicapped and retarded children. He is idealistic and wants to help the children, but he plunges into his work also to avoid the pain of a personal life bereft of companionship and love. The author comments about Pasha's workplace:

> In 1970 when Pasha came to work there were fifteen children in the school. In 1980 there were 100. The percentage of afflicted children has risen. There were several reasons: heredity, the older age of parents, but the main reason was alcoholism. "Wine children." These children grew up, got married, and gave birth to afflicted children. The children of these children were already in the school. A second generation of inferior children.[15]

One of the schoolchildren is a charming thirteen-year-old who has been abandoned by her mother. The mother wants to forget the mistake of her youth and insists that the state has the obligation to care for her child.

Pasha is juxtaposed to his friend Pavlusha, who yearns for the life of the average American, reportedly devoted to "sports, business, and sex" (132). He marries and has affairs on a whim and never keeps a wife longer than six years. When Pasha becomes acquainted with a younger woman named Marina, who is depressed over her victimization by various men, he decides to love her and help her, thereby resolving the emotional difficulties of them both. Marina works for a clothing designer who makes a great deal of money in what amounts to a private business, just as Pavlusha becomes wealthy by doing private work on government time. Pavlusha quickly and easily seduces Marina away from Pasha, who is overcome with resentment and recovers only when he decides to go on with life, as the children do.

Pasha's first step toward dealing with his disappointment is to try to remove the school director, who has used her position to enhance her own circumstances and who has no expectation that the children can become useful members of society. All in attendance at the meeting of the soviet convened to discuss the directorship acknowledge that what Pasha says about the director is true, but they are also quite comfortable with her because she allows them to do as they wish. They muse: *"Perestroika* is *perestroika,* but it isn't clear what will come after it. It's better to leave things just as they are . . . the people were silent" (147). The final words—"the people were silent" (*narod bezmolvstvoval*)—recall the reaction of the people in the concluding scene of Pushkin's *Boris Godunov,* when the people greet the impostor Dmitrii with silence. In this case, however, the hesitancy is overcome and the unexpected takes place: the soviet ("According to the tenets of *perestroika* the worker collective decides everything" [147]) votes to dismiss the director and replaces her with Pasha. Ironically, she becomes a nanny, loves the small children she cares for, and even thanks Pasha for her new job, while he grapples with the school's problems, which are attributed to irresponsible members of society. Among those irresponsible citizens are retarded people who have children year after year, are offered financial incentives to have yet more children, and when they do are hailed as mother heroines.

Pasha eventually meets Marina again, but this time she is accompanied by a three-year-old boy who is the image of Pavlusha. The boy is unmanageable and gives Pasha occasion to comment on the quality of parenting in society and on the absence of social agencies that could be of assistance. Pasha overcomes his personal resentment and discovers that the child responds to love and discipline and is not a problem in the proper hands. This discovery is consistent with his social view that most people can become productive citizens. Marina has left her job in the elegant salon and reports that Pavlusha has been arrested for his activities—all developments that fit snugly in the spirit of *perestroika*. At the end of the story there is some sense that the three of them will be united, that Pasha can care for Marina and help her to be a mother, and that in some way the needs of all three may be met. Here we have a *perestroika* variation on the theme of the affirmation of life.

In another recent story, "Thou Shalt Not Create," Trofimov encounters what he considers to be a near impossibility in the modern Russian experience—a worker who is willing to fix a problem, has the necessary tools and parts, and expects nothing in the way of a bribe or incentive. To Trofimov's utter amazement, the plumber Vitalii simply fixes the faucet and refuses to accept money because he is already being paid a salary. Trofimov is convinced that Vitalii is actually working toward some honor, perhaps to be named to the Brigade of Communist Labor, but Vitalii insists that he is simply doing his job. Vitalii is a vehicle for Tokareva's assessment of life, but the artistic impact of the tale would not be reduced if the commentary on bribes and work were removed and the concluding words about not making unto oneself any graven image stood alone. The social commentary adds essentially nothing to the eventual affirmation of life that in the early stories stood on its merits.

Two stories from the spring of 1991 further demonstrate this development in Tokareva's work. Sidorov, the protagonist of "Kirka and the Officer" ("Kirka i ofitser"), continues the 1980s theme of loyalty in relationships by observing that "the family is a serious matter, just like a garden: he had dug and cultivated and fertilized. There was no time to be distracted by anything else."[16] The distraction comes, however, in the form of a suicide threat in a letter delivered to him by mistake. Sidorov's wife suggests that he meet the girl at the place and time she has designated so that her fate will not be on their consciences. Sidorov is a political education officer at a military hospital and believes firmly in the Party as society's rudder. He opposes a free-market economy, cooperatives, the chaos of the Arbat, and everything else that breaks with the structure and control of the past. The reactionary yet altruistic Sidorov meets Kirka and comes to realize that he is saving the life of a modern and liberated young woman. Kirka seeks love and money and has tried to entice foreigners in the hope of leaving the country. The unlikely companions spend the night in the same room because of a change in the train schedule and are struck by the significant differences between them. The common device of reconciling disparate viewpoints through the potential of love is impeded by Sidorov's devotion to his moral standard. The two talk of life and realize that they agree on little, but they gain some degree of respect and insight from each other. The virtue of Sidorov's political rigidity fades under Kirka's challenges, while her dream of love and travel seems cheap in comparison with the stability produced by his loyalty to his wife. Kirka comes to see the attraction of family life and vows to stand up to the sexual harassment she endures at work at the hands of a thief and speculator who is depicted in the best *perestroika* mode. Sidorov meanwhile wanders about the city, implicitly questioning his beliefs, having fled from what he perceived as Kirka's sexual aggressiveness. The story is consistent with Tokareva's thematic pattern, but Sidorov's politics and the misdeeds of Kirka's co-worker add topicality that does not enhance the work.

"How I Declared War on Japan" ("Kak ia ob''iavil voinu Iaponii") portrays a young poetry-writing misfit who finds himself very out of place in the army. His dream of finding a girl just like his mother is ironic in the military context and emphasizes his position as a comic outcast. When he falls in love with a local girl in the out-of-the-way village where he is stationed and attempts to have a romantic interlude with her, he is comically interrupted in the middle of the night and ordered to type an official declaration of war against Japan. After some hesitation he returns to his sleepy girlfriend and concludes ultimately that "life and a woman are one and the same thing."[17] He has transcended the influence of his mother, both realized and adjusted his dream, and oriented himself in life. The charm and humor of the tale, however, are afflicted with observations about Stalin, the tsar's family, America, and the meat grinder of Soviet society, all of which are endemic to recent events in the former Soviet Union but add nothing to the literary rationale of the work.

Onto her creative history Tokareva has grafted a *glasnost'* and *perestroika* layer that does not produce the intended result. One would not question the legitimacy, even perhaps the urgency, of topicality, yet the result is the replacement of lively captivation by a tendentiousness formerly uncharacteristic of the author. It is as if Tokareva reached back fifty years for the vehicle of her message, unwittingly adopting the heavy hand and the awkward literary mix characteristic of literature past. One may justifiably respond that Rybakov, Dudintsev, Tendriakov, and many other writers born or reborn in the 1980s have the same stylistic tendencies. The contrast of "before" and "after" styles in Tokareva's work is much more dramatic, however, and the results are disappointing. It is fortunate for her art that these topical statements are only interspersed in the text and do not become its foundation either thematically or stylistically. She thus remains one of the important and representative figures of modern Russian literature and continues to give the reader enjoyable and insightful moments.

Notes

1. Victoria Tokareva, "Creativity Is Part of the Instinct for Self-preservation," *Soviet Film*, March 1978, 42.

2. "Gimalaiskii medved'," in *Kogda stalo nemnozhko teplee* (Moscow: Sovetskaia Rossiia, 1972), 85.

3. "Zakon sokhraneniia," in *O tom, chego ne bylo* (Moscow: Molodaia gvardiia, 1969), 87.

4. "Ekhal greka," in *Letaiushchie kacheli* (Moscow: Sovetskii pisatel',
1978), 244.

5. "Letaiushchie kacheli," in *Letaiushchie kacheli*, 157.

6. "Glubokie rodstvenniki," in *Letaiushchie kacheli*, 169.

7. "Nam nuzhno obshchenie," in *Letaiushchie kacheli*, 6, 7.

8. "Mezhdu nebom i zemlei," in *Kogda stalo nemnozhko teplee*, 114.

9. M. Prorokov, review of *Letaiushchie kacheli*, *Nichego osobennogo*,
and *Povesti i rasskazy*, *Oktiabr'*, April 1989, 204.

10. "Liubov' i puteshestviia," in *Nichego osobennogo* (Moscow: Sovetskii
pisatel', 1983), 68.

11. "Koshka na doroge," in *Nichego osobennogo*, 63.

12. "Staraia sobaka," in *Nichego osobennogo*, 93.

13. "Dlinnyi den'," *Novyi mir*, February 1986, 106.

14. "Pervaia popytka," *Novyi mir*, January 1989, 139.

15. "Pasha i Pavlusha," *Oktiabr'*, September 1987, 131.

16. "Kirka i ofitser," *Ogonek*, 1991, no. 10 (March), 14.

17. "Kak ia ob'iavil voinu Iaponii," *Krokodil*, 1991, no. 12 (April), 9.

10

"LEAVING PARADISE" AND *PERESTROIKA*
A Week Like Any Other and *Memorial Day*
by Natal'ia Baranskaia

Thomas Lahusen

> ... experience has fallen in value. And it looks as
> if it is continuing to fall into bottomlessness.
> —Walter Benjamin, "The Storyteller"

Sometimes, publishing a book is like missing a train. That was the experience of the publishing house Sovetskii pisatel' when it released Natal'ia Baranskaia's *Memorial Day (Den' pominoveniia)* in 1989. The book did not become one of the (rare) hits of *perestroika*. And there is a good chance that it will be forgotten even before it has had a chance to be acknowledged: it was not launched by the usual "thick journal" version and its print run was a relatively modest 30,000 copies. The "retrospective" theme of the book did not correspond, as we shall see, to what was generally supposed to be remembered in the late 1980s, in what was still the Soviet Union.

Memorial Day is Natal'ia Baranskaia's first and probably last novel. It might even be the last work that she will publish during her lifetime, as she says melancholically in her "Autobiography without Omissions" ("Avtobiografiia bez umolchanii"), which appeared one year later in an émigré journal. The author's age gives us reason to believe her: Baranskaia was eighty-one years old in 1989. She is better known in the West than at home as the author of the novella *A Week Like Any Other,* whose success is generally attributed to its content, or rather to what could be qualified as its "illocutionary force." Indeed, if any literary work can be said to have helped raise female consciousness in the Soviet Union, it is Baranskaia's story. But its success abroad (it appeared in twenty publications in twelve languages, according to the "Autobiography") contrasts with the author's rather modest fame in her own country and among literary critics, a fact generally explained by the absence of formal sophistication that characterizes her works. If the *Week* "sparked controversy" for a moment, it was "chiefly because of its sociological, rather than literary, value" (Goscilo, *Balancing Acts,* 324). A reevaluation of Baranskaia's *Week Like Any Other* will help to situate her last work in its context: the book called *Memorial Day* includes not only the novel of the same title but also the author's best-seller.

A Week Like Any Other: Literariness and "Life Itself"

There is indeed something peculiar about *A Week Like Any Other* and its author: in some sense both have had an *external* relation to literature. We know that Natal'ia Baranskaia, born in 1908, started to write only after she had to leave her job at the Pushkin Museum in Moscow in 1966, for politico-literary reasons.[1] She joined the living world of belles-lettres in 1969, at the age of sixty-one, with the publication of *A Week Like Any Other* in Aleksandr Tvardovskii's *Novyi mir.* But despite all visibility, her success was not recognized by the profession, as she tells us in her "Autobiography."[2] Since then, her career has been marked by (in her interpretation) a lack of enthusiasm on the part of the Soviet literary establishment. Her first book, a collection of stories for young people published by Molodaia gvardiia (in which *A Week* was not included), took five years—from 1972 to 1977— to appear, with the usual problems encountered at the hands of the censors. Her novella *Liubka* had problems "coming through," and she had to rewrite the ending twice, "conscious that she spoiled it, but trying not to ruin it entirely" ("Avtobiografiia," 138). A collection of two novellas and twenty stories for

Sovremennik took another "five years of ordeal" before it appeared in 1981, this time "almost without editorial interference" (139).[3] Baranskaia's nonfiction *Portret podarennyi drugu,* in which she brings to light some unknown details of Pushkin's life through the story of a portrait and other materials, is obviously related to her earlier activity as a museum archivist and was received with relative indifference. As for *Memorial Day,* Baranskaia's "Autobiography" ends with a poignant address to the "friendly," "understanding," and "receptive" reader.

If we were to give an unfriendly readerly response, we would recall that Baranskaia has been a member of the Writers' Union since 1979, and that many of the writers who joined the union throughout its long existence are now half or completely forgotten. The "understanding" reader could reply that the author is writing at the wrong moment, she is a victim of her time, she is not understood, and literature is full of such examples. Or: she is a woman, and the legitimacy of Russian-Soviet women's literature—if acknowledged as such at all—is limited to a few exceptions, such as Liudmila Petrushevskaia and Tat'iana Tolstaia, to cite two of the most distinguished recent writers, and, moving up in time and perhaps in rank, one would cite Marina Tsvetaeva and Anna Akhmatova; or, turning to memoir writing, perhaps a less "legitimate" type of literature one would cite Evgeniia Ginzburg and Nadezhda Mandel'shtam. . . .

In fact, it is also possible to value the very absence of artistry in a work of art. One could argue that what provoked the success of *A Week Like Any Other* was precisely its lack of sophistication, its striking nonliterariness, its imitation of life itself. It is useful in this connection to recall Jan Mukařovský's theory of aesthetic value:

> If a work is "intended to coincide completely with recognized life-values" it will be "perceived as a fact which is neither aesthetic nor artistic, but simply pretty [Kitsch]" [. . .] . If, on the contrary, a work transgresses too radically all dominant norms and values of the cultural environment in which it appears, it will probably be rejected or simply ignored, thus not generating actual aesthetic value. (Striedter 241)

Natal'ia Baranskaia

The controversy over the politics of gender in *A Week Like Any Other* and its success abroad rule out both complete recognition of life-values and radical transgression. At the same time, this was not literature "like any other." What was it, then? Was it just another instance of the merging of belles-lettres and documentary literature, an avatar of "factography" in the 1960s and 1970s? Edward Brown notes in his *Russian Literature since the Revolution*:

> The documentary value of [Baranskaia's] account of urban life in the seventies will be obvious to anyone who has lived in the Soviet Union, yet in style and structure the work is a negation of documentary prose. Nor is anything ever recollected in tranquillity. Everything is told in a frantic present tense dominated by the verbs for hurrying, worrying, and scurrying. The first person narration is a staccato mimicry of the heroine's life: quick short sentences, incomplete snatches of dialogue, remarks thrown back over the shoulder as one rushes downstairs, anecdotes and one-liners dropped in passing. The story is a magnificent tour de force in the direct embodiment in language of a particular kind of life experience. (320)

Brown's statement calls for further examination. Let us have a closer look at the original version of *A Week Like Any Other* ("Nedelia kak nedelia"), as it appeared in *Novyi mir*. Is Baranskaia's story an example of *skaz*—a well-known Russian literary technique that "involves telling the story, or expressing certain feelings or ideas about the events of the story, from the viewpoint and in the speech style of one of the characters" (Brown 78–79)? Is it characteristic of the renaissance of "polyphony" and "dialogism" that took place in Soviet literature during the 1960s? At first glance, the narrative structure of *A Week Like Any Other* seems desperately traditional and monological: direct discourse prevails overwhelmingly, with almost no trace of narrative "contamination," no mixed modes, such as semi-indirect discourse or "auctorial" *erlebte Rede*, to produce narrative ambiguity. Even if the characters of *A Week Like Any Other* seem not to be waiting for the narrator's permission to go ahead and speak, each voice is properly framed and isolated from the narrator's voice by dialogue tags ("he said," "she answered," "he explained," "she replied" . . .), quotation marks, or other graphic devices, as in any "decent" (socialist) realist prose.

Concerning the register of these voices, functional stylistics would characterize it as fairly standard. What is represented here is undoubtedly Soviet traditional *literaturnost'*, with some addition of "staccato mimicry," produced by the first-person narration and the accumulation of dialogues. It seems that we are light-

years away from the quasi-postmodern textual experiments of an
Andrei Bitov or Sasha Sokolov; the irony and intertextuality of a
Venedikt Erofeev; the polyphonic urban *skaz* of a Iurii Trifonov;
or the rural prose of Vasilii Belov (in his earlier phase), Valentin
Rasputin, or Vasilii Shukshin, all of whom reinvent "heteroglossia" and abandon "authorial narration" in favor of "narrative multiplicity" (Kozhevnikova 13). And yet one observes in Baranskaia's
text a tension between the immediacy of the event and its narration, a tension obtained by a curious alternation of grammatical
times, from present to past and from past to present, often within
a single paragraph and without any apparent reason. One might
argue that this usage is standard in Russian *spoken* language; in any
case, not everything in Baranskaia's story is told in a "frantic present tense," as the following excerpt from Pieta Monks's translation,
with the original forms given in brackets, makes clear:[4]

> Shura explains [present: *raz"iasniaet*] to me in a low voice that
> they are arguing about the fifth question:
> "If you have no children please give the reason: medical evi-
> dence; material circumstances; family situation; personal reasons,
> etc. . . (please underline whichever is relevant)."
> I don't know [present: *ia ne ponimaiu*] what the argument is
> about: we can all answer by underlining "personal reasons". I myself
> would even have underlined "etc. . . ." But it's this question that has
> aroused interest [past: *vsekh zainteresoval*] and even offended [past:
> *zadel*] the childless amongst us.
> Alla Sergeyevna says [past: *opredelila*] that it's incredibly tact-
> less. Shura retorts [past: *vozrazila*] that it's no more so than the
> questionnaire in general.
> Blonde Lusia, having mulled over the part of our conversation
> yesterday that obviously most worried her, "who will cultivate our
> land?" flings herself [past: *brosila*] to the defense of the questionnaire:
> "After all, we must find an answer to our serious, even dangerous,
> demographic crisis."
> Lidya, my rival in the competition for youngest scientific assis-
> tant, who has two adoring suitors, says [past: *skazala*]: "Let married
> women solve the crisis."
> Varvara Petrovna corrects [present: *popravliaet*] Lidya kindly,
> gently. . . . (19–20)

In Beatrice Stillman's translation, by contrast, the alternation of times disappears in favor of a generalized past: "Shura *explained* to me . . . I *didn't* really see what there was to discuss. . . . Alla *called* it "monstrous insensitivity". . . Shura *said* . . . Ludmilla . . . now *rushed* to the questionnaire's defense," and so on. I believe that in unifying the temporal system of the text, both translators missed one of its most interesting features.[5]

What is the reason for the alternation in the Russian original? The *present,* which "naturally" represents what could be called the "plane of reality" or the time of "autobiographical consciousness" (Harris 35), is the time of Ol'ga Nikolaevna living her week. Intermittently, Ol'ga stands back, that is, switches from this present to the past—in order to *narrate* her story, from which there is no escape, because this story is precisely the "Questionnaire for Women," asking her to itemize her life "hour by hour in 'the adopted time unit'." But there is no escape from the present for another—or concomitant—reason: Ol'ga's time is made up of the absence of it: she keeps running against time. During the short time that Ol'ga spends at home, she is constantly cooking, washing, ironing, putting her children to bed (while her husband reads his professional journals). Lack of time also characterizes the distance between home and her work: the buses that are missed or that do not come on time, the time spent in lines, the rare instants when Ol'ga tries to *cheat with time* when she reads a couple of pages of a novel (which the others have already read) between two bus stops or metro stations. There is Ol'ga's literal struggle against the physical manifestations of time: when she gets her hair cut, both males of the story who count in Ol'ga's life—Iakov Petrovich, her boss, and Dima, her husband—notice that she has "become younger"; when she decides to shorten her skirt ("Why should I go around like an old woman with my knees half-covered?"), Dima suggests that she "give up work altogether."

"I'm in a rush. I rush on to the second floor landing and bump into Yakov Petrovich. . . ." This is how the novella begins. It is above all at her workplace that Ol'ga runs out of time: she is late in writing her dissertation; the lab is late and she has to push her own project through, and she wonders whether she can make it by the deadline specified by the plan; she doesn't come on time to the political seminar; and finally, there is the questionnaire: "Who thought up this questionnaire? I turn it round but can't see any information on the compilers" (7). Ol'ga's world is one in which time is abolished, or, better, neutralized: "What week are we meant to work out . . .?" asks one of the women. "Any. . . Aren't they all the same?" answers another. Ol'ga decides to take this week, it is "a week like any other." We now understand better this alternation of times and of discourses (Ol'ga's week and Ol'ga's story about it) in Baranskaia's text. The reason for it is indeed undecidable, and apparently as meaningless as the tautological construction of the original title, "Nedelia kak nedelia," because "this week" is interchangeable with a past that interferes with the present and a present that interferes with the past.

Only at one moment is the interference of times and of discourses interrupted. Wednesday evening, after work, the heroine takes some time to walk aimlessly along the Moscow boulevards. Her thoughts drift toward the time of her first acquaintance with her husband, of their honeymoon. . . . A parenthesis opens in Ol'ga's week, a story within the story, which tells about a happy past that exists no more. The narrating and subjective "I" becomes a narrated, objective, and distant "she." We know that this pronoun introduces impersonal time, the time of history, traditionally used by the novelist (Weinrich 260).[6] The only time that really counts for Ol'ga turns out to be some sort of epic time of the past, without any ties to the present:

> All that was such a long time ago, so dreadfully long ago that it feels as if it wasn't me but some other SHE . . .
> It was like this: SHE saw him, HE saw her, and they fell in love. (30)

> Vse eto bylo, no tak davno, tak uzhasno davno, chto mne kazhetsia, budto eto byla ne ia, a kakaia-to ONA.
> Bylo tak: ONA uvidela ego, ON uvidel ee, i oni poliubili drug druga. (13)

Baranskaia considers her story as "portraying the power of love."[7] In Susan Kay's reading of *A Week Like Any Other,* Ol'ga Voronkova's fairy-tale-like recollection represents not only the mythology of romantic love but also the expression of how the "trap" of patriarchal oppression "was spun" (115–26). Whom should we believe? The author or the critic?

Here is how the parentheses are closed:

> Early one Sunday morning they got on a bus, carrying a backpack and suitcase. They were leaving paradise.
> That had been five years ago. (34)
>
> I shouldn't have walked, my thoughts strayed too far, now I'm late. I run down the escalator. (34)
>
> Rannim voskresnym utrom s riukzakom, s chemodanom on i ona sadilis' v avtobus. Oni pokidali rai.
> Eto bylo piat' let nazad.
>
> Naprasno poshla ia peshkom, razdumalas'. Pozdno! Ia begu vniz po eskalatoru. (40)

"The art of storytelling is reaching its end because the epic side of truth, wisdom, is dying out," writes Benjamin (87). He sees in the rise of the novel one of the earliest symptoms of this decline. Baranskaia's story within the story about *her* and *him*— that is, Ol'ga's "impersonal" recollection of paradise lost— represets the "epic side of truth," the longing for the transcendental home, but with the difference that this "home" (Baranskaia calls it "the power of love") has become ersatz, a cliché, precisely because it takes the novelistic form. The subtle interplay between these discursive instances in *A Week Like Any Other,* between Ol'ga's "personal" narration of timelessness and her "novel," is perhaps what Baranskaia's literary tour de force is all about, giving *form* to its sociological and gendered value.

"And Then the Deluge"

The flashback is not unique to *A Week Like Any Other.* It is, as Kay has shown, a structural device that Baranskaia repeats in later works

(115–16), among them *Memorial Day*. But designation of a device as structural calls for an examination of its place in the general structure of the work. From a structural standpoint, the parenthesis opens Wednesday evening, exactly in the middle of Ol'ga's week, and constitutes therefore its absent climax. Any modification of this scheme may threaten the overall structure. And modifications are always possible, because the story is itself an object situated in time. In fact, Baranskaia's novella, like most Soviet works of literature, has been subject to some textual fluctuations.

Twelve years after its first publication in *Novyi mir*, the text undergoes some noteworthy cosmetic interventions when it appears again in Baranskaia's collection of novellas and short stories, *The Woman with an Umbrella* (*Zhenshchina s zontikom*).[8] The name of the writer Vasilii Aksenov and the title of his work (which Ol'ga reads between two bus stops) have been dropped because in the meantime Aksenov has become a dissident and has emigrated. Among other stylistic "improvements," the colloquial form of a verb is replaced by its standard variant,[9] and an added passage underlines the fact that the "political seminar" for which Ol'ga is late is little more than pure ritual.[10] Another eight years later, in the volume bearing the name of Baranskaia's novel *Memorial Day*, the political seminar gains much more weight, with more than 500 words added in 31 paragraphs of new dialogue. In the *Novyi mir* version, Ol'ga was merely late and apologized; the reader did not learn anything about the content of these *politzaniatiia*. Ol'ga's more active participation in the 1981 (*Woman with an Umbrella*) version is expanded and made explicit in *Memorial Day*, where it culminates in an ideological clash between the heroine and Zachuraev, the political instructor. Here is an excerpt from this final addition, the seminar discussion of whether or not there are "contradictions" in a classless society (my translation):

> I jump up defiantly:
> "So there are no new contradictions? . . . I, for example . . . "
> And then the deluge. . . . A stream, a waterfall of words: I can't make it, we women cannot always make it, the family, our specialty,

the studies, the kids, illness, work, I can't, everything is a mess, the tests aren't finished, I just don't manage, the year is almost over. . . .

Zachuraev tried to stop me:

"The children probably go to kindergarten. . . . Give thanks to the state that helps you by shouldering the major portion of the costs. . . ."

His words only intensified my tirade: emancipation, a deserted hearth, spoiled children, broken families, what's that?—nothing to do with contradiction? Children left alone, without brothers or sisters. The mother with a full-time job, an overload. . . . (299)

Ol′ga ends by asking Zachuraev to excuse her from the political seminar. But such a decision can be made only "by the party committee." There is no doubt that the new version of *A Week Like Any Other* gains in female consciousness. Ol′ga Voronkova's ideological bravado makes her the leader of the "women's lab" against the (male) political establishment.

Are these changes to be attributed to *perestroika?* In a word, yes. Baranskaia says as much in her "Autobiography without Omissions." But there we also learn that the changes in this "last" version are not new; Tvardovskii had omitted them "with her consent" when he published excerpts of the work in *Novyi mir* in 1969, and now she had restored them (144). New or old, the addition concerning the political seminar has important consequences for the structure of the story, because it leaves *A Week Like Any Other* with an additional climax, devaluing—one could even say depressing—the earlier one. What I have called the subtle interplay between the discursive instances of Baranskaia's masterpiece, between the week and the story about it on one hand and the novel of *her* and *him* on the other, is threatened by an *emphasis on the (political) context,* which deprives the previous text of coherence. Should the author have followed the example of Fedor Dostoevskii who never reinserted the censored end of the first part of his *Notes from the Underground?* There is a theory that Dostoevskii opted not to do so in order to prevent his work from having two endings (Todorov 158). This reference to a great author calls for the larger form: let us now turn to *Memorial Day.*

The Wrong Memorial for the Day

One of the critical leitmotifs of *perestroika* was that a time felt to be great needed a major literature, which failed to appear. One of the paradoxes of the era was that *perestroika,* turned toward the new, mainly looked back for inspiration or explanation. Whether the search was for a Soviet Golden Age or for the "originary moment in a trajectory of aberration," it was an era of "memory" (Clark, "Changing Historical Paradigms," 300). Despite Baranskaia's recourse to the "great form," the theme of her novel could not have been more at odds with the times in which it appeared: it evokes the memory of those who gave their lives during the Great Patriotic War (World War II), and most of the novel is devoted to the women who survived. The year Baranskaia's book was published (1989), Germany entered *its* great time, and shortly afterward started negotiations to finance the withdrawal of the Red Army. The Great Patriotic War happened to be the wrong memorial for the day.

The novel begins on the eve of 9 May 1970, the twenty-fifth anniversary of the end of the war. The text is divided into twenty-one parts or chapters, representing the recollections of several women who lost their loved ones between 1941 and 1945. The author-narrator, who enters the diegesis of the novel in the first and last chapters, with some appearances in between, travels with them on a westbound train, heading toward the "brotherly graves." The last sentence of the novel, an inscription on the marble plate marking a soldier's grave, reveals to the reader that the author, too, lost her beloved during World War II: the soldier is identified as Guards Captain Nikolai Nikolaevich Baranskii.

Hence *Memorial Day* is also an autobiography, in which, incidentally, the author wears many masks. One of them is Mariia Nikolaevna Pylaeva, whose testimony takes up about 30 percent of the narrative and displays a great deal of discursive complexity, such as the inclusion—in installments—of letters from her husband at the front and the blurring of chronology and of narrative voices. At a certain point the reader wonders whether Mariia

Nikolaevna's story does not merge with the voice of the author-narrator. The particular *effet de réel* intended by these devices is the suggestion of memory. Paratextual information, such as Baranskaia's "Autobiography" and the critical material based on interviews, confirms that fiction matches reality. The key to interpretation is perhaps that Mariia Nikolaevna "restores ancient books" (6). Or is it the very semantics of her name? "Pylaeva" pertains to "flame" (pylat') and "dust" (pyl'), themselves etymologically related.[11] On board the train travels another—rather enigmatic—character, called "the woman in black" (*zhenshchina v chernom*), who holds red carnations in her hands. In the last chapter we learn that she is the other women's "sorrow," the novel's allegory.

Each chapter after the first represents an episode in the life of one of the widows. Some of these episodes are narrated in the first person, some of them by an omniscient third person, or both. The overall text could be considered a collection of separate stories but for the integrating and unifying elements that hold them together and turn them, more or less successfully, into a novel. Among the devices used to break up the linearity of the episodes and create a more elaborate whole are, as we have seen, the overlapping of stories and the flashback. It is the tension between these centrifugal and centripetal forces in *Memorial Day* that determines the particular genre of Baranskaia's last work and—as I believe—its literary value. Precisely what represented the novel in *A Week Like Any Other* has taken over here, disrupting the precarious equilibrium of the overall structure, the balanced interplay of various discourses, all of which contributed to the originality of Baranskaia's earlier masterpiece, *A Week Like Any Other*.

The Failure of a Soviet Novel

Moscow: sunshine, joy, springtime, the decorations of May Day still in place, red flowers, red stars, red banners. . . . This is how the first chapter, "On the Eve: Flowers and Wreaths," begins.

The novel sets out very much in the manner of a Soviet classic, both in theme and in style. Massive scenes are followed by moral statements about the day when joy and sorrow meet in the commemoration-celebration of a heroic time. The narrative is monumentalized by repetition, emphasis, and the epic use of the present imperfect:

> A slow and solemn procession. The women are walking, the veterans are walking—gray hair, there are orders and decorations on their chests, they travel to the places of the deadly battles with which they are acquainted and which have already become unrecognizable, and from which they escaped by a miracle. The living are going to see the dead.[12]

> Medlennoe torzhestvennoe shestvie. Idut zhenshchiny, idut veterany—sedye golovy, ordena i medali na grudi, edut k mestam znakomym i uzhe neuznavaemym smertnykh boev, gde oni chudom uceleli. Zhivye edut k mertvym. (6)

On the second page this mood culminates in five lines of poetic prose that anticipates the women's state of mind when they head toward the battlefields where their husbands perished. Then the solemn flow of the epic is disrupted by an interview with the seven widows, whose stories make up the bulk of the novel. We learn their names, their social and sometimes geographical origins, their professions, and the reasons for their presence on the train.

The time structure of the first chapter recalls the dual system of narration we encountered in *A Week Like Any Other*. There are similar traces of the present of autobiographical consciousness and the past of narration per se, but in *Memorial Day,* they fail to achieve the same effect because of their isolation among other competing discursive instances. In the first chapter, for example, the author speaks in her own voice, explaining to the reader what this book is all about and thus appropriating the narrative for a nonnarrative purpose—to set forth the ethical project of the book. The purpose of *Memorial Day* is to let future generations know about the blood and tears of war:

We must tell the story of these terrible years, so that our children
and the children of our children, every new generation may feel what
war means [. . .] . To let the children of the distant country beyond
the ocean know that Russians do not, cannot, want a war.

Rasskazyvat' o tekh strashnykh godakh nado, chtoby deti nashi i
deti detei, kazhdoe novoe pokolenie pochuvstvovali, chto znachit
voina. . . . I chtoby deti iz dalekoi zaokeanskoi strany mogli poniat':
russkie voiny ne khotiat. Ne mogut khotet'. (8)

Education of the young, the struggle for peace: Baranskaia's
novel displays from the outset canonical features of socialist realism in its revised, post–Great Patriotic War version.

The struggle for peace, one of the great themes of Soviet writing from the Zhdanov era to Gorbachev,[13] is indeed a recurrent
motif in *Memorial Day:* Until the other widows, Lora Fogel' is
not bound for the grave of her husband—his resting place is
somewhere else. She wants to see the great battlefields in order
to find inspiration for her theme, the ultimate battle against war.
A journalist by profession, she is "attracted by large-scale journalism" ("Loru tianulo k masshtabnoi publitsistike"). Such
masshtabnost', such largeness of scale, also characterizes Baranskaia's novel. We see it represented, for example, in a series of
short italicized texts following a chapter or inserted in the narrative proper, which function as both an epic, parable-like leitmotif
and an inspired commentary on what happens at a lower level of
the story. It is in such a text that our impersonal recollection of
him and *her* reappears, but now the time is set at 22 June 1941
and unfolds toward the future: *he* is leaving for the front, *she*
gives birth to a son, the "race" will be perpetuated ("Pust' rod
nash ne ostanovitsia") (23). The motif of *him* and *her* reappears
in the last chapter, where the dead husbands are resurrected in a
cathartic (and collective) evocation of the widows' dreams. It
literally reaches the level of history a few pages later, when *he*
and *she* become recumbent statues on a fifteenth-century Italian
tomb. Another text in italics, after a chapter headed "And If
Tomorrow the War . . . " (*Esli zavtra voina. . .*), is a parable on

the name Mariia, in which the Virgin Mary and "all mothers of the Earth" embody and sustain the world's peace: "Na materiakh Zemli derzhitsia mir."

The same theme, this time related to Russian folklore, is found in the lyrical invocation of the Russian stove ("Russkaia pech', pech'-matushka . . ."), presented as the symbol of Russian care and motherhood in a passage that recalls the rural prose of Vasilii Belov's *Lad* (*Harmony*). It is found again in Aksin'ia Kuz'minichna's story about a young girl's celebration of spring in her village. Folklore is well represented in *Memorial Day* by a series of "lamentations" (prichitaniia), songs, and poems, some adapted, some contrived. Aksin'ia Kuz'minichna's lament in the last chapter is a true representation of Soviet World War II folklore. It begins:

> He fell, he marched upon us, Hitler, the enemy,
> We didn't know, we didn't foresee, we didn't
>   prepare to fight.
> But he knew, he foresaw, he prepared to fight.
> He strangled and killed, and set on fire. . . .

> Naletel-napal na nas Gitler-vrag,
> My ne znali, ne zhdali, ne sgotovilis'.
> A on znal, on zhdal, on sgotovilsia.
> On dushil-ubival, on ognem palil. . . . (254)

The inclusion of folklore both disrupts and cements the novel. In fact, it increases its epic character because, after all, (pseudo-) folklore and rural prose are more than compatible with the socialist realist canon: they are an integral part of a claim for *narodnost'* (popular-national quality). At the same time, authorial and authoritative narration is fragmented by the multiplicity of narrators, styles, and texts—features also attributed to the village prose of the 1960s and 1970s. Moreover, to continue with Bakhtinian concepts, the issue of carnival may be pertinent to *Memorial Day*. The last chapter of the novel begins with Aksin'ia

Kuz'minichna's pacifist dream about meeting the president of the United States in the White House. She asks him embarrassing questions about the Great Patriotic War and gets shot by a black guard. Unfortunately, the identification of parody or carnival as a narrative device is not confirmed by the tone of the narration or by its justification as a dream that a simple peasant woman such as Aksin'ia might have had.

Finally, and here we move from the discursive to the thematic, on several occasions the novel reminds us of motifs and features in the writings of Baranskaia's contemporary Chingiz Aitmatov. *Memorial Day* and *The Day Lasts More than a Hundred Years* have more in common than (part of) their title: the insertion of parable, the presence of recurrent motifs (the train, for example), the text in italics, religion,[14] folklore, pacifism, and a dominant theme—ecology. The struggle for a natural environment happens to be the natural continuation of the struggle for peace. In the first chapter, one of the women offers her companions some herbal tea and other beverages made from the berries, fruits, and herbs of "our homeland," collected by "knowing people," by "men and women healers" (*vedunami i vedun'iami*), which will calm them, cure them, put them to sleep on board the train, and "vivify memory." We are also told of a paper written by a schoolboy in an Altai village during the war titled "My Homeland Is the Planet Earth," and reminded of our collective guilt for the destruction of the "Russian forest." In the last italicized passage in the novel, the theme is elevated to a parable about the death and resurrection of an apple tree after the frost.

Despite their obvious differences, *Memorial Day* and *The Day Lasts More than a Hundred Years* also have in common a certain heterogeneity of form. The simultaneous presence of fiction and *publitsistika*, a certain roughness of style, can be interpreted at a deeper level as a lack of internal motivation, which weakens their literariness. Is *Memorial Day* yet another example of the mutability of the socialist realist canon (Clark, "Mutability of the Canon")? On the one hand, the *experience,* the *wisdom* of

Baranskaia the story teller seem indeed to be trapped in the ritual form called the "Soviet novel." On the other hand, the novel fails to recreate the canon fully, because experience, though it certainly has fallen in value, has not yet hit bottom. Perhaps the interest of *Memorial Day* lies therefore in its very failure to become a novel. The many stories that it tells have a good chance to be valued as sociology, for their lack of the literary. But they are worth reading.

Notes

1. At the invitation of the poet Joseph Brodsky, Baranskaia had participated in a closed reading at an Akhmatova evening at the museum, and had included a photograph of Anna Akhmatova, Nikolai Gumilev, and their son in an exhibition that was organized on that occasion ("Avtobiografiia," 135–36).

2. "Povest' imela shumnyi uspekh, no ia ostalas' kak-to v storone ot uspekha i ot literaturnoi sredy" ("Avtobiografiia," 136).

3. This volume, *Zhenshchina s zontikom*, included *A Week Like Any Other* with slight but significant modifications, as we shall see.

4. Unless I indicate otherwise, all excerpts from *A Week Like Any Other* are quoted from Monks's translation.

5. Concerning the alternation of present and past in the French version of "Nedelia kak nedelia," as well as the confrontation of Baranskaia's text with contemporary Bakhtinism, see my "Du 'dialogisme.'"

6. See also Benveniste.

7. Goscilo ("Domostroika or Perestroika?" 234) quotes from an interview she conducted with Baranskaia in 1988.

8. This is the version Monks has translated.

9. *Ia ne protivlius'*, for example, becomes *ia ne soprotivliaius'*, and *ia brosaiu* is transformed into a *ia govoriu gromko*.

10. For a detailed analysis of these variants and the significance of rewriting in Soviet literature of the 1960s and 1970s in a sociolinguistic-literary context, see my " 'Parole de l'autre.' "

11. I am grateful to Edna Andrews and Elena Maksimova for attracting my attention to this point.

12. All translations of *Memorial Day* are my own.

13. For an example from the Gorbachev years, see the "Appeal to the Writers of the World," *Literaturnaia gazeta*, 2 June 1986, quoted from Pluksh 360–61.

14. In her "Autobiography" Baranskaia refers explicitly to Aitmatov's novel *The Execution Block* and its religious motifs, which contributed to a change in the social atmosphere that facilitated the publication of *Memorial Day* (143).

References

Aitmatov, Chingiz. *The Day Lasts More than a Hundred Years.* Trans. John French. Bloomington, IN: Indiana University Press, 1983.

Baranskaia, Natal'ia. "Nedelia kak nedelia, povest'." *Novyi mir,* 1969, no. 11, 23–55.

———. *Zhenshchina s zontikom.* Moscow: Sovremennik, 1981.

———. *Portret podarennyi drugu: Ocherki i rasskazy o Pushkine.* Leningrad: Lenizdat, 1983.

———. *Den' pominoveniia.* Moscow: Sovetskii pisatel', 1989.

———. "Avtobiografiia bez umolchanii." *Grani,* 1990, no. 156, 122–48.

Baranskaya, Natalya. "The Alarm Clock in the Cupboard." Trans. Beatrice Stillman. *Redbook,* March 1971.

———. *A Week Like Any Other: Novellas and Stories.* Trans. Pieta Monks. Seattle, WA: Seal Press, 1990.

Belov, Vasilii. *Lad. Ocherki o narodnoi estetike. Izbrannye proizvedeniia v trekh tomakh.* Moscow: Sovremennik, 1984.

Benjamin, Walter. "The Storyteller: Reflections on the Works of Nikolai Leskov." In *Illuminations: Essays and Reflections,* ed. Hannah Arendt, 83–109. New York: Schocken, 1985.

Benveniste, Emile. "Les relations du temps dans le verbe français." In *Problèmes de linguistique générale,* 237–50. Paris: Gallimard, 1966.

Brown, Edward J. *Russian Literature since the Revolution.* Rev. and enl. ed. Cambridge, MA: Harvard University Press, 1982.

Clark, Katerina. "The Mutability of the Canon: Socialist Realism and Chingiz Aitmatov's *I dolshe veka dlitsia den'.*" *Slavic Review* 43, no. 4 (1984): 573–87.

———. "Changing Historical Paradigms in Soviet Culture." In *Late Soviet Culture: From Perestroika to Novostroika,* ed. Thomas Lahusen. Durham, NC: Duke University Press, 1993.

Goscilo, Helena. "Domostroika or Perestroika? The Construction of Womanhood in Soviet Culture under Glasnost." In *Late Soviet Culture: From Perestroika to Novostroika,* ed. Thomas Lahusen. Durham, NC: Duke University Press, 1993.

———, ed. *Balancing Acts: Contemporary Stories by Russian Women.* Bloomington, IN: Indiana University Press, 1989.

Harris, Jane Gary. "Diversity of Discourse: Autobiographical Statements in Theory and Praxis." In *Autobiographical Statements in Twentieth-Century Russian Literature,* ed. Jane Gary Harris. Princeton, NJ: Princeton University Press, 1990.

Kay, Susan. "A Woman's Work." *Irish Slavonic Studies* 8 (1987): 115–26.

Kozhevnikova, N.A. "O sootnoshenii rechi avtora i personazha." In *Iazykovye protsessy sovremennoi russkoi khudozhestvennoi literatury: Proza.* Moscow: Nauka, 1977.

Lahusen, Thomas. "Du dialogisme et de la polyphonie dans deux ouvrages russes des années soixante: *Une semaine comme une autre* de Natal'ja

Baranskaja et *Bilan préalable* de Jurij Trifonov." *Revue d'études slaves* 58, no. 4 (1986): 563–85.

————. "La 'parole de l'autre' dans la littérature soviétique des années 60 et 70: Essai d'analyse sociolinguistique." In *Contributions des savants suisses au Xe congrès international des slavistes à Sofia, septembre 1988*, ed. Peter Brang, 195–211. Slavica Helvetica 28. Bern: Peter Lang, 1988.

Pluksh, P.I., comp. *Literaturnoe dvizhenie sovetskoi èpokhi. Materialy i dokumenty. Khrestomatiia*. Moscow: Prosveshchenie, 1986.

Striedter, Jurij. *Literary Structure, Evolution, and Value: Russian Formalism and Czech Structuralism Reconsidered*. Cambridge, MA: Harvard University Press, 1989.

Todorov, Tzvetan. "Le jeu de l'altérité: *Notes d'un souterrain*." In *Poétique de la prose*, 133–60. Paris: Seuil, 1978.

Weinrich, Harald. *Le temps: Le récit et le commentaire*. Paris: Seuil, 1973.

11

IULIIA VOZNESENSKAIA'S WOMEN
With Love and Squalor

Jerzy Kolodziej

Iuliia Voznesenskaia is a Russian poet and novelist who has lived in Germany since she was exiled by the Soviet government. In addition to her writing, Voznesenskaia has been involved in social causes. In the late 1960s especially after the invasion of Czechoslovakia, and in the 1970s she was active in the dissident movement. In 1976 she and her friends were imprisoned for planning to publish a satirical political journal that they intended to call *Red Dissident*. In prison she wrote *The White Daisy,* about women in labor camps—the first work, she reports, in which she wrote specifically about women. Upon her return to Leningrad, resolved to work for changes in the treatment of women in labor camps, she was invited by Natal´ia Malakhovskaia to join her, Tat´iana Mamonova, and Tat´iana Goricheva in launching a feminist journal. In the fall of 1979 they brought out the first feminist journal in the Soviet Union, *Woman and Russia.* As a result Voznesenskaia was expelled from the country in May 1980; the other three women followed shortly (Morgan 51–54). In emigration Voznesenskaia has published poetry and two novels, *The Women's Decameron (Damskii Dekameron)* in 1986 and *The Star Chernobyl (Zvezda Chernobyl´)* in 1987. *The Women's Decameron* especially repays analysis.

By its very title *The Women's Decameron* invites comparison with Boccaccio's work, and when the two are juxtaposed it quickly becomes apparent that they have many structural elements in common. As in Boccaccio's work, each of ten individuals in Voznesenskaia's text tells a story every day for ten days. Boccaccio's characters quarantine themselves to escape the plague of 1348. Voznesenskaia devises a less drastic situation: ten women in a maternity hospital are quarantined with a skin infection. Both Boccaccio and Voznesenskaia use the devise of the exemplum, demonstrating their theses by offering examples from daily life. The exemplum was widely used in medieval sermons and saints' lives to demonstrate the powers of God's love. Boccaccio used it, as the critic Guido A. Guarino argues, to illustrate "the operation of Nature and the human intellect" (xvi–xvii). Voznesenskaia's work, like Boccaccio's, exemplifies human virtue and vice in tales that celebrate human adaptability. Like Boccaccio's narrators, Voznesenskaia's women tell stories that illustrate previously agreed-upon topics. Most of the themes treated in one work are found also in the other: the happiness and unhappiness of lovers; attained or frustrated goals involving sex or honor or both; women's infidelities and seductions of and by men; generous or noble deeds.

Voznesenskaia has also added a few topics that Boccaccio neglects, such as "Rapists and Their Victims" and "Money and Related Matters"—refinements needed, one assumes, as a concession to the times we live in. The violence and barbarity of men—and occasionally of women—described by Voznesenskaia's narrators are by no means the peccadilloes of lovable rogues or venial sinners. As if to right the balance, Voznesenskaia introduces a topic that is nearly mandatory in Russian literature, "First Love," and her women idealize the concept of romantic love, marriage, and fidelity. Boccaccio's women, in contrast, appear to adhere to the code of courtly love, which idealized illicit liaisons. As one critic ruefully points out, "they are nearly all adulteresses."[1]

Despite its emphasis on the difficulty of women's lives, Voznesenskaia's work shares one outstanding characteristic with Boccaccio's: it brims over with living people and it is life-affirming in its indulgence of human weakness. For both writers great joy can be had in this life, not only in the attainment of lasting

love or in great altruism but also in trickery, deceit, and revenge—in
that part of life which represents escape from conformity.

The thing that most sharply distinguishes Voznesenskaia's
Women's Decameron from Boccaccio's *Decameron,* if one dis-
counts the inevitable disparities in time and setting, is the focus
of the narratives. All of the tales told by Boccaccio's characters
are about other people. The narrators take no personal part in the
stories they relate. Boccaccio is interested in humanity at large,
not in the private or personal. His focus is on the continuum of
human virtue and vice, not on the idiosyncratic behavior of any
individual. Therefore his narrators can only be fascinated voy-
eurs, telling stories about humanity in all of its manifestations.
Voznesenskaia's women, too, tell us anecdotes and stories about
other people, but in half or more of the stories they talk about
themselves. They are involved. As stories about the narrators
alternate with stories about other people, layers of information
are gradually built up about each of the ten women narrators, and
the many other characters and social types to which they introduce us are evaluated in turn both by the narrator and by the
other women in the spirited discussions that follow the tales.

The novelty of *The Women's Decameron* lies in the fact that
the tales are told from the points of view of women. True, seven
of the ten narrators in Boccaccio's *Decameron* are also women,
but their stories are indistinguishable from those told by the men,
and the narrators are all passive. Each of Voznesenskaia's
women has a distinct and active personality. Even when they are
victims, they control the flow of the narrative. In fact, the narrative becomes a glue that facilitates their bonding. As that bond
strengthens, the women undergo changes, as we shall see. The
women's bonding, their sense of solidarity, also determines to
some extent their attitudes toward men. Whatever their views of
men—their attitudes range from love to loathing—the men are
always seen as other; they have no place in the women's value
system, at least so long as the latter are together in the hospital.

One of the distinguishing features of Voznesenskaia's
Decameron is the degree to which it is simultaneously individual

and social, both lyric and epic. According to the critic Edward
Hutton, "in Chaucer the tales often weary us, but the tellers never
do; in Boccaccio the tales never weary us, but the tellers always
do" (x). As a rule, in Latin art the narrative rises out of the
situation, he points out, whereas in English literature the narrative proceeds from character. If we wished to carry the generalization further, we could say that Russian literature also focuses
on character, but it places greater emphasis on social background.
Voznesenskaia's novel not only falls squarely within the Russian
tradition, it also manages to overcome the problem of anemic
plots. She has mastered the art of the quick-paced, well-made
anecdote, and she puts her tales in the mouths of women who
may offend us but never weary us. She places her characters in a
social setting that in itself contributes to their problems.

A reader with even a superficial acquaintance with the facts of
Voznesenskaia's life quickly sees that much of the raw material
of experience that informs the women's stories belongs to
Voznesenskaia herself. Many of the women in the novel are engaged in occupations that Voznesenskaia herself had engaged in
and share experiences that Voznesenskaia reports elsewhere as
her own. Many reflect facets of Voznesenskaia's own personality, her ideas and preoccupations. In this respect her novel is
profoundly personal. Like Larissa, a biologist, and Emma, a theater director, she is a professional. Like Zina, she has spent time
in a prison camp, and one must assume that many of Zina's
experiences are Voznesenskaia's. Like Nelya, she was a music
teacher. Voznesenskaia's two decades in the dissident movement
lend color and dimension to the dissident Galina. Even Voznesenskaia's experience as a metal worker is reflected in her
portrayal of Olga, a shipyard worker. It is Emma, however, who
most resembles her, not only because Emma works in the arts but
also because, like Voznesenskaia, she is a member of the second,
unofficial culture. It is Emma who proposes that the ten women
quarantined in the maternity hospital tell one another stories.
Emma establishes a close connection between herself and
Voznesenskaia by telling the story of the proposed satirical jour-

Iuliia Voznesenskaia

nal *Red Dissident,* and refers to "Julia," a poet now residing in the West, who played a major role in the creation of the journal. She even says that Julia is writing a book about her friends (265).

Her own vivid presence in the novel as alter ego, as character, and as author-narrator provides realistically motivated narration and also suggests that Voznesenskaia is showing her solidarity with these women. It is interesting to note that when Voznesenskaia was

serving time in the camps for her role in *Red Dissident,* she was
told by the women there, with whose help she was able to write
and smuggle out *The White Daisy,* that they were waiting for her
to publish her book (Morgan 53).

The narrator, who calls herself "the author," appears only a
few times in the novel. She dedicates Nelya's story about her
childhood in Auschwitz to Naum Korzhavin (27), and she
"highly recommends" to all women the manner in which
Galina's mother dealt with her husband (20). But we also sense
the narrator's presence in the brief introduction that precedes
each tale and to a lesser degree in the more extensive comments
and banter by the women at the end of each tale. Each introduction provides a factual summary of the story that is to follow and
perhaps a humorous or ironic aside. It is here that the author,
elsewhere content to let the women tell their own stories, most
clearly reveals her personal attitudes. When she introduces
Albina's tale of a drug and sex orgy, for example, she ironically
refers to it as "the sexual revolution in the age of advanced socialism" (20). And when she introduces Zina's story of a village
girl who was seduced and abandoned, she writes: "No one can
accuse us of slandering the Soviet Army, since betrayal of one's
bride and betrayal of one's country—they're as different as chalk
and cheese, as they say in Odessa" (40).

Who are these women and what do they have to tell us? What
are their attitudes and beliefs? They represent a fairly broad cross
section of Russian women, though the majority of them are better
educated than the average. Among them are three university-edu-
cated professionals: Larissa has a doctorate in biology; Emma is
a theater director; Natasha is an engineer. Two other women,
both well educated, are polarized politically: Valentina is a functionary in the city soviet, and Galina strongly supports the dissident cause. Yet another educated woman is Nelya, a sensitive
and shy music teacher. Albina and Zina are not educated, and
though they lead very different lives, they are alike in many
ways. Albina is a flight attendant, a playgirl who is after the good
life. Zina is "a tramp" and "a citizen of no fixed abode." She has

spent considerable time in prison camps. The two women share a cynical attitude toward love and sex; neither is hesitant about using four-letter words. When some of the women seem embarrassed about sharing their first experience of love, Zina asks, "What's there to be shy about? We all love with the same part of the body, don't we?" (4). Albina opines (and I paraphrase) that a man is as good as a certain part of his anatomy (19). Another uneducated woman is Olga, the shipyard worker. Irishka, the secretary to a factory director, is the general favorite of the group.

Of the ten, six are currently married. Albina, Zina, and Larissa have never married; Emma has been married twice. The six married women report that they are happy in their marriages, but some seem to face potential problems. Olga's husband drinks, Galina's husband is a dissident and still in exile, Nelya's husband has already had a heart attack, and Natasha says, "It's frightening how unmanly they [men] have become. A husband in the home is just another child, only greedier" (12). Four of the women are single parents, the professionals (Emma and Larissa) by choice, the uneducated (Albina and Zina) by circumstance.

The individual portraits of these Leningrad women as they emerge from Voznesenskaia's pages bear striking resemblances to those of the thirteen women interviewed by Carola Hansson and Karin Liden in *Moscow Women*. The challenges they face are much the same. The basic problems are the difficulties of balancing work and family roles and of being women in a male-dominated society. Despite the legal equality so tirelessly proclaimed, they receive less pay than men in less prestigious jobs, and when the job is over they perform all of the traditional household tasks. Their difficulties are exacerbated by an irregular and inadequate supply of consumer goods and services and by the cramped quarters in which they live (as recently as 1982 almost a quarter of urban families still occupied communal apartments [Lapidus xi–xii]).

In their tales and in the commentaries afterward Voznesenskaia's women speak primarily about their own lives and about other women's lives. The focus is on women and how they view the world. The novel is about how the Russian woman perceives her society, how she perceives men, and how she perceives her role as a woman. All of these relationships are complex, ambivalent, and often contradictory. Nevertheless, within each of the relationships a dual structure emerges.

In general terms, a woman's relationship both with society and with men is characterized by alienation and powerful antagonisms. With respect to society, she sees herself as both victim and good citizen (though the definition of a good citizen may depend on the woman). As far as men are concerned, she also sees herself as exploited and victimized, but at the same time she nurtures an idealized image of a noble and strong man and a harmonious family unit. Her sense of self is likewise tinged by idealism. She is independent and self-assured, and she sees herself as the equal of any man. Her relationships with other women are characterized by symbiotic caring. She is capable of subordinating her autonomy to the needs of the group and of using her positive qualities of love and compassion for its benefit. The occasional antagonism that flares between women is of a self-protective sort, aroused by competition over a man or over everyday necessities in short supply. The gradual shifts in perception as the ten confined women realize that a special relationship exists among women forms the principal theme within the larger picture of how the Russian woman perceives herself and her environment.

The list of grievances that serve to alienate the women from their society is fairly extensive. Like the Russian religious feminists described by Alix Holt, these women "assume that it is government at the source of the repressive social mechanisms which sets the framework of private as well as public lives, poisoning human relationships and stunting spiritual life" (260). They criticize the social structure as well as the state's treatment of women. The government puts obstacles in Olga's path to prevent her from marrying a German. Not a *real* one, she assures the others, but an East German (5). After they hear a story in which two drunken women brutally murder a man for his money, Voznesenskaia's women bemoan the fact that "every year more and more women are becoming alcoholics" (176). Another story recalls a doctor who says that it would take a lot of influence to get an old woman pensioner with heart trouble into a hospital (187–88). The problem that comes up most often is the housing shortage. We are invited to laugh over fights in communal kitchens (205); over the (no doubt apocryphal) mother-in-law who, after numerous quarrels in the one room she shares with her son and daughter-in-law, chops up the daughter-in-law with an ax and serves her in a soup to her son (206); and over the ingenuity of couples who must strain their powers of imagination to contrive moments of privacy.

Between the hilarious moments we share the women's outrage at the police investigator who refuses to open a rape case because he would be reprimanded if he failed to solve it (153), and at the police officers who do not interfere when a drunken husband tries to kill his wife with an ax ("It's a family matter" [242]), and at the gulag authorities who "treat the women like cattle, and they bullied them, beat them up, and sometimes even raped them" (255). The most extensive criticism, however, is directed at the government's policy regarding mothers. The government is blasted for paying only five rubles a month to help raise a child (12); for the low allotment it gives orphaned children; and for its failure to help women with many children and low-paying jobs to get a better education. One woman suggests that motherhood should qualify one for a pension (251–52). The women's frustration at their inability to influence government policy can be seen when Valentina, the Party functionary, declines to forward the suggestion to her namesake Tereshkova, the woman who is in a position to act on it. "Have you ever heard of her putting in a single word for women?" Valentina retorts. "Of course not, and that's why she's the head of the Committee of Soviet Women" (252).

In view of the amount of criticism these women level against their government, it is somewhat surprising that, with the exception of the dissident Galina, they give it strong support and do not question its authority. Voznesenskaia portrays her women as for the most part apolitical. Natasha and Larissa know about the work of the dissidents, but neither supports them. Valentina and

Olga are politically uninformed. Both believe that in 1968 West Germany "very nearly crossed the border into Czechoslovakia" (247). Their fear of the West is prompted by the fear of war, and they attribute shortages of food and living space to the Soviet Union's need to defend itself (248). Voznesenskaia's own stance toward the Soviet government is highly critical, as she makes clear in the 1979 *Almanac: Woman and Russia*; in what Mary Buckley calls "the strong political flavour of *Mariia 2*, which Voznesenskaia edited" (9); and in her last novel, *Zvezda Chernobyl'*. Her women in *The Women's Decameron*, however, are for the most part good citizens who want peace (". . . let's do without meat and milk, just as long as we don't have war!" [247]) and a better life. If the government cannot provide such essentials as disposable diapers and plastic pants for infants, it should steal them. Emma comments, "Our people are supposed to be involved in industrial espionage, so why couldn't they steal some useful secret instead of always going for electronics?" (1).

The men in the novel, like the government, are also portrayed largely as exploiters. Larissa and Emma, the two most educated and independent women, have washed their hands of them; Albina has turned the tables and uses *them*. The married women, too, are highly critical of men. Not surprisingly, Zina and Albina have the most negative attitudes toward men and are the most skeptical about romantic love. Both of them had their first sexual experiences at the hands of rapists. In fact, we learn that four of the women have been raped, two of them more than once; four others report attempted rapes; one managed to escape from a child molester; and Emma went to bed with a director when he made it clear that this was the only way she would get a film part. "They talk of equal rights for men and women," says Nelya. "What equal rights? What are we—people, or just bait for predators?" (57).

In light of this kind of experience, the degree of hostility directed toward men is hardly surprising. They have no shame, Albina remarks; it all "gets turned into sperm" (214). Zina says, "I'm not going to bore you with all my gripes against men—it

would take too long" (43). Olga, having thought it over, is willing to concede that "you do occasionally get men who are genuine people" (224).

Perhaps these are the men they are thinking of when they idealize
the good man and marriage. The negative and positive attitudes
toward men coexist like parallel universes, without touching. Marriage is the supreme goal in a group of tales that might be called
"Getting a Man at Any Cost." Such is Natasha's story, in which a
seduced and abandoned woman simply goes to Armenia and turns
up on the doorstep of the young man's parents. Olga relates how
cleverly Liuba tricks Pashka—an alcoholic—into marriage. Only
Larissa realizes that her ideal man can never be found, and abandons the search (12). So does Emma, but on moral grounds. In her
efforts to keep her second husband's affections she became aware
that the process was like an addiction and that it was destroying her
as a woman and as an artist (110).

Critics often point out that Voznesenskaia belongs to the camp
of Russian religious feminists, as opposed to the secular feminists headed by Mamonova. It would be a mistake, however, to
place Voznesenskaia within the ranks of those religious feminists
who advocate a "return to the traditional family" or who "accept
the traditional conception of the feminine personality" (Holt 247).
The Women's Decameron makes it clear that Voznesenskaia recognizes the single-mother professional as a legitimate phenomenon. Motherhood is an option for some single women, such as
Larissa and Emma. And none of the other women in the novel
want a "traditional" relationship. A traditional marriage implies a
drunken husband, cruelty, a double work load, and the loss of
self. These women want relationships in which they can be on an
equal footing with their partners. What they crave is an ideal
relationship, and for the majority of them the ideal state is marriage. In this respect they are not radical feminists. They want
men and the social structure to change. Like the women interviewed in *Moscow Women,* they would like to live up to the feminine ideal, to be "the bearers of values, of morality, culture, history,
religion, honesty, and conscience; they are burdened by the respon-

sibilities of perfection itself, and the women berate themselves for their constant inability to live up to this ideal" (Lapidus xvii).

The importance they attach to marriage to the right man is vividly seen in their reaction to Zina's story—the only one that triggers a direct and active response from all the women. On the third day she tells them about her encounter with Igor, whom she left the next morning because he was a good man and she didn't want to ruin his life. On the ninth day she receives a package from Igor, who writes that he has been looking for her and signs himself her "happy husband and father" (236). Galina and Larissa, it turns out, have written Igor a letter. Zina "sat silently on her bed filled with peace and happiness"; the women "exchanged whispers, kept glancing at Zina, and were happy"; and the stories of the ninth and tenth days are about "noble deeds by men and women" and "happiness." The story of Zina—a cynical, foul-mouthed black sheep brought to ruin by men and further victimized by the social system—is more than entertainment or social commentary. It achieves the status of symbol, because through the intervention of women Zina becomes reconciled with men and, potentially, with her society. She can also be said to attain reconciliation with the group of women in the hospital. Whereas earlier the women sympathize with her as with all victims of repression, when she reinforces one of the primary group values by finding the elusive right man, she attains full membership in the group.

Valentina undergoes a similar process. As a Party functionary she is initially treated with some suspicion, and Galina and Albina are downright hostile to her. At first she is so earnestly political that she even politicizes love: "In this country love is a matter of national importance" (4). But the flow of narration sweeps her, too, closer to the other women as she moves from unconscious humor to healthy delight in the ludicrous (a picture of Khrushchev falls on her husband as they make love [68]) to criticism of the Party's policies concerning women (251). In her evolution we see that solidarity among women is more meaningful than blind loyalty to a political institution.

As a group the women in the hospital exert subtle but effective
pressure on the individual members. Undoubtedly Valentina tai-
lors her narratives somewhat to gain the group's acceptance. She
humanizes her tales and introduces elements that indicate her
readiness to compromise with the group's values. Irishka, too,
apparently bows to the group norm: she claims to have slept with
three men, but the women know she is happily married and she
has invented the lovers just to ingratiate herself with them. Yet
despite such pressures, one has the distinct impression that the
women as a group reinforce the feelings that the individual woman has about herself. The group is supportive of single mothers
and empathizes with women who have suffered. The group provides the acceptance and understanding that women as a class do
not receive from men or the state and its institutions. Above all,
the relationships that have been forged among the women in the
hospital (admittedly, an idealized, germfree microcosm of the
real world) do not leave them alienated, victimized, or exploited.
In the hospital they are all equal.

Though the state of affairs that Voznesenskaia describes does
not inspire optimism, her women continue to make the best of a
bad situation. They carry within themselves the cultural load of
the Decembrist wives and the Tat'iana/Natasha tradition: they
are stoic, strong, self-sacrificing, and loving. But they also have a
modern awareness of their subordinate status in society and operate in an ironic mode. For comfort and understanding they turn to
other women. Though many of them remain hopeful and continue to search for the ideal mate with whom they can live on
equal terms, a few have given up the struggle and instead seek
fulfillment in their careers. Ultimately, however, none of the
women is destined to be alone. In acknowledgment of women's
traditional role as lifegivers, Voznesenskaia sets her work in a
maternity hospital.

In the final story of *The Women's Decameron,* which serves as
a kind of epilogue, Irishka briefly sums up each individual as
well as the entire narrative. Her comments represent a reaffirma-
tion of each woman and her special qualities, as well as an affir-

mation of life in all its positive and negative aspects. And yet a longing remains: "I wish life here could be more civilized. I think that we women deserve to have life get a little easier" (302).

Notes

1. The early code of courtly love required not only devotion and complete loyalty to the beloved but also "that the lovers must not be married to one another . . . their love was sensual, illicit and adulterous," in *The Reader's Companion to World Literature,* Calvin S. Brown, ed. (New York: New American Library, 1961), 110.

References

Buckley, Mary. "Soviet Religious Feminism as a Form of Dissent." *Journal of the Liberal Arts,* Fall 1986, 5–12.

Guarino, Guido A. Introduction to *Concerning Famous Women,* by Giovanni Boccaccio, trans. Guido A. Guarino, ix–xxxii. New Brunswick, NJ: Rutgers University Press, 1963.

Hansson, Carola, and Karin Liden, eds. *Moscow Women.* New York: Pantheon, 1983.

Holt, Alix. "The First Soviet Feminists." In *Soviet Sisterhood,* ed. Barbara Holland, 237–65. Bloomington, IN: Indiana University Press, 1985.

Hutton, Edward. Introduction to *The Decameron,* by Giovanni Boccaccio, trans. J.M. Riggs, iv–xvi. New York: Dutton, 1963.

Lapidus, Gail Warshofsky. Introduction to *Moscow Women,* ed. Carola Hansson and Karin Liden, ix–xvii. New York: Pantheon, 1983.

Morgan, Robin. "The First Feminist Exiles from the USSR." *Ms.,* November 1980, 49–56+.

Voznesenskaia, Iuliia. *The Women's Decameron.* Trans. W.B. Linton. Boston, MA: Atlantic Monthly Press, 1986.

12

THE HEARTFELT POETRY OF ELENA SHVARTS

Darra Goldstein

The world of the unseen, with its spirits and demons, takes on nearly tangible form in the verse of the St. Petersburg poet Elena Shvarts. In visions both playful and somber Shvarts conveys a spirituality that derives from intense exploration of the self. Self-exploration is an attempt at purification—or "circumcision," as she terms it.[1] But unlike other poets, who typically choose the intellect or the soul for their poetic conceits, Shvarts makes the heart the very physical locus of her musings. This emphasis on the heart, an organ of the body that traditionally has spiritual significance, lends her work passion in both the religious and sensual meanings of the word.

In many poems this passion reflects the feminine condition, though Shvarts's poetry is in no way politically feminist. Rather, it achieves a maximum degree of self-involvement without lapsing into solipsism. Shvarts explores the lives of women not only through close personal scrutiny but also through two memorable personae. Cynthia, a character influenced by Martial's elegies, is a Roman poet and slaveholder; Lavinia is a heretical but divinely wise nun. Sixteen poems are devoted to Cynthia, whose voice becomes that of Shvarts's muse as it makes universal women's passions and concerns. Lavinia is far less rational than Cynthia, though no less astute. *The Works and Days of Lavinia, a Nun of the Order of the Circumcision of the Heart* is like a fragmentary novel in verse, with Lavinia representing the larger dilemmas of her gender. Through her isolation Lavinia comes to understand

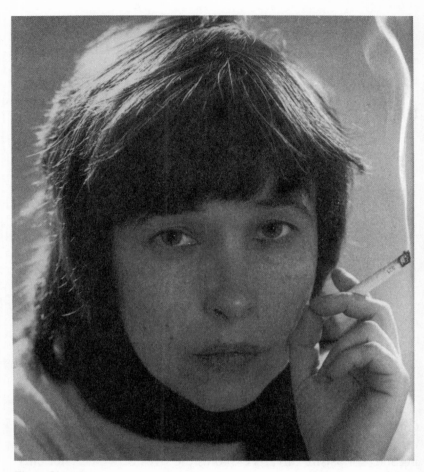

Elena Shvarts

woman's place in the world. "The Virgin is a microcosm," she writes in "A Dark Christmas Song" (*Trudy*, 19), while man is but a man ("Chelovek—on est' muzhchina"). This idea of woman as microcosm provides a working metaphor for much of Shvarts's verse.

Cynthia, a spiteful, vain, and worldly woman, and Lavinia, a nun desperately trying to overcome her sexual desire, are united by the heartfelt pain they experience. Both characters suffer from an abundance of emotion, which at times spills over to cause vexation, embarrassment, or anxiety. Shvarts's own poetic "I" likewise suffers a variety of emotions. Shvarts boldly represents the female microcosm that this range of emotional experience comprises by depicting an entire universe of the interior, replete with inhabitants.[2] The center of this universe is the heart, and Shvarts sets herself apart from other poets by making the term "heartfelt" fully literal. As Shvarts depicts it, the heart is not the valentine typically associated with romantic (or, for that matter, female) poets but an autonomous entity, a vital, pulsating organ that reacts furiously in response to emotions and stimuli. Furthermore, the heart must bear the burden of a difficult, seemingly material life that has been attached to it: "Chto delat' s zhizn'iu nebol'shoiu, / prishitoi k serdtsu moemu" (What is to be done with this small life, / Sewn onto my heart [*Trudy*, 24]). This internal yet extraneous life takes on myriad forms embracing virtually all aspects of the world—human, animal, plant, and material—and makes them a part of the self. More often than not these forms are extremely cumbersome:

> Ia kust iz roz i nezabudok srazu.
> Kak budto mne privil sadovnik dikii
> tiazheluiu tsvetochnuiu prokazu. . .
> > "Zver'-tsvetok" (*Tantsuiushchii David*, 6)

> I am at once a bush of roses and forget-me-nots.
> As if a savage gardener had grafted onto me
> A heavy leprosy of flowers . . .
> > "The Flower-Beast"

Yet the promise of exaltation also exists:

> Vo vnutrennei pustyne mozhno vstretit'
> Sviatogo, Startsa, L'va ili Sebia.
> V pustyne—davka, liudi, tolpy
> I v zhilakh angela poet truba.
> > "V dushe pustynnoi mnogo-mnogo" (*Stikhi*)

In the desert of the interior you can meet
The Saint, the Elder, the Lion, or the Self.
In the desert are throngs, people, crowds
But in the veins the horn of an angel sings.
                "In the desert soul are many, many"

Carrying her literal treatment even further, Shvarts demonstrates the complexity of the interior universe through the inspired imagery of inhabitants of the heart. She provides her most
vivid creations with a dwelling place in Lavinia's heart. Usually
making their presence felt at night, these characters are sometimes terrifying, sometimes reassuring. In a graphic metaphor for
Lavinia's efforts to attain purity and grace, her heart endures
intense physical pain as it experiences violent incursions and
excursions. Lavinia's heart is repeatedly circumcised:

. . . Angel serdtse mne
vdrug vyrezal kontsom kinzhala.
I vot ono skvozit—prolom . . .
                "Svoe muchenie nochnoe" (*Trudy*, 12)
. . . The angel suddenly
cut my heart with the tip of his sword.
And now there's a draft—a gap . . .
                "My nocturnal torments"

With an open hole in her heart, Lavinia is never sure who will
next take up residence there. She senses relief when the Pale
Rider exits (*Trudy*, 12) and the Angel-Wolf steps in (*Trudy*, 14).
Interestingly, the visitors who comfort her most are all masculine
figures, such as the Angel-Wolf, who later metamorphoses into a
lion. In addition to being masculine, both Wolf and Lion represent brute strength, though their brutishness is tempered by habi-
tation in Lavinia's heart. It is tempting to give an overtly sexual
interpretation to these male intrusions. When a nun struggling
against desire is physically invaded by male characters who either ravage or pacify her, the carnal implications seem obvious.

Yet, as we shall see, even though Lavinia endures frequent violations, she does not ultimately end up a victim.

In one affecting poem, the Angel-Wolf emerges from the depths of a literally icy heart to give Lavinia succor, and together they bemoan the pain of the universe. To convey an extended expression of mourning, the poem relies on the repetition of ululant sounds (Russian *y*):

> Mnogo snega palo na serdtse,
> Tresnul i slomalsia led,
> Iz glubokoi temnoi prorubi
> Vyplyl seryi Angel-Volk.
> On zakhlebyvalsia ves',
> Podvyval on—my li, vy li,
> Obnialis' my s nim i vsiu,
> Vsiu Vselennuiu obvyli . . .
>
> "Angel-Volk" (*Trudy*, 14)

> Much snow fell on my heart,
> The ice cracked and broke,
> From a deep, dark ice hole
> The gray Angel-Wolf emerged.
> He was utterly choking,
> He was howling—we, you,
> He and I embraced and howled
> Over all, all the Universe . . .
>
> "The Angel-Wolf"

Despite the Wolf's consoling presence, the poem communicates agitation and unsettling movement—choking, trembling, and arousal (*zakhlebyvalsia, zadrozhalo, vskolykhnulas'*).[3]

The nervous agitation with which events occur in Lavinia's heart is typical of Shvarts's verse, which does not make for quiet reading. Skillfully manipulating poetic form, Shvarts causes the reader to experience a sense of disruption. Much of her poetry relies on a rapid shifting of rhythm and rhyme, creating tension and dynamism in the poems. As Shvarts herself writes in "In

Imitation of Boileau": "I like verse that is like a tram: / clanging and jingling it flies" (Mne nraviatsia stikhi, chto na tramvai pokhozhi: / zvenia i drebezzha, oni letiat [*David*, 7]). Just as she avoids cliché in her pointed treatment of potentially sentimental themes, so Shvarts subjects her verse lines to often jarring alternations, inducing a poetic arhythmia that heightens the discord of the heart.

Not surprisingly, this discord is tied up with the poet's lyrical gift. In "Animus," the poet writes of being besieged by a "harsh god / with burning bloody eye and a snake at his feet." Like the other most powerful residents of the heart, this god is masculine. He tears at the poet's throat with his talons, making her hoarse and endangering her ability to express herself. Through the strong cadence of the poem, the reader feels the internal pounding of the god's fists against the poet's temple. But, paradoxically, this cruel god also offers the possibility of jubilation. Despite her anguish, the poet concludes:

> No kogda na puchke moikh zhil
> On igraet i lapoiu mashet,
> Vse, vse v utrobe zemli
> Zoloto pliashet!
>
> "Animus" (*Stikhi*)

> But when on a bundle of my veins
> He plays and waves his paw,
> All, all the gold in the womb
> Of the earth dances!
>
> "Animus"

Just as angels could suddenly trumpet in the veins, here the life-blood pumping through the veins carries the platelet of redemption to the heart.

Shvarts's metaphor of the heart under siege becomes quite concrete in a number of poems where the heart's inhabitants take their place amid larger edifices. The body that houses them is no

longer merely a body but a church ("Kak budto ia stala sama /
miagkoiu beloiu tserkov'iu" [As if I myself had become / a soft
white church] [*Trudy*, 44]), or even a city. And like churches and
cities, the heart is vulnerable to siege:

> Ia—gorod, i ploshchad', i rynok,
> I mesto dlia tikhikh progulok
> Dlia peripatetikov—dukhov,
> I angel'skii teatr, i sad.
> Ia—gorod, ia—kroshechnyi gorod
> Velikoi Imperii. Ostrov
> V zelenykh moriakh vinograda.
> No chto tak stuchat barabany?
> Vragi podstupili. Osada! . . .
>
> "Chudishche" *(Trudy,* 47)

> I am a city, and a square, and a market,
> And a place for quiet walks
> For peripatetic souls,
> And an angelic theater, and a garden.
> I am a city, I am a tiny city
> Of a Great Empire. An island
> In green seas of grapes.
> But why are drums pounding so?
> Enemies have approached. A siege! . . .
>
> "The Monster"

The heart will be safe only when the poet succeeds in constructing a holy city within, where she can harbor all the sufferings of
the world, having already accepted the agony and ecstasy this
task entails: ". . . i vystroiu v techen'i dolgikh zim / vnutrigrudnoi
Erusalim" (And I shall build over the course of long winters / a
Jerusalem within my breast [*Tantsuiushchii David*, 69]).

"The Monster" helps to clarify Lavinia's relation to the male
despoilers of her heart. In a departure from traditional depiction,
Shvarts portrays woman as the builder of cities, who becomes in

this capacity the guardian of civilization as well as the keeper of the spiritual realm. The barbarian at the gates appears as "the Demon of Temptation," a masculine enemy against whom woman must defend herself and all of womankind. After a fierce battle, woman vanquishes the enemy, emerging "sensitive" and whole, though battered. This poem argues for the multiformity of woman's interior world and her fortitude in protecting it.

While the female heart can contain much of the universe, it continually seeks to encompass more. Simultaneously and paradoxically, it is both a microcosm of the universe and only one small part of it. In expressing the heart's desire to merge fully with the surrounding world, many of Shvarts's poems evince alienation and, in this respect, a highly contemporary consciousness, even when they are set in ancient Rome. Plagued by skepticism and estrangement, Shvarts's personae long to find a place in the natural order of things. They undergo marvelous metamorphoses to grow closer to the natural world, becoming shaggy with fur like a bear or prickly with sedge grass. One of the most complete metamorphoses transforms the poet into a mythical flowering beast. By allowing the human body to experience nonhuman forms, all of these transformations are a way of growing closer to God and Creation. As a wise Greek explains to Cynthia, "the soul is a plant" that eternally transforms itself (*Tantsuiushchii David*, 67). Shvarts implies that the transformations, in turn, will lead to transfiguration.

Trees particularly are kindred to the soul. Their kinship is based on the fundamentally cruciform shape of both human and tree, which suggests that both can endure suffering but also experience redemption. An apple tree follows Lavinia to prayer, her sister in suffering. The tree, in its heartwood, endures loneliness and cold, as does Lavinia in her heart. But epiphany occurs with the promise of the tree's blossoming: "Ty skoro rastsvetesh' tsvetami miagkimi, / Gde krestik zolotoi vnutri kachaetsia" (Soon you will blossom with soft flowers / where the small gold cross within sways [*Trudy* 80]). This blossoming represents the exaltation of spiritual transfiguration. Like the apple tree, Lavinia will blossom once she is blessed with heavenly grace.

One of Shvarts's most provocative poems implies that grace is
easier for women to attain than for men, since women, in becoming mothers, are endowed with automatic purity of heart.

Ia otvedala odnazhdy
moloka moei podrugi,
moloka moei sestry—
ne dlia utolen´ia zhazhdy,
a dlia vol´nosti dushi.
Ona vyzhala iz grudi
levoi v chashku moloko,
i ono v prostoi posude
pelo, penilos´ legko.
Ono pakhlo chem-to ptich´im,
chem-to vol´chim i ovech´im,
bol´she vechnym, chem Put´ Mlechnyi,
bylo teplym i gustym.
Tak kogda-to doch´ v pustyne
starika-otsa poila,
stav i mater´iu emu,
siloi etoi blagostyni
v kolybel´ grob prevratila,
beliznoi prognala t´mu.
Iz protoka vozle serdtsa
napoila ty menia,
ne vampir ia—oi li uzhas—
ono penilos´, zvenia,
sladkim, teplym, vechnym, miagkim,
vremia v ugol vspiat´ tesnia.
          "Vospominanie o strannom ugoshchenii"
                    (*Tantsuiushchii David,* 13)

One day I tasted
the milk of my friend,
the milk of my sister—
not to quench my thirst,

but for freedom of the soul.
From her left breast she squeezed
milk into a cup,
And in the simple vessel
it sang and lightly foamed.
It smelled of something birdlike,
something wolflike, something sheeplike,
more eternal than the Milky Way,
it was warm and thick.
Thus a daughter in the desert
once nursed her old father,
becoming a mother to him,
by force of this benefaction
she turned coffin into cradle,
and banished the dark with whiteness.
From the duct near your heart
you nursed me,
I am no vampire—oh horrors—
it foamed, ringing,
sweet, warm, eternal, soft,
crowding time back into a corner.
                    "Memory of a Strange Refreshment"

    This poem is a paean to woman's ability to nurture selflessly,
whether a child, a father, or a friend. Yet to make her point about
lovingkindness, Shvarts does not settle for a gentle metaphor;
rather, she describes quite literally the sustenance her friend provides, engaging all of the reader's senses: we taste the milk, feel
its warmth, smell its odor, see its whiteness, and hear it ringing in
the cup. Shvarts goes on to evoke the astral imagery of the Milky
Way to emphasize that this sort of selfless love is eternal: time
recedes into a meaningless concept. And in comparing her
friend's milk to birds and beasts, Shvarts alludes to the deep,
underlying bonds between woman and her universe. With its
strong and regular trochaic beat, "Memory of a Strange Refresh-
ment" is atypical of Shvarts's verse. This characteristic, coupled

with the poem's images of purity, intensifies the sense that this is really a strange lullaby, intended to comfort and reassure. And indeed, by partaking of her friend's milk—by sharing sisterly love—the poet gains freedom for her soul. Shvarts treats the subject of motherhood in an entirely new way, without the slightest sentimentality, even as she touts the power of love and the possibility of liberation it offers. Despite the absence of an avowed feminist stance, Shvarts shows herself to be a strong woman's poet.

While those who partake of maternal or sisterly love can experience a kind of redemption, not all women are able to play the role of madonna so easily; certainly not a worldly woman like Cynthia, who is more concerned with lovers than mates, and certainly not a nun like Lavinia, who must work hard to tame her passions, especially at night, when she is visited by demons who try to inflame her desire. These are the kinds of women who interest Shvarts the most, for she does not seek easy solutions. Shvarts is most engaged—and her poetry most engaging—when she grapples with physical or emotional struggle. And since redemption is meaningful only when it is earned with the heart's blood, the heart becomes the battleground where these conflicts are played out.

In her struggle to overcome the vestiges of worldly life, Lavinia endures severe trials, which ultimately impart strength. From an elderly nun she learns that the only way truly to purify oneself is to circumcise the heart, in the process experiencing anguish. But anguish brings insight. In one striking poem Lavinia swallows something sharp in her soup. This foreign object pricks and torments her so greatly that she seeks the advice of a venerated nun, who tells her:

> V obrezannoe serdtse l'etsia Zhizn',
> Liubov' i dukh, i tsarstvie, i sila,
> A chto-to kolet—pliun' i veselis'.
>
> "Staritsa" (*Trudy,* 76)

Into a circumcised heart pours Life,
Love and the spirit, and the kingdom, and strength,

> And if something pricks—spit and rejoice.
>
> "The Elderly Nun"

Elena Shvarts's power as a poet is linked with this same ability to experience dread and deliverance. The poetic eye, at one moment "bound to . . . Divinity," at the next hangs limply "by a bloody thread." Yet this violent emotional tightrope enables the poet to experience "all the pain and glory of the world" (*Tantsuiushchii David,* 7). Engaged in a continual balancing act, she attempts to find a foothold that will allow her to feel secure but not complacent. To a considerable degree the poet's trials and successes represent those of her gender at large, and by reading Shvarts, we can come closer to understanding our own missteps and gambles in the world and finding a formula for equilibrium.

Notes

1. The *Oxford English Dictionary* gives this definition for the figurative meaning of "circumcision": "Spiritual purification by, as it were, cutting away sin." Cf. Rom. 2:29: "Circumcision is that of the heart, in the spirit, and not in the letter." Shvarts uses this verse as one of the epigraphs for *The Works and Days of Lavinia.*

2. In this connection it is interesting to note two poems by male poets that treat the self as a microcosmic entity. In Velimir Khlebnikov's "I and Russia," the body is a country complete with cities, buildings, and residents. Nikolai Zabolotskii, in his long poem "The Trees," sees man as "a tower of birds, / a receptacle of shaggy beasts."

3. This agitation is quite unlike the more regular beating of another heart seized by coldness. Cf. Akhmatova's "Serdtse b'etsia rovno, merno" ("The heart beats evenly, rhythmically").

References

Shvarts, Elena. *Stikhi.* [Poems.] Leningrad: Beseda, 1987.

———. *Tantsuiushchii David.* [The Dancing David.] New York: Russica, 1985.

———. *Trudy i dni Lavinii, monakhinii iz ordena obrezaniia serdtsa (Ot Rozhdestva do Paskhi).* [The Works and Days of Lavinia, a Nun of the Order of the Circumcision of the Heart (from Christmas to Easter).] Ann Arbor, MI: Ardis, 1987.

13

REFLECTIONS, CROOKED MIRRORS, MAGIC THEATERS
Tat'iana Tolstaia's "Peters"

John R. Givens

In a 1989 interview, Tat'iana Tolstaia confirms what is abundantly clear in her prose: language has power.

> Language has existed before us; we are born into language. Language is wiser than we are. . . . Language contains all the ready concepts for the thoughts we come to only later. We think for a year and then find a form of expression: that form was already there in language. Language is an amazing thing: we must approach it with a certain amount of trepidation. . . . (Barta 268)

It is precisely Tolstaia's amazing use of language that has catapulted her to her present height in the Russian literary firmament. While critics were lamenting the death of artistry and of thematic and formal resourcefulness in Soviet prose of the 1970s and early 1980s, Tolstaia and other writers loosely associated with "alternative" or "artistic" prose (*al'ternativnaia, artisticheskaia proza*) were quietly restoring preeminence to the *word* in Russian fiction. Among recent Russian writers it is Tolstaia, however, who has most profoundly explored the creative possibilities offered by the full exposition of the word in artistic utterance. Her "regard for the word," the "accumulation, motion and interdependencies" of her words, and the "almost physical enjoyment" that arises from following them has distinguished Tolstaia in the eyes of critics in Russia and abroad.[1]

Tolstaia's intricate, highly crafted prose, in which the author's and her characters' speech intrude upon each other in often unattributable ways, is famous and, by now, well documented.[2] Reading Tolstaia, we enter into a world of changing tone, nuance, and style, where every comma, hyphen, question mark, or exclamation point is a landmark on the horizon of authorial intention, where common parlance and poetic diction coexist and the author-narrator often cavorts secretly with her drab protagonists in a prose of explosive color. In the world of Tolstaia—and that of her characters—everything depends upon resonance and echo, hidden structures and mutually illuminating inner reflections. "Peters," the story that, in Henry Gifford's words, "alerted the public to Tolstaia's significance" (3), not only offers one of the best examples of the workings of Tolstaia's dense poetics but also works as a key of sorts to Tolstaia's world, a world in which individuals are caught up in the illusions, distortions, ironies, and creative tensions of self-renewing life.

According to Helena Goscilo, the appearance of "Peters" in *Novyi mir* in 1986 was "a major cultural event," firmly establishing Tolstaia's reputation as an exciting new author located outside "mainstream contemporary Soviet fiction" (281). "Peters" has been called "one of Tolstaia's best novellas" (Piskunov and Piskunova 194), singled out for praise even by critics unsympathetic to Tolstaia.[3] The reasons for the universal appeal of "Peters" are complex and stem in part from its title character. Told in an intricate style of shifting and contrasting narrative voices, "Peters" depicts, in episodes, the life from childhood to adulthood of a person on the fringe of normal social discourse. This person, Tolstaia's Peters, never succeeds in establishing meaningful contact with his fellow human beings and finds happiness only when he gives up his dreams and lets life play its games without him. In a way, Tolstaia's creation mirrors the subjects of much of nineteenth-century Russian literature. In his hostile relationship with Leningrad itself, Peters calls to mind Evgenii's clash with Petersburg in Pushkin's *Bronze Horseman*. There is a little of Gogol''s Akakii Akakievich in him, as well as some of Dostoevskii's marginal types. The consequences of Peters's sheltered childhood and overly protective grandmother seem to be distant reflections of the fate of Goncharov's Oblomov. Indeed, these affinities with nineteenth-century Russian literature perhaps endow "Peters" with qualities more immediately accessible to the Russian imagination, thereby accounting for some of the story's pronounced effect on the Russian reading public. Despite these echoes of Russian literary history, however, much more seems to be at work in "Peters."

As might be expected, the further-reaching effects of the story have everything to do with the word; that is, language. In "Peters," after all, Tolstaia tells the story of a person who is constantly thwarted by language. Moreover, an interesting intersection occurs in the story between Tolstaia's need to communicate her text to the world and Peters's need to communicate with his fellow human beings within that text. As his thoughts, fantasies, and perceptions displace the narration, and as other characters' speech is filtered through his discourse within the narration, Peters assumes almost equal footing with Tolstaia's narrator (who may or may not be Tolstaia herself). As the narrator and Peters blend, their goals similarly coincide: both want to break through to an "other"—another human being, a reader. Tolstaia confirmed the importance of such contact in an interview the same year "Peters" was published:

> For me, creative work is an attempt to overcome my own loneliness, to get through to others [*probit'sia k drugim*]. If you stubbornly dig your well, chisel the rock face with hope in the darkness, one way or another you'll come out into the light. I understand creative work to be a self-absorption [*samouglublenie*], a self-immersion [*samopogruzhenie*] that leads not into empty subterranean corridors but to some sort of depth, accessible to everyone. It is at this depth that a special magical contact occurs, a selfless exchange of gifts. (Taroshchina 7)[4]

In such a context, the act of creating—*tvorchestvo*—becomes a means of deliverance from isolation. It also serves as a palliative of sorts for such isolation. The writer is provided solace in composition. The writing endows its unlikely subject—in this case, Peters—with the bright colors of a wonderful life. At the same time, some communication is achieved, the evidence for which is the written text in the hands of the reader. Language, then, assumes a role of heightened importance in Tolstaia's story, for it not only enables the writer to communicate her fiction but also gives voice to the fictions created in Peters's mind.

By consciously exploiting the creative potential of language in a story about a person who is constantly defeated by language, Tolstaia establishes a unique paradox. As paradoxes tend to be, this one is revealing. We, as readers of Tolstaia's fiction, discover the saving possibilities of language even as we read in Peters and his fictions the warning that language itself is not to blame for our miswielding of it. Language may be the repository for all the ready-made concepts for our utterances, yet we still need to choose the suitable utterance at the right time. The ability to do so unerringly distinguishes the artist; the inability to do so at all reveals the social outcast.

If we let these considerations guide our reading of "Peters," we will see how language simultaneously haunts Tolstaia's protagonist even as Tolstaia herself exploits its rich expressive possibilities to inform not only "Peters" but her philosophy of writing as a whole.[5]

Peters's name offers the first clue to the workings of language in the story. Peters is "Peters" and not "Petr" because of his grandmother's wish that he learn German. The *s* (short for *sudar'*, or "sir") is appended to "Peter" because as a child Peters finds that presenting himself in a way that was adopted in the nineteenth century as a sign of respect is endearing and amusing. That the childish nickname sticks with him as an adult marks him linguistically as an oddity. Peters seems doomed from the beginning to discomfort or dysfunction within his own language. Burdened with a foreign name, he experiences a foreigner's linguistic isolation. Part of the problem is that the ridiculous nickname impedes Peters's healthy maturation into an adult. Indeed, the connection between his impaired language and his incomplete maturation is most tellingly chronicled in Peters's disastrous attempts to elicit the attention of the opposite sex. The incredible ineptness of Peters's real-life utterances in such instances contrasts sharply with the rich verbal fabric of his imagination, communicated through quasi-direct discourse in a syntactically and grammatically freighted prose. The disparity between Peters's language in the "real" world and that of his fantasy world naturally originates in his childhood, the time when language is acquired.

The child Peters is raised by his grandmother, who tightly controls his home environment. We learn that his mother has run away to warmer climes with a scoundrel and that his father, who takes no interest in him, spends his time with "easy women" (*zhenshchiny legkogo povedeniia* [170]). Listening to the adults, Peters imagines the scoundrel to be "a black man sitting under a banana tree," and, owing to his childish confusion as to the dual meaning of the word *legkii* ("easy" and "light"), he fantasizes a visit from his father and his *legkie* women, who, being "light," would actually fly in the air (170).

From his earliest thoughts about his father's *legkie* women, the life of the imagination becomes for Peters a means of coping with the harsh realities of life. Peters's first fantasies as an adult concern imagined trysts with future lovers. They are filtered in the narrative through Peters's eyes, and are rendered in a language that both betrays Peters's quasi-direct intrusion into the narration and reflects the fine-tuned workings of his well-developed fantasy life. Peters imagines reading Schiller in German to his lover as a prelude to kisses, tears, and the dawn, as in Fet's poem "Shepot, robkoe dykhan'e, treli solov'ia."[6] Significantly, however, Peters chooses to communicate with his lover in a foreign language and uses a verbless Russian poem to capture the essence of his tryst. The possibility for communication is accordingly hampered. Peters himself admits that the lover is not even supposed to know German.[7] Furthermore, Fet's verbless poem seems to foreshadow not only Peters's inability to overcome his passivity (verbs = action) but also his difficulty forming Russian verbs later in the story.[8] It is no wonder that none of Peters's dates turn out well, even in his imagination.

In the last of these imagined trysts, Peters's voice intrudes into the text for the first time in utterances not set off by quotation marks, but reported in the first person singular. "I mozhet byt' dazhe zhenius'" and such colloquial expressions as "A chto?" and "Nu i chto takogo?" mark Peters's new and direct involvement in the narration. In other imagined encounters with Faina and Valentina, Peters is also present within the narration, his utterances often not marked typographically. Phrases such as "ostav'te ee mne" (174) and "stisnu zuby i poidu naprolom . . . Pridu—uznaiu. . . . Proshchai Valentina . . . " (181) pepper the text, as do phrases whose *tone* indicates Peters's presence in the narration ("Khoroshee mesto!" [181], "Nu chto zhe. Inache i byt' ne moglo" [182], and so on).

Indirect reflections of Peters's perceptions recur in the text just as often as do direct intrusions into it that betray Peters's presence. A bad dream Peters has provides a good example.

> Sleep came and invited him into its trapdoors and corridors, named meetings on secret staircases, locked doors and rebuilt familiar buildings, frightening him with closets, bimbos, bubonic sores, black tambourines; it led him down dark passages and pushed him into a stuffy room where, behind a table, shaggy and smirking, twiddling his thumbs, there sat the expert in many bad things.
>
> Peters thrashed about in his sheets, begged for forgiveness, and, forgiven this time, again sank down to the bottom until morning, all tangled up in the reflections of the crooked mirrors of a magic theater. (173)

The Russian alliteration and assonance of Peters's dream are striking: "pugaia chulanami, babami, chumnymi bubonami, chernymi bubnami, bystro vel po temnym perekhodom." The plosives and hushers combine to create a rocking, whispered pitch that vividly evokes Peters's nightmare encounter with the "expert in many bad things." This verbal display is maintained in the next paragraph: "bilsia v prostyniakh, prosil proshcheniia, i, proshchennyi na etot raz, pogruzhalsia . . . putaias'. . . ." For Tolstaia (and for Peters; after all, it is *his* dream), language—the text, the levels of narrative discourse, character speech—becomes the crooked mirror in which we are shown the reflections of a magic theater: the world of dreams, hopes, and life itself.

Like a crooked mirror, language—art—is necessarily a distortion, an approximation of intent. Tolstaia in a 1991 interview explains that just as the smallest of our intents can never be realized exactly as we imagine, so our larger expectations are also, of necessity, either over- or underfulfilled, usually the latter. Daily errands, work, career plans, the text of a story turn out in ways we do not expect. According to Tolstaia, this "state of expectation" (*sostoianie ozhidaniia*) is precisely what makes up "the drama of life" ("eto i est' drama chelovecheskoi zhizni").[9] The disparity between expectation and realization torments Peters, whose every dream seems to fail him, although the language in which these failures are communicated is ever pregnant with poetic possibilities.

Indeed, the "distortions" of Tolstaia's crooked mirror are often quite beautiful. It is not surprising that submerged poems surface within the story, as if attesting to the sustained tension between the poetry of the text and the prose of its subject. Let us consider the following passage.

> They were celebrating New Year's at work. Peters bustled about, cutting out paper snowflakes the size of saucers and pasting them onto the library windows. He hung pink tinsel, became tangled up in its metallic rain, in his dreams and desires, while Christmas tree lights were reflected in his screwed-up eyes. It smelled of fir and horseradish. Snow drifted into the crack of the window. (174)

Here the hazy skeleton of a poem emerges from out of the poetic narrative, where whole lines have their own inner meter and rhyme:[10]

> 1 bumazhnye snezhinki razmerom s bliudtse
> 2 nakleival ikh na bibliotechnye okna

3 razveshival rozovuiu mishuru
4 putalsia v metallicheskom dozhde
5 putalsia v mechtakh i zhelaniiakh
6 malen'kie elochnye lampochki
7 pakhlo khvoei i khrenom
8 v otkrytuiu fortochku nametalo snezhnuiu krupku

Sounds are repeated and resound in rhythm, incidental rhyme
occurs (lines 1 and 2), one phrase echoes another's linguistic and
grammatical structure (see especially lines 4 and 5), and words and
syllables find their mirror images reflected within the same phrase
(notice the *mal-lam* opposition of line 6). These echoes and reflections are, of course, central to the poetics of the text, whose style
reproduces not only the distorting qualities of mirrors but also those
of the imagination and human expectations. Moreover, the poetic
quality of the prose, the inner reflections of sounds and letters also
mirror the entangled narration, in which the narrator's voice is har-
monized with those of Peters and others who enter the text.

Armed with such knowledge, we can better sort out and appreciate the individual voices of the narration, as when Peters overhears a conversation between two girls.

> The girls were gabbing about love, of course, and Peters over-
> heard the story of one Irochka, who had been going out with a
> comrade from brotherly Yemen, or maybe Kuwait, with the idea of
> marrying him. Irochka had heard that over there, in the sandy steppes
> of the Arab countries, oil was as plentiful as berries and any decent
> man was a millionaire and flew his own plane with a golden john. It
> was this golden john that drove Irochka nuts. She had grown up in
> the Yaroslav district where the lady's room was three walls with an
> open fourth looking out onto a pea field—the kind of "expansive
> landscape" of Repin's paintings. But the Arab wasn't itching to get
> hitched, and when Irochka hit him up, he said something like "And
> wouldn't you like one upside the head!" and so forth, and he threw
> her and all her shabby belongings out. (179–80)

Suddenly the language of the narration becomes extremely conversational. In the span of four sentences we encounter more

words and expressions indicative of conversational speech
(*razgovornaia rech'*) than in the entire story up to this point:
*shchebetat', nekii, kadrit', slikhat', nefti—kak kliukvi, muzhik,
svodit' s uma, zhenit'sia ne chesat'sia, postavit' vopros rebrom,
a po kha ne kho, privet tete, ubogie shmotki.* We understand,
however, that this change in language is entirely appropriate.
After all, we are hearing the girls' conversation as it is filtered
through Peters's perceptions. Peters obviously does not talk this
way. His voice, marked by the participle clauses and involved
syntax that inhere in the language of his fancy, reenters the narration immediately after the reported conversation.

> The girls didn't notice Peters and he listened and pitied this un-
> known Irochka and he imagined first those Yaroslav expanses of pea
> fields, bordered [*opushennye*] on the horizon by dark, wolfish for-
> ests, thawing [*taiushchimi*] under the blue brightness of the northern
> sun, then the dry rustle of millions of grains of sand, the turgid
> pressure of a desert storm, the brown light filtering through the mor-
> tal murk, the forgotten [*zabytye*] white palaces, covered [*zanesennye*]
> by the deadly dust or bewitched [*zakoldovannye*] by long-dead
> [*davno-umershimi*] wizards. (180)

Language, then, is exploited on many levels in the story. Even
if we disregard the textual play of language embedded in "Peters," the story's plot itself raises language as an issue. After all,
Peters pins many of his hopes on learning German as a means of
finally communicating with the opposite sex. Time and again he
laments not knowing the language.

> Ah, if only he had studied German when he had the chance! Oh,
> then, probably. . . Oh, then, of course. . . Such a difficult language, it
> lisps and smacks and rustles in the mouth, O Tannenbaum!, no one,
> probably, even really knows it. . . . But Peters would learn it and
> amaze his amour. . . . (177)

But Peters's expectations are too high. His own Russian language, divorced from the embellishment of his imagination and
forced into a real-world utterance, fails him, and, in a revealing

fashion, dooms his plans to learn German before he even makes it to his tutor's apartment. Peters sets off for his first tutorial with Elizaveta Frantsevna, vowing: "No ia napriagus; ia pobediu! . . . Pobediu. Pobezhdu. Pobezhu" (But I'll put my back into it! I'll concur it! Conquer. Concur. Conquur [180–81]). His difficulty in trying to conjugate the verb *pobedit'* (to conquer, master), which cannot be conjugated in the first person singular, foreshadows his failure to learn German—indeed, his failure to communicate meaningfully at all in the real world. His "Pobediu. Pobezhdu. Pobezhu," while covering all of the linguistically logical variants, is nonetheless nonsense.

If language fails Peters in the real world, however, it rescues him in his imagination. Although not explicitly attributed to Peters, the language that conveys Peters's flights of fancy—language bursting with participles and intricate subordinate clauses—is certainly a linguistic reflection of his mental processes and is correspondingly dependent upon Peters for its coloring, tone, and final form. In those passages communicating the workings of Peters's imagination the author's speech intersects with the character's. The language of the story suddenly wholly belongs neither to the narrator proper (be she Tolstaia or some other persona) nor to Peters. When Faina, for instance, waves a mitten at Peters, his imagination is fired in a poetic tribute:

> In his ears there beat festive bells and his eyes were suddenly opened to the previously unforeseeable. All roads led to Faina, all winds trumpeted her glory, cried out her dark name and flew off above steep slate roofs, above towers and spires, snaked into snowy plaits and flung themselves at her feet. All of the city, all the islands—the waters and the shores, the statues and the gardens, the bridges and the gratings, the wrought-iron roses and horses—everything flowed into a ring, weaving a thunderous winter wreath for his beloved. (175)

We realize that this poetic text, though it reflects Peters's feelings, is not his direct speech. A shift in narration occurs that marks this passage linguistically as quasi-direct discourse.

In this regard, anthropomorphisms, which are frequently encountered in Tolstaia's prose, become especially important in "Peters," as they serve to betray the intrusion of Peters's perceptions into the text. The evening Peters finds out what Faina really thinks of him, for example, is described as "consumptive" (*chakhotochnyi* [175]). One spring day Peters watches the wind "build, change, rebuild" Valentina's hair-do (177). The posted handbills advertising Peters's desire to learn German have fluttering "pseudopods" (*lozhnonozhki* [177]). The autumnal Leningrad weather repays Peters's hatred of it by spitting on him with icy spray from thundering rooftops, spouting a colorless stream of dark water in his eyes, sticking especially deep and wet puddles under his feet, and whipping him with rainy blows to his face and body (178). Clammy buildings stumble across Peters at night and the wind dances tuberculosis-threatening figure 8s around his wet feet (178). In each instance, the narration, channeled through Peters's unique optic lens, incorporates those peculiarities of perception that belong to Peters himself.

But Peters's imagination does more than simply distort. It also lets him slip invisibly into other people's lives, as in the conversation he overhears in the restaurant:

> The girls turned to the story of the complex relations between Ol'ia and Valerii, about shameless Aniuta, and Peters, sipping bullion, pricked up his ears and, invisible, entered into this other person's story. He brushed up against somebody's secrets, even stood, holding his breath, at the very door of those secrets. He sensed, smelled, and felt everything as in a magic cinema. Maddeningly close—just stretch out your hand—were glimpses of faces, tears in wounded eyes, explosions of smiles, sun in hair causing green and rose sparks, dust in sunbeams and the heat of warmed parquet squeaking nearby in this other, happy and real life. (180)

Here, through the "magic cinema" (*volshebnoe kino*) of his fancy, Peters participates in "real life" (*zhivaia zhizn'*). Like the "magic theater" of his dreams and its crooked mirrors, this magic cinema embellishes "real" life, simultaneously transforming its

prose into the poetry of art. When the two girls leave the restaurant, for instance, they float out (*vyplyli*) into the rain and rise
into the heavens, their transparent umbrellas a sign of "another,
higher existence" (180). The waitress rushes by Peters's table
like a desert sandstorm (a perception that is beautifully consistent
with the workings of Peters's imagination—he has just been
thinking about desert storms and Yemen); she snatches twenty
dirty plates in one smooth motion and then "dissolves into the
air" (180). Indeed, as if in a painting by Chagall, people throughout the story are dissolving, floating or flying away, fluttering in
and out of buildings, or are being carried away on the wind. Even
Elizaveta Frantsevna floats like a seal or water nymph, "legko
bormochushchaia na sumrachnom germanskom narechii" (181).
According to the logic of Peters's imagination and its appropriation of the narrative, it is entirely fitting that Frantsevna float
"like a water nymph" (*undinoi* [181]). After all, the word already
has a German connotation for Peters because of his earlier imagined reading of Schiller, in which, at least for Peters, dark oaks
and water nymphs abound. Also, Frantsevna is easily/lightly
(*legko*) mumbling German. She floats because, in Peters's mind,
there is some permanent semantic confusion between the two
meanings of *legkost'*.

These intersections between authorial speech and Peters's
quasi-direct narrative discourse prepare us for Peters's important
encounter with the "butterfly-girl" (*devochka-motylek*), an event
that provides the climactic crisis in the story. In this encounter,
Peters's language discomfort and dysfunction reach their peak of
intensity. En route to Frantsevna's apartment, Peters stops by a
restaurant for a cocktail and appetizers. Peters's assessment of
the place—*khoroshee mesto,* repeated three times (once with an
exclamation point, once with an added *khoroshee*)—announces
his quasi-appropriation of narrative discourse. Indeed, it is after
his last *khoroshee, khoroshee mesto* that the *chudnaia peri,* the
letuchii tsvetok, appears *pod loktem ego. . . iz vozdukha* (181–82).
Through Peters's eyes we see her red-green dress as an explosion
of tiny flames, her eyelashes as tiny, fluttering wings. This ethe-

real creature (Peters calls her an "angel" [182]) is yet another of Peters's floating, heavenly visions, and Peters, naturally, is initially scared of frightening it away. More to the point, Peters is *afraid to begin talking* ("On makhnul, chtoby dali eshche rozovogo spirta, *boias' zagovorit'*" [182; my emphasis]). Speaking, of course, would shatter his vision. More precisely, Peters's real-world utterance—divorced from the rich linguistic environment of his dreams and expectations—would fall incredibly short of his hopes.

This lingual catastrophe, however, proves inevitable. Indeed, Peters's very first utterance is framed by a pair of vision-dooming, throat-clearing "ahems" (*kkhem*) and does not move beyond mention of his childhood bunny or German lessons. Moreover, no real communication takes place between Peters and his "peri," who leaves after tricking him out of his wallet. We realize here, of course, that Peters's "angel" is no more ethereal than his father's "floating women," indeed, is one and the same: a *zhenshchina legkogo povedeniia*—a prostitute. Peters's expectations are crushed by the leaden weight of his own tied tongue. While others float away, he remains marooned on earth. Life flows around him like "an impetuous flood around a heavy pile of rocks" (180).

As might be expected, the disparity between Peters's expectations of a wonderful life and his actual situation finds its resonance in the repetition of the phrase *prekrasnaia zhizn'* itself. Tolstaia chose *prekrasnaia zhizn'* as the original title not only of "Peters" but also of her collection *"On the Golden Porch"* (*"Na zolotom kryl'tse sideli . . . ,"* 1987). Against her wishes, however, Tolstaia's editors changed the title.[11] The phrase plays an interesting role in the story, where it occurs three times. Despite its ironic tone in a tale that in many respects chronicles a life that is anything but "wonderful," the phrase does not seem to mock Peters's dreams, self-delusions, or misperceptions. Rather, it underscores the more universal inequality commonly perceived between what we expect and what we get.

The phrase first occurs when Peters, as a child, emerges from the confines of his grandmother's apartment to go to a New Year's party—his first contact with other children. Peters can hardly contain his excitement. He rushes to make friends—"a wonderful life was beginning" (*nachinalas' prekrasnaia zhizn'* [171]). He meets a girl with warts and follows devotedly at her heels until she abandons him, at which point he starts running in circles and screaming. The exhilaration of his "wonderful life," however, is crushed when his grandmother hustles him home, away from "contaminating" contact with other children.

Peters continues to anticipate his "wonderful life" as an adult. And indeed, it comes again. After his setback with Faina, a "new spring" comes when Peters becomes attracted to the "small, shamelessly young" Valentina (*malen'kaia bezbozhnaia molodaia* [177]). Life, Peters thinks, is wonderful again (*zhizn' prekrasna* [178]). Indeed, as with the girl with warts, Peters follows childlike at Valentina's heels (*po piatam*). The incongruity, however, between Peters—now older and as flabby as ever—and *prekrasnaia Valentina* (179)—whose youth the text constantly emphasizes (*bezbozhnaia molodaia, takaia molodaia, bystraia i molodaia*) and whom *iunoshi* (youths) constantly attend—dooms Peters's expectations from the start. Standing in a downpour, waiting to present Valentina a bouquet of flowers, Peters understands that it is "stupid and too late to study German, that wonderful Valentina, raised among sporty, springy youths, would only laugh and step right through him," and that "fiery passions and light steps, fast dances and jumps" are "not for him in this world" (179). At this turning point Peters simultaneously gives up the German language (symbolic of his attempts to contact the opposite sex) and Valentina (who is a symbol of the unattainable "wonderful life"). Girls who are literally bouncing with life are incompatible with Peters, whose grandmother forbids him to jump and shout as a child and who is too "heavy and wide in the waist" (179) as an adult. Indeed, disillusioned by the impossibility of a relationship with Valentina, Peters completes the parallel between his past experience with the girl with warts and his present failure with Valentina by thinking despairingly that he should have just "married his own grandmother and quietly rotted away" (179).

Life is *prekrasnaia* only for other children and only at the end of the story, when Peters realizes that it simply goes on with or without him. New children replace old adults. Life begins again and each new childhood is filled with promise. It is only Peters's childhood that does not turn out, only Peters who is trapped in the failure of childhood games.

Indeed, the one childhood game that most specifically links Peters with both linguistic dysfunction and an incapacity to form sexual relationships is the card game Black Peter (*Chernyi Peter*). The game is taught to Peters by his grandmother and involves collecting animals into male and female pairs in order to learn their German names. Only the cat, Black Peter, has no mate, and anyone left holding him at the end of the game is the loser. Peters, of course, often ends up with the black cat, who becomes his enigmatic namesake. With his strange German name, he is almost pre-ordained to be life's Black Peter, the card without a mate. Here Tolstaia makes the connection in Peters's mind between the German language and successful courtship explicit. The consequences for Peters's healthy sexual development are severe.

Language, as we have seen, can be distorted. Peters's childish understanding of the German language translates into his childish understanding of the most perplexing of adult games— courtship. Peters's inability to succeed in real-life matchmaking is emphasized by the childish turns of his adult reasoning. His plea to Faina's imagined fiancé employs such childish logic.

> . . . Leave Faina, leave her to me. What's it to you? You can find somebody else, you know how. But I don't. My mama ran away with a scoundrel, Papa is floating in the sky with blue women, Grandmother ate up Grandfather with rice porridge, ate up my childhood, my only childhood, and little girls with warts don't want to sit on the couch with me. Give me at least *something,* huh? (174)

Unsuccessful attempts at suicide and wild thoughts of murder grimly underscore both Peters's amorous failures and the seriousness of his language dysfunction. The suicide attempt after his unrealized affair with Faina is thwarted because the gas in the stove with which Peters intends to kill himself has been shut off. His humiliation and impotence are complete. The murder of his German tutor that Peters fleetingly considers after the robbery by the prostitute is meant to avenge all of his unsuccessful relationships with women. Peters's vow to kill Frantsevna on behalf of "all the . . . tonguetied and incoherent" (*vsekh . . . kosnoiazychnykh i bestolkovykh*) directly links his sexual deficiency with language inadequacy.

As we have seen, Peters's language inadequacy has its roots in his childhood. His grandmother haunts all of his adult relationships with other women. Indeed, Peters's idea of murdering Frantsevna can be viewed as an attempt to avoid the quasi-oedipal relationship with his grandmother that he fears is his lot. If Black Peter, the German lessons, and his stuffed bunny are the childhood baggage that fatally encumber Peters as an adult, then his grandmother, as provider of such baggage, is the one figure Peters must excise from his life before he can achieve adult independence. By wanting to kill Frantsevna (who is a *bystraia zavitaia babul'ka* [184]), Peters reveals a death wish against his grandmother, confirming his desire to gain his freedom from her at last. Such freedom, however, is not easily purchased. The idea of killing Frantsevna passes as quickly as it came and in the end Peters indeed fulfills his quasi-oedipal destiny by marrying a "cold, hard woman with big legs" who, like his grandmother, leads him around by the hand (185).

With the appearance of the woman with big legs, the story quickly concludes. The grandmother/wife, who soon leaves him, seems to fulfill only one function in the story: the total negation of Peters's "wonderful life." Under her watchful eye Peters figuratively dismantles the dreams and expectations of his childhood by cutting up a "chicken-youth" (*kurinyi-iunosha* [185]) that she buys for dinner. In cutting up the chicken, Peters erases all memory that it was born, fluttered its young wings, and dreamed of a cock's comb, and now would never know green grass, pearly grain, golden dawns, and the "happy round eye of a girlfriend" (185–86): all in all, a striking evocation of Peters's own unhappy biography.

At this point in the story, it is obvious that Tolstaia's verbal web is spinning itself out. No overt moral is offered up. No conclusive ending is presented. Complaints that Tolstaia either cannot write endings[12] or that they are "tacked on"[13] arise precisely because Tolstaia often chooses not to end her stories with a bang. "Peters" especially ends on an ambiguous note—either in the middle of Peters's reawakening to life or at the end of his utter resignation to its "cruel games." The threefold repetition of *prekrasnaia* at the end of the story is possibly ironic, perhaps life-affirming, or maybe only an indicator of a child's simple repetition of words. The last notion offers intriguing possibilities for interpretation. The final narrational utterance of the story is certainly delivered through Peters's quasi-direct discourse and is colored by his perceptions of the children playing in the courtyard below him. Peters himself has completed a movement of sorts away from adult social intercourse back to a child's charmed isolation. Indeed, "something long forgotten, something young and trusting," smiles within him (186). Although Peters does not come out to play, neither does he totally withdraw. Quite the contrary, he flings open the window. He realizes that life will always tease and run by, will always dazzle even the dullest of its children with its explosive, magical colors regardless of whether the vague promises of these bright explosions will ever be actually fulfilled.

In this respect, Tolstaia's theme here intersects her methodology. Life—like language—is filled with possibilities. How we seize those possibilities depends upon us. Like the personification of life in the story, which peers into Peters's window and teases him, Tolstaia is playful but dry-eyed in her narration. The floridness of her prose, with its frolicking turns, illuminates the drab and the remarkable alike and sets them in opposition. Creative pretension is accordingly defeated in the crooked mirror of Tolstaia's authorial vision, which reflects the magic theater of life only according to its own peculiar properties. Peters, for instance, is both held up to pity and singled out for ridicule, yet his story ends without the obvious intrusive touch of the author's hand. Rather, his life story is simply *displaced* from the narrative, ostensibly by the arrival on the scene of the "new children" *(novye deti),* but also because his story has simply lost its ability to sustain the energy required by Tolstaia's metaphorically charged, poetically enjambed, narrationally entangled prose. As one critic puts it, at the conclusion of Tolstaia's stories (including "Peters") her metaphors "simply *supplant* reality and subordinate it to themselves" (metafory prosto *vytesniaiut* real'nost' i podchiniaiut ee sebe) (Lipovetskii 14).

Peters gives up on his dreams and expectations and lets life play its games without him, but his linguistic isolation is tempered by the inviting gesture of his open window at story's end.[14] In gratefully smiling at life (a "new, golden spring" [186]), Peters releases it—and, by extension, Tolstaia—to play its magical games elsewhere without him. As at the conclusions of several others of Tolstaia's stories, our attention is not focused on any decisive resolution but rather is simply aimed away from the present tale. In the story "Liubish', ne liubish' " ("Loves Me, Loves Me Not"), for example, the departure of the hated nanny Mar'yvanna is jauntily dismissed by the child narrator with the story's closing statement, "U nas vperedi leto" ("We've got summer ahead"). "Fakir" ("The Fakir") ends with an anthem to the suburbs and the "first bluish ice in the deep impression of another's footprint"—an instance in which Tolstaia literally steps away from one story into the next, from one utterance toward its successor. In "Peters" the reader is released from Peters's room to the outside world. His story is over, but life, "indifferent, ungrateful, deceitful, mocking, senseless, alien," and "wonderful, wonderful, wonderful," goes on. And so proceeds Tolstaia's art.

Notes

1. Bakhnov 227; Vasilevskii 256; Lipovetskii 12.
2. See Nevzgliadova and especially Helena Goscilo's ground-breaking study "Tat'iana Tolstaia's 'Dome of Many-Coloured Glass.' "
3. See, e.g., Murav'eva 116.
4. All translations are mine.

5. My analysis reflects notions put forward by Mikhail Bakhtin in "The Problem of the Text," in *Speech Genres and Other Late Essays*, ed. Caryl Emerson and Michael Holquist, trans. Vern W. McGee, 103–31 (Austin, TX: University of Texas Press, 1986). I also make use of Bakhtin's idea of *nesobstvenno-priamaia rech'*"—the "intrusion of the emotional aspects of someone else's speech into the syntactic system of authorial speech (ellipsis, questions, exclamations)" (319)—as it is outlined in his essay "Discourse in the Novel," in *The Dialogic Imagination*, trans. Caryl Emerson and Michael Holquist, 259–422 (Austin, TX: University of Texas Press, 1981).

6. My thanks to Marina Ledkovsky for correcting my misinterpretation of these lines in an earlier draft of this paper.

7. Peters says, "She, of course, doesn't—*can't*—understand anything, but that's not important" (Ona nichego, konechno, ne ponimaet i ponimat' ne mozhet, no nevazhno [172]). His attitude here only underscores the depth of his language dysfunction.

8. I am grateful to Helena Goscilo for these observations.

9. Tolstaia, personal interview, 5 February 1991.

10. In comments after a reading in Seattle, Washington, on 2 February 1991, Tolstaia directly addressed the place of poetry in her prose. She admitted preserving strict metrical and aural contrasts in writing certain stories, even when doing so required her to sacrifice semantic accuracy in the name of poetic effect.

11. Tolstaia, personal interview, 5 February 1991.

12. M. Zolotonosov claims that Tolstaia suffers from "unresolved doubts about her right as a writer [to address] man's moral requirements or ethical imperatives. Hence the uncertainty of her endings, which either smack of literary devices or are simply missing altogether" (nerazreshennye somneniia v svoem pisatel'skom prave na moral'nuiu trebovatel'nost' k cheloveku, na eticheskie imperativy. Otsiuda i neuverennost' v finalakh, ot kotorykh libo 'pakhnet chernilami,' libo ikh prosto net [60]).

13. Zolotonosov claims that the ending to "Peters" is *"prikleen"* (58). For other interpretations, see Goscilo, "Tolstajan Love" esp. 46; Spivak 201–2; Piskunov and Piskunova, esp. 194.

14. Interpretations of the conclusion to "Peters" vary greatly. Two diametrically opposed assessments are noted here. In "Tolstajan Love" Goscilo argues that Peters has made a transition to "a new phase of existence": "The story's ending celebrates the new Adam, the dawn of Peters's authentic life" (46). Galya Diment of the University of Washington, however, links Peters's forceful opening of the window to the earlier episode when he thought of flinging himself from the window, a common form of suicide in the Soviet Union. That time Peters decided to kill himself with gas instead because he did not want to ruin the wonderful job he had done of taping up the windows for the winter (176). Now it is spring. Diment therefore concludes that Peters is again contemplating suicide at the end of the story (personal communication).

References

Bakhnov, Leonid. "Chelovek so storony." *Znamia*, 1988, no. 7, 226–28.

Barta, Peter I. "The Author, the Cultural Tradition, and Glasnost: An Interview with Tatyana Tolstaya." *Russian Language Journal*, 1990, nos. 147–49, 265–83.

Gifford, Henry. "The Real Thing." *New York Review of Books*, 1 June 1989, 3–6.

Goscilo, Helena. "Tat'iana Tolstaia's 'Dome of Many-Coloured Glass': The World Refracted through Multiple Perspectives." *Slavic Review* 47, no. 2 (1988): 280–90.

————. "Tolstajan Love as Surface Text." *Slavic and East European Journal* 34, no. 1 (1990): 40–52.

Lipovetskii, M. " 'Svobody chernaia rabota': Ob 'artisticheskoi proze' novogo pokoleniia." *Voprosy literatury*, 1989, no. 9, 3–45.

Murav'eva, Irina. "Dva imeni." *Grani*, 1989, no. 43, 99–133.

Nevzgliadova, Elena. "Eta prekrasnaia zhizn'." *Avrora*, 1986, no. 10, 110–20.

Piskunov, V., and S. Piskunova. "Uroki zazerkal'ia." *Oktiabr'*, 1988, no. 8, 188–98.

Spivak, P. "Vo sne i naiavu." *Oktiabr'*, 1988, no. 2, 201–3.

Taroshchina, S. "Ten' na zakate." *Literaturnaia gazeta*, 1986, no. 30 (23 July), 7.

Tolstaia, Tat'iana. "Peters." In *"Na zolotom kryl'tse sideli . . . ,"* 169–86. Moscow: Molodaia gvardiia, 1987.

Vasilevskii, Andrei. "Nochi kholodni." *Druzhba narodov*, 1988, no. 7, 256–58.

Zolotonosov, M. "Mechty i fantomy." *Literaturnoe obozrenie*, 1987, no. 4, 58–61.

INDEX

271